Charles Seale-Hayne Library
University of Plymouth
(01752) 588 588
LibraryandITenquiries@plymouth.ac.uk

IMAGERY, LANGUAGE, AND VISUO-SPATIAL THINKING

Imagery, language, and visuo-spatial thinking

edited by

Michel Denis
Université de Paris-Sud, France

Robert H. Logie
University of Aberdeen, UK

Cesare Cornoldi
Università di Padova, Italy

Manuel de Vega
University of La Laguna, Tenerife, Canary Islands

Johannes Engelkamp
University of Saarland, Germany

PSYCHOLOGY PRESS
ALERE FLAMMAM
Taylor & Francis Group

First published 2001 by Psychology Press Ltd
27 Church Road, Hove, East Sussex, BN3 2FA

www.psypress.co.uk

Simultaneously published in the USA and Canada
by Taylor & Francis Inc
325 Chestnut Street, Suite 800, Philadelphia, PA 19106

Psychology Press is part of the Taylor & Francis Group

British Library Cataloguing in Publication Data
A catalogue record for this book is available from the British Library

Library of Congress Cataloging in Publication Data
Imagery, language, and visuo-spatial thinking / edited by Michel Denis . . . [et al.].
    p. cm. — (Current issues in thinking & reasoning)
  Includes bibliographical references and index.
  ISBN 1–84169–236–0
    1. Imagery (Psychology). 2. Visualization. 3. Psycholinguistics. I. Denis, Michel,
  1943– II. Series.
  BF367.I4625 2000
  152.14′2—dc21   00–044566

Cover design by Joyce Chester
Typeset by Graphicraft Limited, Hong Kong
Printed and bound in Great Britain by Biddles Ltd, Guildford and King's Lynn

Contents

List of contributors

David P. Carey, Department of Psychology, University of Aberdeen, Aberdeen AB24 2UB, UK

Marguerite Cocude, Groupe Cognition Humaine, LIMSI-CNRS, Université de Paris-Sud, BP 133, 91403 Orsay Cedex, France

Cesare Cornoldi, Dipartimento di Psicologia Generale, Università di Padova, Via Venezia 8, 35131 Padova, Italy

Marie-Paule Daniel, Groupe Cognition Humaine, LIMSI-CNRS, Université de Paris-Sud, BP 133, 91403 Orsay Cedex, France

Rossana De Beni, Dipartimento di Psicologia Generale, Università di Padova, Via Venezia 8, 35131 Padova, Italy

Doris Dehn, Department of Psychology, University of Saarland, Saarbrücken, Germany

Michel Denis, Groupe Cognition Humaine, LIMSI-CNRS, Université de Paris-Sud, BP 133, 91403 Orsay Cedex, France

Manuel de Vega, Department of Cognitive Psychology, University of La Laguna, Tenerife, Canary Islands, Spain

Johannes Engelkamp, Department of Psychology, University of Saarland, Saarbrücken, Germany

Sylvie Fontaine, Groupe Cognition Humaine, LIMSI-CNRS, Université de Paris-Sud, BP 133, 91403 Orsay Cedex, France

Olivier Ghaëm, Groupe Cognition Humaine, LIMSI-CNRS, Université de Paris-Sud, BP 133, 91403 Orsay Cedex, France

Robert H. Logie, Department of Psychology, University of Aberdeen, Aberdeen AB24 2UB, UK

Emmanuel Mellet, GIN-Cyceron, Boulevard Henri-Becquerel, BP 5229, 14074 Caen Cedex, France

Francesca Pazzaglia, Dipartimento di Psicologia Generale, Università di Padova, Via Venezia 8, Padova, Italy

David Pearson, Department of Psychology, University of Aberdeen, Aberdeen AB24 2UB, UK

Louise Phillips, Department of Psychology, University of Aberdeen, Aberdeen AB24 2UB, UK

Oliver Turnbull, School of Psychology, University of Wales Bangor, 39 College Road, Bangor, Gwynedd LL57 2DG, UK

Maria José Rodrigo, Department of Cognitive Psychology, University of La Laguna, Tenerife, Canary Islands, Spain

Susan Rudkin, Department of Psychology, University of Aberdeen, Aberdeen AB24 2UB, UK

Tomaso Vecchi, Sezione di Psicologia, Università degli Studi di Pavia, P.za Botta 6, 27100 Pavia, Italy

Hubert Zimmer, Department of Psychology, University of Saarland, Saarbrücken, Germany

PREFACE

Imagery, language, and visuo-spatial thinking: *E pluribus unum*

Robert H. Logie and Michel Denis

Visual imagery and visuo-spatial memory play key roles in the higher cognitive functions of mental representation, of creative thinking, and of planning complex actions, as well as contributing to understanding of differences in mental ability. This volume presents discussions of current theories and empirical endeavours driving these dynamic areas of research. Each chapter is jointly authored by leading European researchers from five different laboratories (Orsay, France; Aberdeen, Scotland; Padova, Italy; La Laguna, Canary Islands; and Saarbrucken, Germany) which have been part of a significant, and extended collaborative effort within the context of a European Union funded partnership under the Human Capital and Mobility Programme. The programme allowed a level of scientific interaction and exchange of scientific personnel that is extremely rare in cognitive psychology, enabling the significant co-ordinated effort of five physically distant and distinct laboratories to be devoted to complementary scientific questions. The achievements of this partnership have been disseminated in the scientific literature, through the now well established biennial European Workshop on Imagery and Cognition, and through the European Society for Cognitive Psychology as well as at national and international conferences in Europe and in North America. This volume collates the disseminated work in the form of theoretical and empirical reviews while taking advantage of the medium to extend theory, to report ongoing work, to speculate a little, and to explore a few possible areas of application as well as of science.

The focus is on recent research across European laboratories, but each chapter has clear pointers to the highly influential data and theory from North America that have dominated thinking on imagery since the early 1970s, allowing the more recent European as well as American work to be set in context. The involvement in each chapter of authors from different laboratories offers a degree of coherence and cross-referencing that would be difficult to achieve with independent contributions. The chapters each address key aspects of the properties and functions of imagery as basic components of human visuo-spatial thinking, from mental discovery to helping plan actions and routes, from making sense of and remembering our immediate environment through to generating pictures in our mind from verbal descriptions of scenes or people, and from the discussion of how individuals differ in their ability to use imagery through to the neuropsychological and neuroanatomical correlates of imaging in the brain.

In Chapter 1, David Pearson, Rossana De Beni, and Cesare Cornoldi address fundamental questions as to how mental images are generated, maintained, scanned, and transformed, as well as how images appear to support the processes of mental discovery. The questions have been explored within the context of quite different theoretical frameworks, notably the computational model developed by Kosslyn and his colleagues, and the working memory model developed by Baddeley, Hitch, Logie, and others. The chapter illustrates clearly how each model addresses different empirical questions, with the former conceived as a model of mental imagery while the latter is a model of part of the cognitive system which supports a range of cognitive tasks, including the generation, maintenance, and transformation of images.

In Chapter 2, Tomaso Vecchi, Louise Phillips, and Cesare Cornoldi explore the individual differences in visuo-spatial working memory that might serve as indicants of mental ability. They discuss research on imagery in the maturing minds of children and in individuals facing learning disability, on visuo-spatial cognition in the ageing minds of adults, on the nature and use of imagery in the blind, on visuo-spatial ability in adults who have suffered cognitive impairment following brain damage, and on the impact of cognitive expertise on the use of imagery strategies. The theoretical discussions again include the Kosslyn model and visuo-spatial working memory, but there is in addition a new theoretical perspective based on whether imagery tasks have a dynamic or a passive emphasis.

Chapter 3 examines the importance of implicit or explicit aspects of cognitive representation, with a detailed treatment by Johannes Engelkamp, Hubert Zimmer, and Manuel de Vega of the perceptual and conceptual coding of words and pictures. Images involve both the surface features of objects and scenes and the meanings and associates of objects in the scene. In implicit memory tests in which a subsequent memory test is not expected, memory performance is typically dependent on physical properties and largely independent of conceptual processing. This led researchers to assume that physical properties of stimuli are decisive in implicit tests, whereas meaning is decisive in explicit tests where participants are aware that memory for the material will be assessed. However, it turns out that meaning also plays a role in implicit tests and that physical properties can be retrieved in explicit tests. This chapter offers an explanation that draws on the perceptual–conceptual distinction as well as on the construct of episodic integration and on the specific mode of retrieval in explicit tests.

In Chapter 4, Oliver Turnbull, Michel Denis, Emmanuel Mellet, Olivier Ghaëm, and David Carey discuss some of the detailed studies of cognitive impairment in people who have suffered from brain damage, as well as some of the recent studies using both neuroscience and neuroimaging techniques to examine the neuronatomical correlates of mental imagery. This is a fascinating combination of neuropsychological and brain-imaging techniques that is starting to reveal not only the functional organisation of imagery, its links with perception and how it breaks down following brain damage, but also the mapping of these important cognitive functions onto areas and pathways in the brain. The structures of the occipito-parietal system (the dorsal "where" or "how" stream) appear to be involved in deriving information about the spatial location of objects, and the process of visually guided action. In contrast, the structures of the occipito-temporal system (the ventral "what" stream) seem to be involved in deriving information about the identity of objects, from the process of object recognition. The evidence converges on the general conclusion that object recognition and spatial abilities are achieved by relatively independent neural systems.

The principles that govern the links between language and the mental representation of space are explored in Chapter 5 by Manuel de Vega, Marguerite Cocude, Michel Denis, Maria José Rodrigo, and Hubert Zimmer. These researchers discuss the forms of spatial representations that people generate following their perceptual experience or following a verbal description. One part of the discussion is focused on the sensory-motor system that appears to involve fine-grained representations that have the properties of Euclidean space. This is thought to govern navigation in the environment, and the grasping and manipulation of objects. A second aspect of the discussion is of a system thought to direct pointing to objects in the current environment. The mental imagery system forms a third topic, referring to a spatial simulation system that allows people to build Euclidean representations of layouts and mental analogies of movement such as rotation and scanning, and this mental simulation appears somewhat independent of the current perceptual environment. A fourth element is the topological system, thought to be associated with the comprehension and production of verbal descriptions involving categorical and relational representations of space. Finally, there is discussion of a metaphorical system that permits the mapping of complex verbally based relations into spatial relations. The chapter describes and evaluates the wealth of experimental evidence addressing all of these five proposed aspects of the links between language and visuo-spatial cognition and how the different levels of representation are thought to interact.

Chapter 6 explores experiments, theory and potential applications to navigation. Michel Denis, Marie-Paule Daniel, Sylvie Fontaine, and Francesca Pazzaglia discuss how people use a variety of sources of information for constructing their spatial knowledge: navigation through their environment, visual inspection of surrounding space, processing of cartographic information, and processing of verbal descriptions of spatial environments. The use of this last source of information requires a close link between the processing of language and the visuo-spatial representational system. Although both systems have quite different structural and functional properties, they cooperate efficiently in a wide range of natural contexts. The authors review empirical data collected in experiments on the production and comprehension of spatial discourse, with special reference to situations where language is used for the purpose of providing navigational aids in unfamiliar environments. Cognitive processes involved in the production of route directions are analysed experimentally in an attempt to identify the factors that determine effective communication. The experiments involve judges' ratings of the effectiveness of verbal route descriptions and also the use of the route descriptions in navigating through complex urban environments, including the labyrinthine streets and alleyways of Venice.

In Chapter 7, Robert Logie, Johannes Engelkamp, Doris Dehn, and Susan Rudkin complete the book by discussing research findings that point to links between physical enactment, imagined enactment, and memory for actions. Some of this literature has focused on the association between actions and aspects of episodic and semantic memory. A parallel theoretical development has been the suggestion that one component of working memory (as discussed in Chapters 1 and 2) provides cognitive support for the planning of actions and immediate memory for movements. The authors address the possible theoretical contributions that can be drawn from the working memory literature to account for aspects of memory for actions. In so doing, they explore the role of working memory in remembering and planning actions, as well as the associations between working memory and long-term storage.

A common theme throughout the book is the development of theories of visuo-spatial thinking in the context of thorough experimentation. The result is a volume that intends to serve a tutorial function through thoughtful reviews of each sub-area, as well as offering a coherent statement of current developments. The human cognitive system appears to comprise interacting, specialist subsystems that can successfully address a wide range of everyday cognitive tasks. This book has arisen from interacting, specialist subgroups of researchers coming from different scientific cultures in different laboratories in different countries. The common object of their study, visuo-spatial cognition, is complex and diverse, and the insights achieved thus far have capitalised on the diversity of approaches and expertise that the authors represent. We hope that this volume will be persuasive in illustrating the level of scientific productivity that can be achieved through orchestrated international collaboration.

ACKNOWLEDGEMENTS

We gratefully acknowledge the support of the European Union Human Capital and Mobility Programme contract number CHRXCT940509, without which our collaborative efforts would have been much less productive. The research described was also supported by a significant number of national grants for individual projects. We are grateful to Caroline Osborne at Psychology Press and to the series editor, Ken Gilhooly, for their willingness to commission this book and for their patience in awaiting its completion. We also thank the many friends and colleagues with whom we have had numerous stimulating discussions and by whom we have been inspired, but who are not represented among the authors in this book.

CHAPTER ONE

The generation, maintenance, and transformation of visuo-spatial mental images

David Pearson
University of Aberdeen, UK

Rossana De Beni
Università degli Studi di Padova, Italy

Cesare Cornoldi
Università degli Studi di Padova, Italy

INTRODUCTION

In the last 30 years, imagery research has developed in many different directions, with different approaches, methodologies, types of observations, and phenomena. Visuo-spatial mental imagery phenomena may be classified into many different categories, including fantasy, hypnagogic imagery, hallucinations etc. In the present chapter we will focus on the involvement of mental imagery during visuo-spatial thinking. It is well known (e.g., Denis, 1989) that mental imagery can offer critical support to a variety of thinking processes, including spatial reasoning, problem solving using analogical representations, or mental discovery of novel or emergent properties. In order to implement these or similar processes, the human mind often spontaneously generates and manipulates mental images. Such manipulations can be of varying types, including the scanning, zooming, or transforming of images, but all require that the mental image be *maintained* during the time required for the relative manipulatory operations to be carried out.

In this chapter we will examine different alternatives concerning the cognitive architecture involved in the use of mental imagery, including the potential role played by visuo-spatial working memory. The properties of mental images and the processes involved during their generation will be discussed in relation to the different types of mental image that can occur during thinking, and the nature of the processes that may underlie their maintenance. We will then move on to consider important examples of mental manipulation, including the rotation and scanning of images, and imaged transformations of size and colour. Finally, the chapter will end by examining the involvement of mental imagery in aspects of creative thought, and in particular during the discovery of novel or emergent properties of objects or patterns based on the manipulation of visual mental images.

IMAGE GENERATION AND THE FORMAT OF LONG-TERM MEMORY INFORMATION

In this chapter we distinguish between mental images that consist of visual traces loaded directly from perceptual experience, and mental images that are generated using long-term information without any reliance on external visual support. There are also intermediate cases, such as images that are based on transformed visual input (see later section on mental synthesis), as well as images in sensory modalities other than vision, such as those that occur during auditory imagery (see Reisberg, 1992).

In some cases the image-generation process appears almost automatic and outside the voluntary control of the participant. A famous example of this concerns the author Marcel Proust, who reported being overwhelmed by a complex series of recollections apparently evoked by the experience of eating a cake that went on to form the basis of his great novel cycle *Remembrance of Things Past*. In other cases participants' goals and metacognition clearly guide the implementation of an image-generation plan (Cornoldi, De Beni, & Giusberti, 1996). For example, if people have to imagine the shortest way of reaching a particular place, they can direct their image-generation process according to both the nature of the task (i.e., should they drive or walk?), and to their particular metacognition (i.e., what kind of image would be most adequate for answering this question?).

Both automatic and controlled image generation use information retrieved from long-term memory. There has been considerable debate concerning the nature of the long-term information that is used for generating mental images. In the early 1970s two radical and opposing views were presented. The propositional view (e.g., Pylyshyn, 1973) assumed that both long-term information and conscious representation were always based on a unique amodal propositional format. In contrast, the dual-system view (e.g., Paivio's dual-code theory, 1971) assumed the existence of both linguistic and non-verbal modal formats in long-term memory and conscious representation. Subsequently different authors have proposed an intermediate position which assumes that long-term information can consist of a unique amodal format, while the conscious mental image has a format more related to the properties of the medium used during the implementation of the representation (Kosslyn, 1980; see also Marschark & Cornoldi, 1990).

As regards the format of long-term information, the computer metaphor has often been applied to show that a single type of information can be used for generating representations of different formats (e.g., Kosslyn, 1980). However, any psychological theory of imagery must offer an explanation for why mental images are sometimes directly and automatically generated with either highly specific modal information (such as a specific odour or colour), or else a predefined imaginal organisation (such as a prototypical image of a dog), or even a combination of both characteristics.

We cannot exclude the possibility that long-term memory can maintain to some extent the sensory properties of a stimulus. Cases of involuntary memories being primed (even after very long periods of time) by re-exposure to the same sensations experienced during learning (such as Proust's experience described earlier) suggest that the memory pattern code can in some way be related to memories for specific sensory information.

The possibility that this sensory information persists, or at least can be retrieved after long periods of time, seems to depend on its original repeated exposure during conditions of high activation. Mandler and Ritchey (1977) have argued that in general visual memories appear subject to decay functions which produce a rapid loss of specific sensory information, while more general schematic information is maintained. This suggests that visual memories may initially maintain elements encoded during perceptual exposure, but that these elements are then progressively subjected to processes of transformation and integration within long-term memory which result in an increasing loss of specific sensory details (see also Hitch, Brandimonte, & Walker, 1995; Cornoldi, De Beni, Giusberti, & Massironi, 1998; differential effects of long-term and short-term memory images were also found by Ishai & Sagi, 1997).

In summary, it can be seen that understanding the organisation of long-term memory is important to account both for which information is used during the image generation process, and also for how this information is accessed and retrieved. This issue is returned to later on in the chapter, following a discussion of the nature of medium in which mental images are represented.

THE IMAGE MEDIUM: VISUO-SPATIAL WORKING MEMORY OR A VISUAL BUFFER?

In the 1980s different positions were presented for describing the cognitive system(s) involved during the generation and manipulation of mental images. Baddeley (1986) separately considered short-term visual memory and image representation, but seemed to suggest that in both cases the same system was involved, i.e., the visuo-spatial component of working memory. Kosslyn (1980) postulated the existence of a specific system, the visual buffer, that possesses strong analogical properties. Despite the fact that Kosslyn did not consider its relationship with working memory, the two systems appear to share many characteristics (Logie, 1991). Two arguments seemed to support this conclusion:

(a) if working memory is the system involved in maintaining information used in mental activity, images must *by definition* be within this system; and (b) if mental images have specific properties, they must be held within the working memory subsystem that preserves these properties.

However, although it may be apparent that mental images are maintained within the working memory system, it is much less clear specifically which *components* of working memory may be involved. The model of working memory proposed by Baddeley and Hitch (1974; Baddeley, 1986) is a tripartite system that comprises three separate components; a central executive, a phonological loop, and a visuo-spatial sketchpad. The loop and sketchpad are both modality-specific "slave systems", the former implemented during the retention of verbal speech-based material, the latter during the retention of visuo-spatial material. The central executive is a modality-free system that supervises the operation of the slave systems, and is also assumed to be involved during strategy selection and the planning of complex cognitive tasks (Gilhooly, Logie, Wetherick, & Wynn, 1993; Toms, Morris, & Ward, 1993).

Both of the slave systems of working memory have themselves been fractionated into two inter-related components. The phonological loop consists of a passive phonological store and an active articulatory rehearsal mechanism (Baddeley & Lewis, 1981). A similar distinction has also been made within visuo-spatial working memory (VSWM), in which a passive visual cache is supported by an active "inner scribe" spatial rehearsal mechanism (Logie, 1995; Logie & Pearson, 1997). Information held in the visual cache is subject to decay unless maintained, and also subject to interference from new visual input entering the store. The active inner scribe mechanism is responsible for rehearsing the contents of the visual cache, and is also involved during the planning and execution of movement. Although spatial locations can be stored within the cache in the form of a static visual image (Smyth & Pendleton, 1989), the storage of *sequential* locations or movements requires the operation of the inner scribe. The scribe also extracts information from the visual cache to allow for targeted movement. Hence, any concurrent movement to discrete spatial locations can result in a disruption of the visuo-spatial rehearsal mechanism (Baddeley, Grant, Wight, & Thomson, 1975; Quinn & Ralston, 1986).

According to a revised model of VSWM (Logie, 1995; Pearson, Logie, & Gilhooly, 1999), the visual cache is considered a separate component from the visual buffer in which conscious mental images are represented. During the performance of a mental imagery task the visual cache and inner scribe can function as temporary stores for visual and spatial material, providing a means to transfer additional information to and from the visual buffer. Information held in each of the slave systems can be extracted by the central executive component and utilised during the completion of various cognitive tasks, as can semantic information held in long-term memory. Mental imagery therefore occupies the resources of the working memory system as a whole, rather than being specifically the province of the visuo-spatial sketchpad, which functions as a temporary store for information outwith the conscious image.

In fact much evidence has been accumulated showing that different imagery processes differentially involve a working memory system. For example, it has been shown that a concurrent task (spatial tapping) that typically interferes with VSWM activity does not interfere with mental imagery, whereas a task typically interfering with the central executive (random generation) may interfere with imaginal activity (Logie, 1995; see also Bruyer & Scailquin, 1998). Furthermore the passive storage function of the visual cache cannot easily be identified with the active role played by Kosslyn's visual buffer, and only part of the stored information within VSWM need actually be utilised during imaginal activity. These results may be better interpreted if we use different descriptions of VSWM (see other chapters in this book), and also if we consider different aspects of a generated image.

The generation and maintenance of a mental image involves not only storage processes, but also *active* processes. The quality and/or quantity of these processes can vary according to the nature of the task both between images and within an image. Three different, though partially overlapping, aspects of an image can be used to explain this last point. First, images, like percepts, can be organised (without voluntary intervention of the participant) into a figure and a background. The figure is more activated than the background, but the background remains included in the representation. Second, an attentional window (Kosslyn, 1980) can emphasise and improve the quality of the representation of certain parts of the image, even if the other parts remain present. Third, this process can be made highly selective by "zooming in" on some parts of the image while excluding other parts from the buffer (and potentially holding them highly accessible in a separate VSWM store; Logie, 1995).

The problem of the capacity of the image medium is therefore related to the problem of defining the systems that are implicated and of defining the critical variables within the system. In principle, exceeding that capacity can imply either a loss of information or a reduction in the quality of the representation.

Kosslyn does not directly specify the cognitive resources underlying image maintenance, although he does state that they are *not* the same "top-down" hypothesis-testing mechanisms that function during image generation. This theoretical position can argue in favour of either a fractionation of activity related to VSWM and imagery processes (Logie, 1995; Pearson, Logie, & Green, 1996; Pearson et al., 1999), or a continuum-based model that assumes that this activity can be differentiated along a vertical and a horizontal continuum (see Vecchi, Phillips, & Cornoldi, Chapter 2, this volume). The vertical continuum progresses from low-activity processes (such as the automatic retrieval of highly available mental images), through intermediate-activity processes (such as simple image maintenance), to highly active processes (represented by complex manipulations and transformations of mental images). The horizontal continuum describes the range of variations in the format of material and representation, suggesting that information treated in VSWM and mental imagery can be located more or less further away on the continuum from other modalities of representation. For example, Cornoldi et al. (1998) assumed that visual traces are more distant from verbal and conceptual representations than mental images generated from long-term memory. Furthermore, generated images become even closer to conceptual representations if they were generated along a semantic pathway. Cornoldi et al. (1998) asked a group of participants to remember geometrical patterns of different colours (red, yellow, and blue) or of similar colours (different variations of blue). In one condition (visual trace) the figures had been seen earlier, in another condition they were generated from verbal instructions, and in a final condition (conceptual generated image) they were generated with reference to colours of world objects. Figure 1.1 shows how, in the last condition, the recall of shape, size, and colour of the patterns was enhanced and was less sensitive to a visual similarity effect.

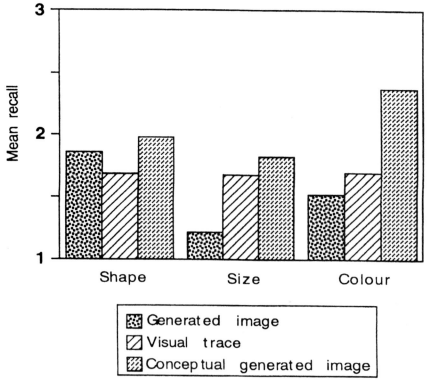

Figure 1.1.   Mean numbers of characteristics recalled by the generated image group, visual trace group, and conceptual generated image group for stimuli of similar colours (data from Cornoldi et al., 1998). Reprinted with permission.

There are a growing number of studies that have argued for an empirical distinction between generation and maintenance processes within visual imagery (e.g., Cocude, Charlot, & Denis, 1997; Cocude & Denis, 1988; Uhl et al., 1990; Wallace & Hofelich, 1992). Although such a distinction is persuasive, in terms of the working memory model it would appear that the maintenance of a conscious image requires the operation of attentionally based components of working memory. This need not be the case for the maintenance of visual material outwith the conscious image, as this could be maintained by the operation of visual cache which is functionally independent of the visual buffer (Logie, 1995; Pearson et al., 1999).

IMAGE GENERATION

The initial image-generation process must be highly flexible. It may also be highly automatised if we accept, as proposed by Kosslyn (1994), that image activation can also be an extreme form of priming, of the sort used when one expects to see a specific object or part during perception. It is only at this point that the most-activated pattern-activation subsystem engenders an image within the visual buffer. Pattern activation seems related to its conceptual representation (Kosslyn, 1994; Rosch et al., 1976). Moreover, the image-generation process appears sequential, beginning with a global image which is stronger because it has been activated more often. In a second phase the image can be enriched with details that make it closer to visual experience. This position is in agreement with the observation that people can generate either very general, low-resolution images, or rich specific images. General images are more often generated in standard conditions, take less time to be generated, are less memorable, and are rated by subjects as less vivid (Cornoldi, De Beni, & Pra Baldi, 1989; Helstrup, Cornoldi, & De Beni, 1997; see also De Beni & Pazzaglia, 1995).

The position illustrated here might explain why people can have more stable representations of objects that they have seen many times from different perspectives, and why a generated mental image can be different from each of these preceding experiences. From our perspective, however, the organisation of knowledge requires far more integrated information. The task of generating an image takes place within a particular context of knowledge activation and task demands, which influences the sources of information involved in the generation process. Not only the specific pattern code, but also the related pathways and other implicated nodes are activated at the same time, producing a representation that uses a mixture of different information. In some cases this mixture is particularly rich, whereas in other cases stimulus characteristics and/or task demands can reduce the contribution of less specific sources of information. For example, the generation of an image of a specific monument (e.g., the tower of Pisa) or of a rigidly defined form (e.g., a circle) can require fewer diverse sources of information than the images of a dog, or of a chimeric figure such as a centaur, which can have a higher degree of stimulus variability (see also Anderson & Helstrup, 1993).

In Kosslyn's (1994) view, the image-generation process is more complex when multipart images must be generated. Stored perceptual units must be integrated to form the image. In generating a multipart image we operate sequentially, first accessing the foundation part, which is the portion of the shape that is indexed by the spatial relation associated with a to-be-imaged part or property. Once the part or the property is properly positioned, the generative attentional mechanism (attention window) encodes a new pattern. At this point the attention window is adjusted and the appropriate representation is activated to project feedback into the visual buffer. Increases in detail and time processing will determine an increase in the quality of the image, although it is not clear whether this directly affects the subjective impression of vividness by a subject.

In concluding this section, it must be added that subsequent processes will be differentiated according to the *type* of image the subject generates. For this reason it is important that we consider the research concerning the differentiation of mental images.

TYPES OF MENTAL IMAGES

The literature on imagery has proposed to distinguish between different types of image representations which have different implications for neurological structure (Kosslyn, 1994) and for psychological functioning. For example, convergent evidence has been obtained for a distinction between visual and spatial representation (e.g., Farah, Hammond, Levine, & Calvanio, 1988). Within the spatial type of representation, important distinctions have been proposed between coordinate and categorical representations (Kosslyn, 1994), spatial simultaneous and spatial sequential representations (Pazzaglia & Cornoldi, 1999) etc.

We will focus here on differences concerning degree of specification, contextualisation, and involvement of personal and autobiographical information in mental images. An image may be general or specific according to its degree of specification; e.g., we can generate a very general image of a car, not strictly related to a brand and/or model, or a very specific image of a car, such as a Ferrari 312. The standard generation process will usually start from a general image, but it may also directly retrieve a specific image in cases of very familiar representations associated with frequent experiences. The specific image is more often the result of successive enrichment of a more general image, and the specific elements can be accessed very rapidly if strictly associated with the basic representation (e.g., a dog collar), or they can be the result of a highly controlled and strategic search in memory (e.g., a Lucerne chalet). A particular case of specification of an image is represented by its personalisation, with the inclusion of specific "self-reference" elements; i.e., an image of *my* umbrella or the presumably more synaesthetic image of myself *below* an umbrella.

Episodic autobiographical images apparently involve the retrieval of already available episodic traces consequent to autobiographical events, but may also involve a lot of constructive activity. They must be distinguished from the more general case of autobiographic images, which can be defined as images representing not only an episode of a subject's past life (Cornoldi et al., 1989; Groninger & Groninger, 1984) but also the subject him/herself interacting with an object (Rogers, 1980) or objects belonging to the subject (Helstrup et al., 1997). In fact, a distinction can be made between images referenced to a single episode of the subject's life (episodic autobiographical images) and images involving the subject him/herself without a precise episodic reference (autobiographic images; De Beni & Pazzaglia, 1995). For example, an autobiographic image generated in response to a cue word (e.g., "river") will involve a process to some extent similar to the specification and contextualisation processes already described, but with the peculiar enrichment represented by the involvement of the self-schema. In contrast, the generation of an episodic autobiographical image seems to follow a different pathway, in that it requires the search of appropriate information in an autobiographical memory system, leading to the choice of those memories that are considered the most representative and appropriate. The retrieval of autobiographical memories, even in the absence of specific instructions, seems to be strictly associated with the use of mental imagery (Brewer, 1988), as if the accessing of these memories automatically requires the generation of imagery.

PROPERTIES OF THE MENTAL IMAGE

Mental images may be described and defined according to various dimensions. For example, Raspotnig (1997) found that emotionally positive images were consistently reported as being more colourful, richer in shape and focus, and more vivid than negative images. The subjective vividness of an image has been the characteristic most widely examined in the literature. According to Cornoldi et al. (1992), image vividness has been only intuitively defined, as if instructing subjects to generate vivid images causes them to focus on a primitive dimension immediately comprehensible although not wholly definable to them. Despite the subjectivity and biases associated with rating the vividness of imagery, and despite the influence of individual differences, focus of rating, and type of image (e.g., specific images are rated as being more vivid than others), the dimension appears to represent a central property of the generated image.

Vividness intuition sometimes refers to two aspects: (a) the extent to which the image approaches actual visual experience; and (b) the luminosity and clarity of the image. In order to analyse the vividness dimension, Cornoldi et al. (1992) studied the role of some characteristics of images which may play a critical role in determining the impression of vividness. Six fundamental characteristics were identified by means of comparative examinations of subjects' reports of mental images. These characteristics were: specificity, richness of detail, colour, saliency, shape and contour, and context. All of these characteristics appeared to be related to the vividness of an image, but their individual contributions varied depending on the task demands. In particular, shape and contour were the best predictors of vividness. Cornoldi et al. (1991) synthesised the results of the research by concluding that, when images are generated using only one characteristic at a time, any of the six characteristics influences vividness ratings of images to a similar extent. Furthermore, when an image generated and rated in vividness has to be successively analysed with reference to the six characteristics, then the six characteristics have differential effects. Some of them, especially shape and contour, were more likely to influence vividness than others. These data suggest that complexity (or richness in detail) is not particularly critical for the vividness experience. In fact, specific images are richer than general images and they are also rated as more vivid; however, in other cases an increase of complexity, especially when it exceeds the capacity limitation of the image buffer, may produce a loss of the quality of the image. Therefore, during the sequential process of image generation, it is possible that the subject reaches an optimal level of resolution, which is subsequently lost. The image resolution may influence aspects other than the richness of detail, such as the clarity of the shape contour, how well the shape is designed, the image colour, the salience of the core figure with respect to its background, etc.

Baddeley and Andrade (1998) proposed (a) that visual and auditory images reflect the operation of visual and auditory working memory slave systems, and (b) that a vivid image reflects a rich and detailed representation (or else the potential to access a great deal of sensory detail). Therefore they predicted that a concurrent visuo-spatial task would disrupt the representation of a visual image, hence reducing the perceived vividness, whereas a phonological task such as articulatory suppression would reduce the perceived vividness of an auditory image. Predictions were confirmed, especially in the case of novel stimuli. With more familiar stimuli, the vividness ratings were more affected by other variables, such as active (e.g., a cat climbing a tree) vs. static (e.g., a lion in a zoo) or conventionality vs. bizarreness (e.g., a car dissolving), than by the nature of the concurrent task. Images that were meaningful, static, or sensible were rated as significantly more vivid than respectively nonsense, active, or bizarre images. These last results, which were not influenced by the nature of the involvement of working memory, require an examination of the role of long-term memory. The authors suggest that in these cases VSWM can be involved to a small extent, as the subjects' ratings are affected by the judgement of the quantity of related sensory information which, although not activated, can be accessed easily.

IMAGE MAINTENANCE

Once an image has been generated, it will then typically be used as a basis for further cognitive processing. This can include using imagery as a mediator during learning (Quinn & McConnell, 1996a, b; Richardson, 1985, 1998), using images of depicted objects in order to make comparative judgements of selected attributes (Engelkamp, Mohr, & Logie, 1995; Paivio & te Linde, 1980), or manipulating imagery in order to discover novel combinations or insights (Finke, 1990; Pearson et al., 1996) etc. The most simple active processes concern the effort devoted to maintaining a mental image.

A mental image is subject to a rapid decay, and it has even been estimated that the average duration of generated images can be only 250 ms (Kosslyn, 1994). Hence, typically an image will have to be *maintained* prior to and during any transformation procedure taking place. Maintenance processes are particularly critical in mental imagery as they are necessary both during the sequential generation of the image (for maintaining the already generated parts) and during their manipulation. If maintenance processes are not activated we can expect that the image will decay rapidly. Mellet, Tzourio, Denis, and Mazoyer (1995) found that the generation–maintenance of a mental image is specific with respect to other visual activities, such as visual scanning. They found that the generation–maintenance of the mental exploration of a map involved the right occipital cortex, but not bilaterally the visual area, as was the case for the visual exploration of a map.

The specific role of maintenance processes has been demonstrated and measured both for mental images (e.g., Cocude & Denis, 1988; Kosslyn, 1994) and for visual traces (e.g., Watkins, Peynircioglu, & Brems, 1984), but we do not know to what extent they are similar, nor are the underlying mechanisms clear. Two views of the maintenance process, i.e. simple serial scanning and simple regeneration, must be rejected. The simple scanning view implies that the image is serially scanned and refreshed, but does not consider the fact that an image is typically organised with more central and more peripheral parts; consequently if a sequential scanning mechanism is involved, it follows a priority sequence which does not correspond to a serial exhaustive process. Furthermore the organisation of an image is of units of different size and relevance, with the implication that scanning for maintenance should be considered more "wandering" and should involve *significant* units rather than single units of the mental screen. The regeneration view involves a priority principle, as the order of refreshment is not simply related to a spatial sequence; but it assumes that this order reflects the order by which the parts of the image were originally assembled during the generation process. The regeneration process should require less cognitive resources, as the necessary information is already available; but it would involve the same sequence of construction, an assumption that seems too strong in consideration of the fact that the progressive construction of an image may have changed the priority of its elements.

Therefore, it is probable that the maintenance activity involves a variety of heterogeneous processes, which partly mirror the generation processes and simple scanning activity, but which are still capable of respecting the organisation and differential importance of elements of the image.

It has been observed (Cocude et al., 1997; Cocude & Denis, 1988; Pazzaglia & Cornoldi, 1999) that people experience difficulty in maintaining a mental image for more than a few seconds, and this occurs to a different extent for different individuals. This difficulty in maintaining images does not appear to mirror the facility by which people can maintain for longer periods of time verbal information through verbal rehearsal, or visuo-spatial information that is not represented by a conscious image. This could reflect the higher quantity of attentional resources required for carrying out the image-maintenance operations, and this could have an adaptive function, in that the maintenance of an image could be less useful than its manipulation. However, it is also possible that the difficulty in maintaining an image is due in part to its complexity in comparison to other material, such as the temporary retention of digit strings in verbal short-term memory.

It is not clear how the image fades and how the subject reacts to the risk of losing the image, such as whether he or she tends to modify it in order to make it more persistent (by inducing a movement or a change of perspective etc.). However, introspective evidence suggests that, even if active maintenance processes are carried out, it is difficult to maintain an image for a long time without changing its characteristics.

As we have already mentioned, maintenance processes may be considered by different theoretical approaches. A particularly influential theoretical position has been proposed by Kosslyn. In Kosslyn's computational model of visual imagery (Kosslyn, 1980, 1994) such maintenance is an extension of the image-generation process, rather than a separate procedure in its own right. Image generation involves the priming of perceptual units stored within pattern activation subsystems, which are responsible for the activation of analogue-like representations held within long-term visual memory. There are two such pattern-activation subsystems; an exemplar subsystem which is used during the generation of images with specific parts; and a category subsystem which is utilised if the image is more prototypical in nature. Kosslyn has claimed that image generation from these pattern-activation subsystems is an extreme form of the same kind of priming that occurs when we expect to see a specific object or part of an object during normal perception (Rosch, 1975; Warren & Morton, 1982). During the generation of an image from visual memory, mapping functions are established between the individual perceptual units in the pattern-activation subsystems and the visual buffer. If the image needs to be maintained for more than 250 ms, then these functions are continually reactivated, thereby refreshing the configuration of activity within the visual buffer and preserving it from decay.

Kosslyn distinguishes visual-memory-based image generation from attention-based image generation, in which a spatial image is created via the incremental movement of an attention window across the visual buffer. Maintenance of such an image is dependent on the continued focusing of attention on the appropriate activated regions of the buffer. Kosslyn claims that the processes involved in both the maintenance of visual-memory-based and attention-based images adapt quickly, making it increasingly difficult to maintain a visuo-spatial image accurately within the buffer over time.

Kosslyn has termed the temporary maintenance of information across the various components of the imagery system as comprising a form of "working memory" (Kosslyn, 1994). However, the temporary retention of visuo-spatial material is seen as an integral part of the image-generation process, rather than as a separate process in its own right. As discussed previously, an alternative to this is to conceive of working memory as comprising a number of storage systems that, although involved during image processing, remain *functionally separate* from the image-generation process (Logie, 1995; Pearson et al., 1999; Pearson et al., 1996).

In conclusion, in the consideration of the maintenance issue, a direct equation of the working memory model with Kosslyn's computational theory is not appropriate, as both have developed in order to address different empirical issues. The emphasis within the working memory literature has been mainly on the temporary retention of visual and/or spatial material over short periods of time, whereas the computational model literature has focused more on the image processes themselves, in particular those involved during image generation and image transformation. Although the computational model does address the issue of image maintenance within the visual buffer, it is not clear whether such maintenance is directly compatible with the rehearsal of visuo-spatial material within working memory.

MENTAL ROTATION AND MENTAL SCANNING

We will now move on to consider the manipulation and transformation of mental images. One of the most extensively researched types of image transformation is that of mental rotation. The initial work in this area was carried out by Shepard and Metzler (1971), who presented subjects with pictures of pairs of three-dimensional objects. The second item of each pair would either be a rotated version of the first item, or instead a rotated version of a *mirror image* of the first item. During testing subjects were required to determine whether each pair of items depicted identical or mirror-reversed objects. A typical example of findings from such a procedure is that response time for each trial is linearly related to the degree of angular disparity between the two depicted items. This effect has proved to be highly replicable across a range of different stimuli (Cooper, 1991; Cooper & Podgorny, 1976; Cooper & Shepard, 1973; Corballis, 1986), and has been used by some to argue for the existence of an analogue-based rotation procedure, in which mental representations of items are gradually transformed through intermediate states in a fashion analogous to the actual physical manipulation of real objects (Paivio, 1991; Shepard & Cooper, 1982).

Although currently the existence of some form of mental rotation procedure is widely accepted, its relationship to visual imagery is more open to question. In the computational model of imagery (Kosslyn, 1987, 1994), mental rotation is characterised as being a form of *motion-added* transformation, in which an image of an object previously viewed in a static situation is incrementally transformed so as to simulate movement (this is distinguished from *motion-encoded* transformations, in which visual memories of previously encoded dynamic movements are reactivated and displayed within the visual buffer). Motion-added transformations are dependent on the anticipated consequences of actions; i.e., because real objects have to move through trajectories, the mental movement of objects will also follow this pattern, and therefore mental rotation consists of a series of incremental transformations.

Mental rotation of abstract shapes appears to involve both spatial and executive components of working memory. As the capacity of working memory is limited, it should be expected that mental rotation will be adversely affected by any increases in cognitive load. An early study carried out by Rock (1973) found that subjects became less accurate in making judgements about rotated items as the complexity of the items was increased. Corballis (1986) reported that subjects are generally slower in performing the mental rotation of letters while maintaining a concurrent verbal or visual memory load. More recently, Bauer and Jolicoeur (1996) have shown that subjects take longer to rotate mentally three-dimensional items compared to equivalent two-dimensional representations of the same items. All of these findings are consistent with the notion that the conscious manipulation of mental images is dependent on the general resources of a memory system, while the rotation procedure itself requires the operation of a modality-specific spatial component (Logie & Salway, 1990).

A critical role of mental imagery has also been shown for mental scanning procedures, in which subjects are required to imagine moving from one point on an image to another (for a very complete review, see Denis & Kosslyn, 1999). Kosslyn, Ball, and Reiser (1978) asked subjects to memorise a map of a fictitious island on which were depicted various geographical landmarks. Subjects were subsequently asked to generate an image of this island and then imagine moving from one specified geographical location to another. As with the mental rotation studies, subjects' scanning time was found to increase proportionally with the physical distance between landmarks depicted on the actual map.

Kosslyn et al. (1978) argued from these findings that imagery functions as an analogue representation during scanning tasks, although critics again countered with the charge that subjects were instead merely simulating what they would *expect* to occur during the scanning of an actual percept (Baddeley, 1990; Denis & Carfantan, 1985; Pylyshyn, 1981; for a metacognitive analysis of the scanning task, see Cornoldi et al., 1996). This interpretation seems less likely, however, for a series of scanning experiments carried out by Finke and Pinker (1982, 1983) in which no explicit instructions to adopt an imagery strategy were ever given. Despite this, subjects' response times continued to increase linearly with represented distance between start and target points, and in subsequent questioning the majority of subjects reported spontaneously adopting an imagery strategy in order to complete the task.

In Kosslyn's computational theory of imagery, scanning *within* an image requires the shifting of an attention window across the visual buffer. However, it is also possible that attention and focusing are differently directed or that scanning is made "off screen", moving to parts of an image that were not previously "visible" within the conscious image (Kosslyn, 1978, 1980). This requires an actual transformation of the contents of the visual buffer. As with other forms of image transformation, this can take the form of either motion-encoded or motion-added movement. In the former an image is scanned in a manner analogous to how the depicted object was scanned during encoding; i.e., a series of images are generated that represent the sequence of visual memories encoded during initial perception. In the latter case, which is most likely to occur while scanning a novel image, new representations of the parts of an object being scanned are primed in the pattern-activation subsystems, which then results in their generation within the visual buffer.

Kosslyn also links image scanning to systematic eye movements, based on work reported by Brandt et al. who found that subjects tended to move their eyes while scanning mental images (see Brandt & Stark, 1997). Such eye movements serve either to index visual memories encoded at specific locations on the image (motion-encoded scanning), or to alter representations within a spatiotopic mapping subsystem linked to pattern-activation subsystems (motion-added scanning). Some support for a link between eye movement and image transformation is provided by Irwin and Carlson-Radvansky (1996), who report that mental rotation is suppressed during saccadic eye movements in a primed mental rotation task.

Eye movements have also featured in the working memory literature, where Baddeley has suggested that the eye movement system may be used to rehearse and maintain information held within visuo-spatial working memory. In a study carried out with Idzikowski, Dimbleby, and Park (reported in Baddeley, 1986), it was found that eye movements produced by visual tracking selectively interfered with performance of the Brooks Matrix task. Pearson (1999) has reported that concurrent spatial tapping selectively interferes with subjects' ability to scan mentally between two landmarks on a mental image of an island, but does not disrupt the replacement of an image of a landmark with a new one. Baddeley has argued that the rehearsal of spatial material within working memory may be dependent on implicit motor processes such as those involved during such eye or hand movements, in an analogous fashion to the rehearsal of verbal material via an active articulatory mechanism during verbal working memory. However, the problems we discussed earlier in relation to the nature of the visuo-spatial rehearsal processes also apply to the case of mental scanning. Smyth and Scholey (1994a, b) have instead argued that spatial rehearsal may be dependent on shifts in spatial *attention* rather than implicit motor processes, and this view could also be used for examining the scanning issue. In one study (1994a), they found that spatial span (as measured by a computerised version of Corsi Blocks) could be disrupted simply by requiring subjects to attend to visual or auditory signals presented in varying locations (see also Cornoldi, Cortesi, & Preti, 1991). This disruption was increased if subjects were asked to make an additional motor (pointing in the direction of the signal) or categorical (indicating whether signals were presented left or right) response to the signals.

In a following study, Smyth and Scholey (1994b) found no significant relationship between the time taken to move between targets on a computerised version of Corsi Blocks and spatial memory span. This lack of a relationship between movement time and spatial span is in contrast to the "word length effect" demonstrated for verbal working memory (Baddeley, Thomson, & Buchanan, 1975), and may suggest that the inner scribe component is not linked to overt responding in the same way as the articulatory loop. One potential criticism of the Smyth and Scholey study is that the distances between the targets on the Corsi Blocks task were not sufficiently large to produce a significant reduction in spatial span, and clearly the issue will require further research before firm conclusions can be drawn.

SIZE AND COLOUR TRANSFORMATIONS

As with mental rotation and mental scanning, Kosslyn conceives of "zooming" (increasing the extent of an image in the visual buffer) as being an *incremental* process, in which an image is shifted through various intermediate stages before reaching the desired scale. It automatically occurs in situations in which the resolution limits of the visual buffer obscure parts or characteristics that are implicit within the global image. Kosslyn distinguishes a zoom transformation from a size-scaling transformation, as the former involves a change in perceived *distance*, whereas the latter results in a change in perceived *size*. Although it might be expected that both types of transformation produce the same result within the visual buffer, studies have shown that imaged size and imaged distance can be experimentally manipulated. Roth and Kosslyn (1988) asked subjects to generate a visual image of the pattern represented in Figure 1.2, which was specified as depicting either a pyramid or a mineshaft. Subjects then had to judge whether a series of visually presented dots would fall on or off specified parts of their image. Roth and Kosslyn found that subjects' response times were significantly more sensitive to imaged distance than imaged size when they conceived the pattern as either a pyramid or mineshaft, but that there was no such effect when *perceptual* judgements of the pattern were made.

Image transformation need not necessarily involve altering size or orientation, as the *colour* of an imaged object can also be readily manipulated. Watkins and Schiano (1982) asked subjects to imagine various black and white familiar and abstract figures as if they were "painted" in a specific colour shade. In a subsequent surprise recognition test, subjects performed much better with items that were presented in the same colour shade they had previously imaged, suggesting that

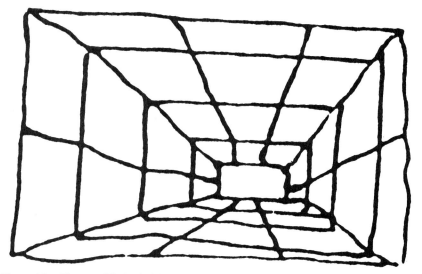

Figure 1.2.   The pyramid/mineshaft figure (from Roth & Kosslyn, 1988). Reprinted with permission.

the colour transformation had been encoded along with the representation of the figure. In another experiment Watkins and Schiano found that it was only the actual colour that aided recognition memory rather than a verbal label representing the colour, suggesting that the results cannot be accounted for purely in terms of verbal association.

MENTAL SYNTHESIS

The maintenance and transformation of visual images normally occurs as part of some other cognitive activity, such as creative design (Reed, 1993), scientific reasoning (Gardner, 1993), or general problem solving (Antonietti & Baldo, 1994). This final section will focus on mental synthesis, in which discrete parts in an image are transformed and manipulated in order to form novel patterns or allow novel insights. The technique of "combinatory play" advocated by Einstein (Ghiselin, 1952) is an often-cited example of such mental synthesis, and discoveries based on image transformation have also been attributed to Kekule, Faraday, and Feynman among others (Finke, 1993).

Some of the most influential research in this area has been carried out by Ronald Finke and his colleagues. In one experiment Finke, Pinker, and Farah (1989) asked subjects to carry out a series of transformations on imaged figures in response to verbally presented instructions. The suggested transformations were designed so that the final imaged pattern would resemble a familiar object or symbol, and the experiment was intended to determine whether it was possible for the subjects to make novel interpretations of the transformed figures purely on the basis of imagery alone. Finke et al. found that subjects correctly followed the verbal instructions on 59.7% of the trials, and that out of these 58.1% of the final figures were correctly identified. In a series of follow-up studies, Finke et al. demonstrated that the discoveries could *only* be successfully made using imagery, as subjects were unable to anticipate the end result on the basis of the starting stimuli or verbal instructions alone.

Using the Finke et al. procedure just described, Pearson et al. (1996) carried out a series of experiments investigating the role that working memory may play during such an imagery task. An example of the instructions and related transformations is presented in Figure 1.3. Subjects were asked to carry out the image-manipulation task either on its own or concurrently with a range of secondary tasks known to interfere selectively with the different components of the working

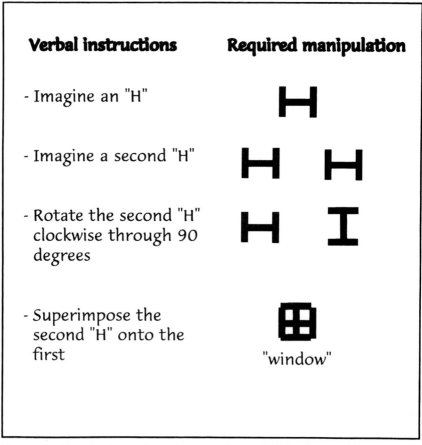

Figure 1.3. Example of instructions and corresponding manipulations for the guided image transformation task (from Pearson et al., 1996).

memory system. Articulatory suppression and spatial tapping were used to target the resources of the phonological loop and visuo-spatial sketchpad respectively, while two forms of random generation task (oral random number generation and random key tapping) were used to target the central executive component.

Neither articulatory suppression nor spatial tapping produced a significant effect on the number of trials correctly identified, while both of the random generation tasks produced a significant decrement in performance. These findings are consistent with the hypothesis that the Finke et al. image-manipulation task has a high executive load, but places only minimal demands on the verbal and visuo-spatial slave systems of the working memory system.

One potential weakness of the Finke et al. procedure, however, is that subjects only transform their images in response to *explicit* verbal instructions from the experimenter. Furthermore, the "discoveries" they can make from their images are only those predetermined by the experimenter; hence the task lacks the type of creative, unexpected discovery process described by people such as Einstein and Kekule in their accounts of mental synthesis. In an attempt to rectify this weakness, Finke went on to develop the creative visual synthesis task, in which subjects are not so constrained in either the transformations or discoveries they can make using their imagery (Anderson & Helstrup, 1993; Finke & Slayton, 1988; Roskos-Ewoldsen, 1998). In the initial stage of the synthesis task subjects were presented with 15 symbols, each of which was associated with a verbal label (i.e., "circle", "capital D" etc.) First of all subjects were required to learn the 15 symbols so that they could accurately image each of them in response to only the verbal name. Following this, on each experimental trial subjects were presented with three of the verbal names selected randomly from the set of 15. Subjects were then given two minutes to imagine manipulating the given symbols so as to form a *recognisable* object or pattern. The only constraint on the image trans-formations that they could carry out was that subjects could not alter the form of the presented symbols (e.g., stretch the circle into an oval). Overall, subjects managed to produce recognisable patterns on around 40% of the presented trials. Furthermore, Finke and Slayton demonstrated that neither the experimenter nor the subjects themselves were capable of predicting the final result of the synthesis on the basis of the presented symbols alone, supporting the claim that the novel discoveries were being made using imagery alone.

Following the Pearson et al. study described previously, Pearson, Logie, and Gilhooly (1999) have examined the role that the slave systems of working memory may play during the creative visual synthesis task. Subjects were required to perform a five-symbol version of the synthesis task either alone or concurrently with one of three secondary tasks. Some examples of the kind of patterns created by subjects are given in Figure 1.4. Articulatory suppression and spatial tapping were used to occupy the resources of the phonological loop and inner scribe respectively. The third secondary task was a dynamic visual noise display based on the work of Quinn and McConnell (1996a, b; McConnell & Quinn, 1996),

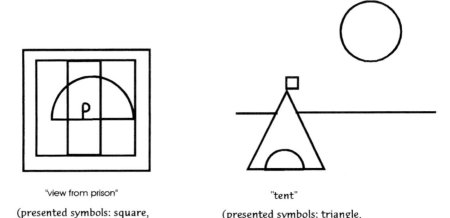

"view from prison"   "tent"

(presented symbols: square,   (presented symbols: triangle,
rectangle, square, D, P)   circle, D, square, line)

Figure 1.4. Examples of presented symbols and resulting synthesised patterns (data taken from Pearson et al., 1999).

which was intended to target selectively the operation of the passive visual cache component.

Unlike the mental manipulation task described earlier, the synthesis task placed heavy demands on the slave systems of working memory. Previous studies had indicated that on an average trial subjects would carry out a number of transformations upon the presented symbols, combining them in a series of different positions and orientations until a final satisfactory pattern was achieved. Protocols collected by Pearson et al. suggested that it is only towards the end of the synthesis process that all five symbols become integrated within the conscious image. Concurrent spatial tapping significantly reduced the number of legitimate patterns that subjects produced during the mental synthesis task. As many of the image transformations carried out on the symbols involve rotating them into new orientations, this is consistent with the theory that the inner scribe component of VSWM is involved during dynamic image processes such as mental rotation (Logie & Salway, 1990; see also Pearson, 1999). More recently, Pearson, Logie, and Gilhooly (1998) have found substantial dual-task interference if creative synthesis is performed concurrently with a secondary task thought to demand executive resources, such as oral random generation. Significant disruption was evident for both three- and five-part synthesis trials, and there was also a significant reduction in subjects' *conscious* experience of imagery during dual-task conditions. Taken together, these studies are supportive of the argument presented earlier that the conscious maintenance of imagery is largely a function of the central executive component of working memory, whereas the slave systems are implemented mainly during tasks that require additional verbal or visuo-spatial storage outwith the conscious image itself. Pearson et al. (1999) also found that concurrent articulatory suppression produced a highly disruptive effect on the synthesis task, significantly affecting not only the number of legitimate patterns subjects produced, but also the number of presented symbols that they could correctly recall. This suggests that during the synthesis task subjects utilise the phonological loop in order to maintain the verbal labels of the five symbols, and thereby induce better control over visuo-spatial thinking.

One further prediction could be that the visual cache would be responsible for storing the contents of the conscious image, assuming that the cache performs the same function as the visual buffer in Kosslyn's computational model. However, the results of the study did not support this. There was no significant effect of concurrent visual noise on the number of legitimate patterns produced, the memory for the shapes themselves, or on the degree of rated correspondence between the verbal labels and their associated drawings. These results do not appear consistent with the claim that the passive visuo-spatial component of working memory is involved during the generation and manipulation of visual images, or that visual images are maintained within the visual cache (i.e., Baddeley, 1986, 1988; Quinn & McConnell, 1996a, b). However, theoretically the passive visual store featured in the work of Quinn and McConnell appears more akin to Kosslyn's visual buffer than the visual cache described by Logie and Pearson. Within this theoretical framework it therefore remains uncertain whether the dynamic visual noise display specifically disrupts the operation of a passive visual store (as claimed by Quinn & McConnell, 1996a), or instead interferes with an imagery subsystem which is independent of the visuo-spatial sketchpad. This problem stems from the fact that significant disruption by visual noise has currently been demonstrated mainly with imagery tasks such as pegword mnemonics or method of loci, rather than visual short-term memory tasks such as matrix span (Phillips & Christie, 1977a, b) or the retention of colour shade (Logie & Marchetti, 1991).

Another issue that has continued to provoke debate among researchers in the area is the role that stimulus support may play during image discoveries. Stimulus support is essentially anything that externally represents aspects of the imagery process, whether it be paper and pencil or a computer-based graphics package. Many of the anecdotal accounts of creative imagery also mention the use of stimulus support; for example, Picasso produced 45 preparatory compositions during his painting of *Guernica* (Gardner, 1993), and Watson and Crick utilised both image manipulation and physical manipulation of cardboard models of molecules during their investigations into the structure of DNA (Shepard & Cooper, 1982).

Experimental studies have also indicated that stimulus support can aid subjects during image-discovery tasks. Chambers and Reisberg (1985) found that although subjects found it very difficult to reinterpret the classic duck/rabbit figure using imagery alone, their success rate was significantly improved when they were allowed to draw their image on a piece of paper. Similarly, Pearson et al. (1996) found that subjects' performance on the Finke et al. (1989) image-manipulation task was significantly better when they were viewing drawings of their completed images rather than the actual images themselves.

Reisberg (1996; Reisberg & Logie, 1993) has accounted for the effects found in research on image interpretation in terms of a mental reference frame which constrains the types of discoveries that can be made from a visual image. Reisberg argues that images, unlike percepts, cannot be inherently ambiguous, but instead are always interpreted within the context of a specific frame of reference that specifies how the image should be understood; i.e., which part is the "front", which the "back" and so on. In the case of forming an image of the duck/rabbit figure (Chambers & Reisberg, 1985; Reisberg & Chambers, 1991), the reference frame will cause the image to be interpreted either as a duck *or* a rabbit, but not both. A successful reinterpretation of the figure requires a reference frame reversal, where the coordinates in which the image is interpreted are reassigned. Reisberg and Chambers (1991) found that subjects' drawings of their images of the duck/rabbit figure were distorted depending on the reference frame in which the image was interpreted, i.e., those who encoded the figure as representing a duck would tend to emphasise the "beak" aspects of the figure more and de-emphasise the bump on the figure that represents the rabbit's mouth.

CONCLUSIONS

This chapter has discussed some of the literature that has investigated the cognitive processes that underlie the generation, maintenance, and transformation of visuo-spatial images. These processes have important implications for the comprehension of thinking, as mental imagery plays a relevant part in much cognitive activity. In the chapter we have considered the critical steps and variables associated with the use of mental imagery. In particular, the mental image-generation process is seen as very important and complex, especially when the generated image is not the simple by-product of a recent visual experience. To this purpose, we have stressed the need for distinguishing between visual traces and generated images. We have focused on the contribution of long-term memory to mental images, and of the controlled processes guiding image generation. We have also observed that generated images may be of different types corresponding to partially different generation processes. A subsequent point has been to examine how a mental image can be described, and its main properties. Despite its popularity, the usefulness of the vividness dimension requires deep consideration, and the problems associated with the construct have been discussed.

We have also considered the nature of the operations carried out on mental images, starting with the apparently simple operation of image maintenance, and moving to more complex manipulations, such as rotation, scanning, and feature transformation. The analysis of these processes has been made with particular reference to two theoretical approaches which have been successful in tackling these problems, i.e., the computational model of imagery (Kosslyn, 1980, 1987, 1994) and the working memory model (Baddeley, 1986; Logie, 1995). Although both theories make reference to image maintenance and image transformation, it can be seen that the models are not entirely compatible, as both have evolved in order to address different empirical questions. Although previously the visuo-spatial sketchpad has been characterised as being responsible for the generation and maintenance of visual images (Baddeley & Lieberman, 1980), we have discussed the position that argues instead that such imagery processes could be better assigned either to more active and controlled components of the working memory system (Vecchi & Cornoldi, 1999) or to the central executive component of working memory, with the visual cache functioning only as a temporary storage system for material outwith the conscious image (Pearson et al., 1999). One advantage of the working memory model is that it attempts to separate storage and processing functions within a cognitive task, while such a separation is much less clear within the computational model. The working memory model also provides a framework within which to account for how verbal encoding and storage may interact with the use of imagery, which is an aspect of imagery not clearly addressed by the computational model. On the other hand, although many of the transformations that occur during imagery tend just to be attributed to either spatial or executive components within working memory, Kosslyn has provided a much more detailed analysis of what processes and subsystems may underlie activities such as image rotation, scanning, or size scaling. Future developments in the area will need to take into account the empirical findings from both approaches, while also adopting caution in assuming any direct equivalence between the various structures and mechanisms specified by both models.

REFERENCES

Anderson, R.E., & Helstrup, T. (1993). Visual discovery in mind and on paper. *Memory and Cognition, 21*, 283–293.

Antonietti, A., & Baldo, S. (1994). Undergraduates' conceptions about the cognitive functions of mental imagery. *Perceptual and Motor Skills, 78*, 167–170.

Baddeley, A.D. (1986). *Working memory*. Oxford: Oxford University Press.

Baddeley, A.D. (1988). Imagery and working memory. In M. Denis, J. Engelkamp, & J.T.E. Richardson (Eds.), *Cognitive and neuropsychological approaches to mental imagery* (pp. 169–180). Dordrecht: Martinus Nijhoff Publishers.

Baddeley, A.D. (1990). *Human memory: Theory and practice*. Hove, UK: Lawrence Erlbaum Associates Ltd.

Baddeley, A.D., & Andrade, J. (1998). Working memory and consciousness: An empirical approach. In M.A. Conway, S.E. Gathercole, & C. Cornoldi (Eds.), *Theories of memory, Vol. II*. Hove, UK: The Psychology Press.

Baddeley, A.D., Grant, S., Wight, E., & Thomson, N. (1975). Imagery and visual working memory. In P.M.A. Rabbitt & S. Dornic (Eds.), *Attention and performance* V (pp. 205–217). London: Academic Press.

Baddeley, A.D., & Hitch, G. (1974). Working memory. In G.H. Bower (Ed.), *Recent advances in learning and motivation*, Vol. 8. New York: Academic Press.

Baddeley, A.D., & Lewis, V.J. (1981). Inner active processes in reading: The inner voice, the inner ear and the inner eye. In A.M. Lesgold & C.A. Perfetti (Eds.), *Interactive processes in reading* (pp. 107–129). Hillsdale, NJ: Lawrence Erlbaum Associates Inc.

Baddeley, A.D., & Lieberman, K. (1980). Spatial working memory. In R.S. Nickerson (Ed.), *Attention and performance VIII* (pp. 521–539). Hillsdale, NJ: Lawrence Erlbaum Associates Inc.

Baddeley, A.D., Thomson, N., & Buchanan, M. (1975). Word length and the structure of short-term memory. *Journal of Verbal Learning and Verbal Behavior, 14*, 575–589.

Bauer, B., & Jolicoeur, P. (1996). Stimulus dimensionality effects in mental rotation. *Journal of Experimental Psychology: Human Perception and Performance, 22*, 82–94.

Brandt, S.A., & Stark, L.W. (1997). Spontaneous eye movements during visual imagery reflect the content of the visual scene. *Journal of Cognitive Neuroscience, 9*(1), 27–38.

Brewer, W.F. (1988). A qualitative analysis of the recalls of randomly sampled autobiographical events. In M.M. Gruneberg, P.E. Morris, & R.N. Sykes (Eds.), *Practical aspects of memory, Vol. I: Memory in everyday life* (pp. 263–268). Chichester, UK: John Wiley & Sons.

Bruyer, R., & Scailquin, J.C. (1998). The visuospatial sketchpad for mental images: Testing the multicomponent model of working memory. *Acta Psychologica, 98*, 17–36.

Chambers, D., & Reisberg, D. (1985). Can mental images be ambiguous? *Journal of Experimental Psychology: Human Perception and Performance, 11*, 317–328.

Cocude, M., Charlot, V., & Denis, M. (1997). Latency and duration of visual mental images in normal and depressed subjects. *Journal of Mental Imagery, 21*, 127–142.

Cocude, M., & Denis, M. (1988). Measuring the temporal characteristics of visual images. *Journal of Mental Imagery, 12*, 89–101.

Cooper, L.A. (1991). Dissociable aspects of the mental representation of visual objects. In R.H. Logie & M. Denis (Eds.), *Mental images in human cognition* (pp. 3–34). Amsterdam: North-Holland.

Cooper, L.A., & Podgorny, P. (1976). Mental transformations and visual comparison processes: Effects of complexity and similarity. *Journal of Experimental Psychology: Human Perception and Performance, 2*, 503–514.

Cooper, L.A., & Shepard, R.N. (1973). Chronometric studies of the rotation of mental images. In W.G. Chase (Ed.), *Visual information processing.* New York: Academic Press.

Corballis, M.C. (1986). Is mental rotation controlled or automatic? *Memory and Cognition, 14*, 124–128.

Cornoldi, C., Cortesi, A., & Preti, D. (1991). Individual differences in the capacity limitations of visuospatial short-term memory: Research on sighted and totally congenitally blind people. *Memory and Cognition, 19*, 459–468.

Cornoldi, C., De Beni, R., Cavedon, A., Mazzoni, G., Giusberti, F., & Marucci, F. (1992). How can a vivid image be described? Characteristics influencing vividness judgments and the relationship between vividness and memory. *Journal of Mental Imagery, 16*, 89–108.

Cornoldi, C., De Beni, R., & Giusberti, F. (1996). Meta-imagery: Conceptualization of mental imagery and its relationship with cognitive behaviour. *Psychologische Beiträge, 38*, 484–499.

Cornoldi, C., De Beni, R., Giusberti, F., Marucci, F., Massironi, M., & Mazzoni, G. (1991). The study of vividness of images. In R.H. Logie & M. Denis (Eds.), *Mental images in human cognition* (pp. 305–312). Amsterdam: North-Holland.

Cornoldi, C., De Beni, R., Giusberti, F., & Massironi, M. (1998). Memory and imagery: A visual trace is not a mental image. In M.A. Conway, S.E. Gathercole, & C. Cornoldi (Eds.), *Theories of memory, Vol. II.* Hove, UK: Psychology Press.

Cornoldi, C., De Beni, R., & Pra Baldi, A. (1989). Generation and retrieval of general, specific and autobiographic images representing concrete nouns. *Acta Psychologica, 72*, 25–39.

De Beni, R., & Pazzaglia, F. (1995). Memory for different kinds of mental images: Role of contextual and autobiographic variables. *Neuropsychologia, 33*, 1359–1371.

Denis, M. (1989). *Image and cognition.* Paris: Presses Universitaires de France.

Denis, M., & Carfantan, M. (1985). People's knowledge about images. *Cognition, 20*, 49–60.

Denis, M., & Kosslyn, S.M. (1999). Scanning visual mental images: A window on the mind. *Current Psychology of Cognition, 18*, 409–466.

Engelkamp, J., Mohr, G., & Logie, R.H. (1995). Memory for size relations and selective interference. *European Journal of Cognitive Psychology, 7*(3), 239–260.

Farah, M.J., Hammond, K.M., Levine, D.N., & Calvanio, R. (1988). Visual and spatial mental imagery: Dissociable systems of representation. *Cognitive Psychology, 20*, 439–462.

Finke, R. (1990). *Creative imagery: Discoveries and inventions in visualization.* Hillsdale, NJ: Lawrence Erlbaum Associates Inc.

Finke, R. (1993). Mental imagery and creative discovery. In B. Roskos-Ewoldsen, M.J. Intons-Peterson, & R.E. Anderson (Eds.), *Imagery, creativity, and discovery: A cognitive perspective* (pp. 255–286). Amsterdam: North-Holland.

Finke, R., & Pinker, S. (1982). Spontaneous imagery scanning in mental extrapolation. *Journal of Experimental Psychology: Human Perception and Performance, 8*, 142–147.

Finke, R., & Pinker, S. (1983). Directional scanning of remembered visual patterns. *Journal of Experimental Psychology: Learning, Memory, and Cognition, 9*, 398–410.

Finke, R., Pinker, S., & Farah, M.J. (1989). Reinterpreting visual patterns in mental imagery. *Cognitive Science, 13*, 51–78.

Finke, R., & Slayton, K. (1988). Explorations of creative visual synthesis in mental imagery. *Memory and Cognition, 16*, 252–257.

Gardner, H. (1993). *Creating minds.* New York: BasicBooks.

Ghiselin, B. (1952). *The creative process.* New York: Mentor.

Gilhooly, K.J., Logie, R.H., Wetherick, N.E., & Wynn, V. (1993). Working memory and strategies in syllogistic reasoning. *Memory and Cognition, 21*, 115–124.

Groninger, L.D., & Groninger, L.K. (1984). Autobiographical memories: Their relation to images, definitions, and word recognition. *Journal of Experimental Psychology: Learning, Memory and Cognition, 10*, 745–755.

Helstrup, T., Cornoldi, C., & De Beni, R. (1997). Mental images: Specific or general, personal or impersonal? *Scandinavian Journal of Psychology, 38*, 189–197.

Hitch, G.J., Brandimonte, M.A., & Walker, P. (1995). Two types of representation in visual memory: Evidence from the effects of stimulus contrast on image combination. *Memory and Cognition, 23*, 147–156.

Irwin, D.E., & Carlson-Radvansky, L.A. (1996). Cognitive suppression during saccadic eye movements. *Psychological Science, 7*, 83–88.

Ishai, A., & Sagi, D. (1997). Visual imagery: Effects of short- and long-term memory. *Journal of Cognitive Neuroscience, 9*, 734–742.

Kosslyn, S.M. (1978). Measuring the visual angle of the mind's eye. *Cognitive Psychology, 10*, 356–389.

Kosslyn, S.M. (1980). *Image and mind.* Cambridge, MA: Harvard University Press.

Kosslyn, S.M. (1987). Seeing and imagining in the cerebral hemispheres: A computational approach. *Psychological Review, 94*, 148–175.

Kosslyn, S.M. (1994). *Image and brain.* Cambridge, MA: MIT Press.

Kosslyn, S.M., Ball, T.M., & Reiser, B.J. (1978). Visual images preserve metric spatial information: Evidence from studies of image scanning. *Journal of Experimental Psychology: Human Perception and Performance, 4*, 47–60.

Logie, R.H. (1991). Visuo-spatial short-term memory: Visual working memory or visual buffer? In C. Cornoldi & M. McDaniel (Eds.), *Imagery and cognition* (pp. 77–102). New York: Springer-Verlag.

Logie, R.H. (1995). *Visuo-spatial working memory.* Hove, UK: Lawrence Erlbaum Associates Ltd.

Logie, R.H., & Marchetti, C. (1991). Visuo-spatial working memory: Visual, spatial, or central executive? In R.H. Logie & M. Denis (Eds.), *Mental images in human cognition* (pp. 105–115). Amsterdam: North-Holland.

Logie, R.H., & Pearson, D.G. (1997). The inner eye and the inner scribe of visuo-spatial working memory: Evidence from developmental fractionation. *European Journal of Cognitive Psychology, 9*, 241–257.

Logie, R.H., & Salway, A.F.S. (1990). Working memory and modes of thinking: A secondary task approach. In K. Gilhooly, M. Keane, R. Logie, & G. Erdos (Eds.), *Lines of thinking: Reflections on the psychology of thought, Vol. 2* (pp. 99–113). Chichester, UK: Wiley.

Mandler, J.M., & Ritchey, G.H. (1977). Long-term memory for pictures. *Journal of Experimental Psychology: Human Learning and Memory, 3*, 386–396.

Marschark, M., & Cornoldi, C. (1990). Imagery and verbal memory. In C. Cornoldi & M. McDaniel (Eds.), *Imagery and cognition*. New York: Springer-Verlag.

McConnell, J., & Quinn, J.G. (1996). Interference at the encoding and maintenance of visual information. *Psychologische Beiträge*, *38*, 343–354.

Mellet, E., Tzourio, N., Denis, M., & Mazoyer, B. (1995). A positron emission tomography study of visual and mental spatial exploration. *Journal of Cognitive Neuroscience*, *7*, 433–445.

Paivio, A. (1991). *Images in mind: The evolution of a theory*. Hemel Hempstead, UK: Harvester Wheatsheaf.

Paivio, A., & te Linde, J. (1980). Symbolic comparisons of objects on color attributes. *Journal of Experimental Psychology: Human Perception and Performance*, *6*, 652–661.

Pazzaglia, F., & Cornoldi, C. (1999). The role of distinct components of visuospatial working memory in processing the texts. *Memory*, *7*, 19–41.

Pearson, D.G. (1999). Mental scanning and spatial processes: A role for an inner scribe? *Current Psychology of Cognition*, *18*, 564–573.

Pearson, D.G., Logie, R.H., & Gilhooly, K. (1998). *Creative synthesis and executive resources: The impact of computer-based stimulus support*. Paper presented at the 15th Annual BPS Cognitive Psychology Section Conference, Bristol, UK. [Abstract in *Proceedings of The British Psychological Society*, *7*(1), 44. Leicester, UK: BPS.]

Pearson, D.G., Logie, R.H., & Gilhooly, K. (1999). Verbal representations and spatial manipulation during mental synthesis. *European Journal of Cognitive Psychology*, *11*, 295–314.

Pearson, D.G., Logie, R.H., & Green, C. (1996). Mental manipulation, visual working memory, and executive processes. *Psychologische Beiträge*, *38*, 324–342.

Phillips, W.A., & Christie, D.F.M. (1977a). Components of visual memory. *Quarterly Journal of Experimental Psychology*, *29*, 117–133.

Phillips, W.A., & Christie, D.F.M. (1977b). Interference with visualization. *Quarterly Journal of Experimental Psychology*, *29*, 637–650.

Pylyshyn, Z.W. (1981). The imagery debate: Analogue media versus tacit knowledge. *Psychological Review*, *87*, 16–45.

Quinn, J.G., & McConnell, J. (1996a). Irrelevant pictures in visual working memory. *Quarterly Journal of Experimental Psychology*, *49*A, 200–215.

Quinn, J.G., & McConnell, J. (1996b). Exploring the passive visual store. *Psychologische Beiträge*, *38*, 355–367.

Quinn, J.G., & Ralston, G.E. (1986). Movement and attention in visual working memory. *Quarterly Journal of Experimental Psychology*, *38*(A), 689–703.

Raspotnig, M.A. (1997). Subcomponents of imagery and their influence on emotional memories. *Journal of Mental Imagery*, *21*, 135–146.

Reed, S.K. (1993). Imagery and discovery. In B. Roskos-Ewoldsen, M.J. Intons-Peterson, & R. Anderson (Eds.), *Imagery, creativity and discovery: A cognitive perspective*. Amsterdam: North-Holland.

Reisberg, D. (Ed.) (1992). *Auditory imagery*. Hillsdale, NJ: Lawrence Erlbaum Associates Inc.

Reisberg, D. (1996). The nonambiguity of mental images. In C. Cornoldi, R.H. Logie, M.A. Brandimonte, G. Kaufmann, & D. Reisberg (Eds.), *Stretching the imagination: Representation and transformation in mental imagery*. New York: Oxford University Press.

Reisberg, D., & Chambers, D. (1991). Neither pictures nor propositions: What can we learn from a mental image? *Canadian Journal of Psychology*, *45*, 288–302.

Reisberg, D., & Logie, R.H. (1993). The ins and outs of visual working memory: Overcoming the limits on learning from imagery, In M. Intons-Peterson, B. Roskos-Ewoldsen, & R. Anderson (Eds.), *Imagery, creativity, and discovery: A cognitive approach* (pp. 39–76). Amsterdam: Elsevier.

Richardson, J.T.E. (1985). Converging operations and reported mediators in the investigation of mental imagery. *British Journal of Psychology*, *76*, 205–214.

Richardson, J.T.E. (1998). The availability and effectiveness of reported mediators in associative learning: A historical review and an experimental investigation. *Psychonomic Bulletin and Review*, *5*, 597–614.

Rock, I. (1973). *Orientation and form*. New York: Academic Press.

Rogers, T.B. (1980). A model of the self as an aspect of the human information processing system. In N. Cantor & J. H. Kihlstrom (Eds.), *Personality, cognition, and social interaction*. Hillsdale, NJ: Lawrence Erlbaum Associates Inc.

Rosch, E. (1975). The nature of mental codes for color categories. *Journal of Experimental Psychology: Human Perception and Performance*, *1*, 303–322.

Rosch, E., Mervis, C.B., Gray, W.D., Johnson, D.M., & Boyes-Braem, P. (1976). Basic objects in natural categories. *Cognitive Psychology*, *8*, 382–439.

Roskos-Ewoldsen, B. (1998). Recognizing emergent properties of images and percepts: The role of perceptual goodness in imaginal and perceptual discovery. *Journal of Mental Imagery*, *22*, 183–212.

Roth, J.R., & Kosslyn, S.M. (1988). Construction of the third dimension in mental imagery. *Cognitive Psychology*, *20*, 344–361.

Shepard, R.N., & Cooper, L.A. (1982). *Mental images and their transformations*. Cambridge, MA: MIT Press.

Shepard, R.N., & Metzler, J. (1971). Mental rotation of three dimensional objects. *Science*, *171*, 701–703.

Smyth, M.M., & Pendleton, L.R. (1989). Working memory for movements. *Quarterly Journal of Experimental Psychology*, *41*(A), 235–250.

Smyth, M.M., & Scholey, K.A. (1994a). Interference in spatial immediate memory. *Memory and Cognition*, *22*, 1–13.

Smyth, M.M., & Scholey, K.A. (1994b). Characteristics of spatial memory: Is there an analogy to the word length, based on movement time? *Quarterly Journal of Experimental Psychology*, *47*A, 91–117.

Toms, M., Morris, N., & Ward, D. (1993). Working memory and conditional reasoning. *Quarterly Journal of Experimental Psychology*, *46*A, 679–699.

Uhl, F.G., Goldenberg, G., Lang, W., Lindinger, G., Steiner, M., & Deecke, L. (1990). Cerebral correlates of imagining colours, faces, and a map–II. Negative cortical DC potentials. *Neuropsychologia*, *28*, 81–93.

Vecchi, T., & Cornoldi, C. (1999). Passive storage and active manipulation in visuo-spatial working memory: Further evidence from the study of age differences. *European Journal of Cognitive Psychology*, *11*, 391–406.

Wallace, B., & Hofelich, B.G. (1992). Process generalization and the prediction of performance on mental imagery tasks. *Memory and Cognition*, *20*, 695–704.

Warren, C., & Morton, J. (1982). The effects of priming on picture recognition. *British Journal of Psychology*, *73*, 117–129.

Watkins, M.J., Peynircioglu, Z.F., & Brems, D.J. (1984). Pictorial rehearsal. *Memory and Cognition*, *12*, 553–557.

Watkins, M.J., & Schiano, D.J. (1982). Chromatic imaging: An effect of mental colouring on recognition memory. *Canadian Journal of Psychology*, *36*, 291–299.

CHAPTER TWO

Individual differences in visuo-spatial working memory

Tomaso Vecchi
Università degli Studi di Pavia, Italy

Louise H. Phillips
University of Aberdeen, UK

Cesare Cornoldi
Università degli Studi di Padova, Italy

THE NOTION OF VSWM

Visuo-spatial working memory (VSWM) is the term that identifies the system involved in short-term retention and processing of visuo-spatial material. The concept of a visuo-spatial working memory system is closely linked to the working memory model proposed by Baddeley and Hitch (1974; Baddeley, 1986). In this chapter we will use the term simply as a way to define a system that is able to memorise and process visuo-spatial material, either deriving from sensory perception or from long-term storage systems. From this perspective, the Baddeley and Hitch model (1974; and later modifications such as Logie, 1995) is one of the possible interpretations and later we will describe the most plausible alternatives.

The existence of a specific visuo-spatial system has been demonstrated in recent years although its characteristics are still to be defined in detail. Studies of individual differences have greatly enlarged our knowledge of visuo-spatial processes both by differentiating independent subsystems and by showing the way the system develops and works.

This chapter will focus on reviewing evidence so far reported by individual-differences studies towards the definition of the architecture of VSWM, and its possible implications for the understanding of a general cognitive resources

29

theory in cognitive functioning. In particular, we will consider the development of VSWM in children; the evolution that occurs with ageing, and studies showing a selective impairment of visuo-spatial processing either following cerebral damage (i.e., neuropsychological case studies), specific cognitive syndromes (e.g., non-verbal learning disability), or physiological impairments (i.e., blindness). The description of such evidence gives the opportunity to describe the difficulty of assessing visuo-spatial ability, and to report some examples of tests and procedures that have been used in the investigation of VSWM. In conclusion, we will relate this large body of evidence to the theories of VSWM and of brain functioning as well as to education and cognitive rehabilitation techniques.

Evidence in favour of a specific visuo-spatial system

The working memory model proposed by Baddeley and Hitch (Baddeley, 1986; Baddeley & Hitch, 1974) interprets human memory not only as a system capable of retaining information but also as a structure able to organise, manipulate, and transform long-term stored material as well as sensory inputs. This model has been widely confirmed in its general structure, and working memory has been found to be involved in the execution of mathematical tasks (e.g., Logie & Baddeley, 1987; Logie, Gilhooly, & Wynn, 1994), text comprehension (e.g., Baddeley & Lewis, 1981; Just & Carpenter, 1992), problem solving (e.g., Gilhooly, Logie, Wetherick, & Wynn, 1993; Phillips et al., 1999; Saariluoma, 1991), learning tasks (e.g., Baddeley, Papagno, & Vallar, 1988; Gathercole & Baddeley, 1989), and visuo-spatial processing tasks (e.g., Cornoldi, 1995; Logie, 1995). The original formulation of this model includes a central executive, to coordinate and organise the different processes, and a number of subsidiary systems, more closely related to sensory inputs and less demanding in terms of cognitive resources. Baddeley (1986) identified two such subsystems and described them in more detail: the articulatory loop, for elaboration of verbal material, and the visuo-spatial sketchpad, for processing of visuo-spatial information. The articulatory loop has been extensively investigated but the structure of the visuo-spatial sketchpad was little explored until the end of the last decade (e.g., Logie, 1986, 1989). New findings have led to reformulations of the original model with a new theoretical perspective on visuo-spatial working memory (Cornoldi, 1995; Logie, 1995). This visuo-spatial system is capable of organising complex functions, such as mental imagery, as well as maintaining the visual and spatial information used in everyday activities (e.g., analysing the position of objects, their colour and shape).

Initial evidence of the existence of a specific visuo-spatial system came from the studies carried out by Brooks in the late 1960s (1967, 1968). These experiments required subjects to perform two tasks simultaneously, and verified the extent to which different pairs of tasks could be successfully carried out or

selectively interfered with each other. Brooks' aim was to distinguish the processing of visual and verbal information: if visual and verbal processes rely on different components, then two verbal (or visual) tasks presented together should interfere more than tasks tapping different components.

Brooks showed selective interference effects, thus providing evidence for two separate verbal and visuo-spatial subsystems in working memory, and pioneered the use of the dual-task paradigm. Subseqently, Logie, Zucco, and Baddeley (1990) demonstrated the existence of specific limited visuo-spatial resources, independent from central processing. Phillips and Christie (1977a, b; and see also Phillips, 1983) proposed a general, non-modality-specific use of central components of memory on the basis of the existence of an interfering effect between visual and arithmetic tasks. To re-interpret the Phillips and Christie results, Logie et al. (1990) used two main tasks, verbal span, and visuo-spatial span, and two interfering tasks, namely arithmetic sums and composition of visual matrices. The results confirmed that a visual task could be disturbed by the execution of arithmetic but to a lesser extent than by the concurrent composition of visual matrices. This result confirms once again the existence of a specific visuo-spatial system and does not seem to be due to a general trade-off of attentional resources. In fact, the decrease in performance in the case of a visual and a verbal task executed together was minimal, as has been reported previously (Baddeley, 1986). On the contrary, the presence of a strong selective interference effect confirms the existence of specific subsystems.

The experimental evidence is also supported by neuropsychological evidence: The patient ELD described by Hanley, Young, and Pearson (1991) presented a selective deficit in the processing of visuo-spatial material. This deficit did not involve long-term memory for visuo-spatial information acquired prior to the lesion. ELD was impaired in performing tasks such as mental rotation, imagery mnemonics, or Brooks' tasks; however, his performance in verbal tasks was within the range of control subjects. The double dissociation between verbal and visuo-spatial processing is completed by patient PV (Vallar & Baddeley, 1984), who performed flawlessly in visuo-spatial tasks but showed a deficit in tasks requiring phonological storage or mental rehearsal of verbal material.

Theoretical models of VSWM

As we have pointed out, the characteristics of visuo-spatial processes have been investigated only recently and, consequently, the relations between different theoretical models of VSWM have also been largely unexplored. The different approaches vary in terms of the internal structure of the visuo-spatial system, degree of independence of the different subsystems, and the relation between the system and other components of short-term or long-term memory. However, a complete review of the existing models is not the aim of the present chapter and we will only present a brief account of the three cognitive models of VSWM that, in our view, best represent the scientific debate in this field: the multi-component model (Baddeley, 1986; Logie, 1995), the distributed "continuum" model (Cornoldi, 1995), and the mental imagery model (Kosslyn, 1994).

Multicomponent model. Since the late 1960s, two complementary experimental techniques have become very popular among cognitive scientists: double dissociation in neuropsychology and selective interference in experimental psychology (for a detailed description of these techniques see Shallice, 1988, and Baddeley, 1986, respectively). The underlying theoretical assumption is that different cognitive functions are performed by different systems in the brain that work with a high degree of independence. This view is evident in the formulation of the working memory model, where the central executive, articulatory loop, and visuo-spatial sketchpad are independent structures, and a strong effort has been devoted to identifying the relation between tasks and systems.

In this field of research the most influential hypothesis for the architecture of the visuo-spatial working memory (as an alternative to the term 'sketchpad') was formulated by Logie (1995). He maintained the original architecture of working memory as postulated by Baddeley and Hitch (1974) and concentrated his attention on the characteristics of the visuo-spatial working memory system. Logie postulated the visuo-spatial working memory system as being independent from the central executive and the articulatory loop, and being divided into two major components, one for the processing of visual material and the other for processing of spatial information. The other major innovation from Baddeley's original hypothesis is that the route from visual perception, and possibly from all sources of external stimuli, is via long-term semantic knowledge and representations. The central executive is closely related to higher functions, such as mental imagery, and in such cases it coordinates and draws on the material temporarily stored in the visual and spatial subsystems.

Distributed "continuum" model. An alternative view which has been proposed by Cornoldi and Vecchi (2000; Cornoldi, 1995) is that working memory processes vary according to: (1) the nature of the to-be-processed information, and (2) the amount of active information processing required. At the level of passive peripheral processing, different types of information are processed independently, reflecting the different sensory modalities of the material. At this level, cognitive systems are relatively autonomous and domain-specific. In contrast, more active information processing utilises domain-independent techniques, and interconnections between different sensory systems. The model therefore includes a vertical continuum reflecting the amount of active processing required by a task, dependent on the requirements for information manipulation, coordination, and integration.

This model is illustrated in Figure 2.1 and comprises horizontal dimensions reflecting the distinction between separate peripheral systems, and a vertical

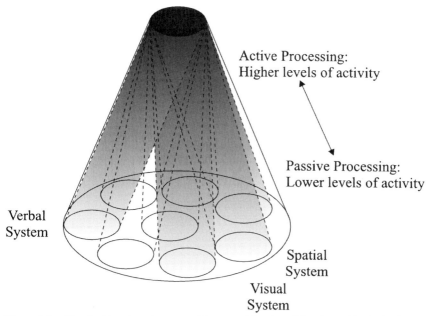

Active Processing:
Higher levels of activity

Passive Processing:
Lower levels of activity

Verbal
System

Spatial
System

Visual
System

Figure 2.1.   The distributed continuum model proposed by Cornoldi and Vecchi. The horizontal continuum represents differences between the specific information (e.g., verbal and visuo-spatial information), while the vertical continuum represents differences in the specific processes (e.g., passive and active processes).

dimension that reflects the amount of active processing required in a task. The dissociation between verbal and visuo-spatial processes in working memory is reflected in the horizontal dimensions of the model by the distance between the systems involved. In a similar fashion, the closer association between visual and spatial processes in VSWM is indicated by the relatively small distance between the correspondent areas of the model.

Tasks are positioned along the vertical continuum on the basis of the amount of active processing that is required to carry out the task. Even relatively passive tasks, such as verbal or spatial span, may require some sort of active processing, probably in the form of mental rehearsal. However, active processing demands are low and such tasks can be positioned close to the passive pole of the continuum. When the information has to be transformed, modified, or integrated, then a higher amount of active processing is required. The inter-relations between different types of tasks represented by the horizontal continuum decrease as the active processing demands rise.

Mental imagery model.   This model develops a theory proposed by Kosslyn in 1980. In Kosslyn's view, mental imagery processes are directly related to visual perception processes with which they share most of their properties. Kosslyn's recent attempt to "solve the imagery debate" (Kosslyn, 1994) is focused on two aims: to investigate the properties of the image itself and to relate mental representations to other cognitive processes, such as memory or reasoning. However, the former issue is much better addressed than the second, and the most interesting part of the theory explains how mental images are generated, the properties of the images, and the neurophysiological evidence that high-level vision and mental imagery share areas of neural substrates. This model is closely related to the neuropsychological and neurophysiological literature that identified mental imagery essentially in the processes of recognition, identification, or manipulation of objects. From this point it provides a very detailed description of all image properties and, consequently, of all the subsystems that must be involved.

Distinctions within VSWM

A large proportion of research into the architecture of VSWM has been focused on the possibility of distinguishing several subcomponents of the system. In particular, research has investigated the differentiation between visual and spatial subcomponents (and also within the spatial component, the distinction between categorical and coordinate spatial information, and between tasks involving sequential and simultaneous spatial processing), and between passive storage and active elaboration of visuo-spatial information.

Visual and spatial processing in VSWM.   In 1982, Ungerleider and Mishkin demonstrated that processing the characteristics of objects is related to two different neural pathways: specifically, the elaboration of "what" the object is, and the elaboration of "where" the object is with relation to spatial coordinates (ventral and dorsal neural pathways, respectively). These studies were carried out on primates, and showed that the characteristics of an object are separately analysed from the spatial relations of the object; the two neural pathways are independent starting from the retina, through the geniculate nuclei, and up to the associative areas of the cerebral cortex. This result has led to the hypothesis that visual and spatial processing could be distinguished at a higher level, in terms of cognitive operations of VSWM. A few studies have confirmed this hypothesis both in experimental paradigms using normal subjects and in neuropsychological studies by analysing the performance of brain-damaged patients.

Using experimental paradigms Robert Logie and collaborators (Logie, 1986, 1989; Logie & Marchetti, 1991) carried out some significant studies to differentiate, within the VSWM system, the existence of separate visual and spatial components. Logie and Marchetti (1991) relied on the technique of selective interference: a primary visual task (e.g., the recall of coloured shape) or spatial task (e.g., the recall of sequence of movements) was paired with a visual secondary task (e.g., the visual presentation of irrelevant material) or spatial secondary task (e.g., the movement of the arm of the subject in a box). Overall, the results have shown that visual and spatial tasks rely on different components, because they are subject to selective interference with the secondary task tapping the same modality.

In the neuropsychological context several studies have investigated visuo-spatial processing, but a double dissociation between visual and spatial processing has been demonstrated only recently. In 1988, Farah, Hammond, Levine, and Calvanio described a patient, LH, showing a deficit in visual tasks, such as shape, colour or size judgements; conversely, LH performed flawlessly in spatial tasks, such as recall of spatial pathway or Brooks' task (1968). In contrast, Luzzatti et al. (1998) described the patient EP presenting a deficit in spatial tasks associated with a diagnosis of topographical amnesia, as described by De Renzi, Faglioni, and Villa (1977), associated with a normal performance in visual tasks.

Taken together, these results indicate that the distinction reported by Ungerleider and Mishkin (1982; see also Levine, Warach, & Farah, 1985) in the peripheral processing of visual and spatial stimuli is replicated at higher processing levels; in particular, VSWM comprises two subsystems at least partially independent for processing visual and spatial information.

Recent research has also suggested that it is possible to fragment, in a more articulated way, the structure of VSWM: in particular the spatial component has been investigated in order to distinguish the processing of coordinate and categorical spatial information, and to distinguish between spatial sequential and simultaneous processing. Kosslyn (1994; Kosslyn et al., 1995) suggested that the elaboration of categorical spatial relations (e.g., right of, above) is independent from the analysis of coordinate spatial relations (e.g., spatial information that is related to a specific metric measure) both in terms of cognitive processes and in terms of anatomical localisation. Furthermore, Pazzaglia and Cornoldi (1999) hypothesise a distinction between spatially based sequential tasks (e.g., the Corsi blocks) and simultaneous tasks (e.g., the recall of the position of objects simultaneously presented in a matrix).

Passive storage and active processing in VSWM. As we suggested earlier, VSWM processes may be distinguished according to the degree of associated activity. In particular, there may be a distinction between (1) the simple recall of previously acquired information, and (2) the integration and manipulation of information to produce an output that is substantially different from the original inputs (whether coming from sensory perception or long-term storage). As outlined in more detail later in this chapter, passive storage functions may be relatively spared in people who have experienced a decrease in their active VSWM abilities (Cornoldi, 1995; Vecchi, Monticelli, & Cornoldi, 1995), whereas active processing functions are more sensitive to deterioration and to individual differences (e.g., Salthouse & Mitchell, 1989; Vecchi, 1998). These effects cannot simply be interpreted in terms of higher complexity of the active tasks, as both passive and active tasks can vary in complexity to an extent that makes either overload the system capacity. Moreover, Cornoldi and Rigoni (1999) presented a single-case study of a child with non-verbal learning disability who performed well on active measures of mental rotation and transformation, but poorly on passive recall of visuo-spatial matrices or spatial positions.

There is unlikely to be a pure dichotomy between passive storage and active processing in VSWM. Many active VSWM tasks may be dependent in part on passive visuo-spatial memory. This would explain why very few selective deficits of passive visuo-spatial processes have been reported. A patient with a selective deficit of active processing of visuo-spatial materials is reported by Morton and Morris (1995). The patient suffered a left parieto-occipital lesion, and presented a selective deficit in the visuo-spatial rotation and scanning of figures with a spared performance in more peripheral tasks.

Also, as we have suggested, it is possible to hypothesise that passive and active processes are positioned along a continuum of processing where passive storage, closely related to modality-specific sensory systems, is fairly independent from central processes; on the other hand, the more that stimuli have to be integrated, modified or transformed, the greater the demands on central/coordinative functions.

The distinction between passive storage and active processing has been found to be particularly relevant in individual-differences studies, e.g., in predicting visuo-spatial abilities in the case of developmental modifications, gender differences, or congenitally blind limitations. Such results will be described in detail in the following sections and thus will not be outlined here.

Assessment of VSWM

In order to look at the nature of differences in visuo-spatial working memory it is important to have reliable and valid methods of assessment. In fact there are no standardised tests of VSWM, and no agreed format that such tests should follow. A number of tests of visuo-spatial *short-term memory* are available, e.g., the Corsi block test, the Doors and People test (Baddeley, Emslie, & Nimmo-Smith, 1994), the Visual Patterns test (Della Sala, Gray, Baddeley, & Wilson, 1997). These correspond more to the idea of "passive visuo-spatial processing" outlined earlier, as they do not require an active manipulation of stimuli. Of course, most memory tasks require some sort of active processing in the form of mental rehearsal. However, the lack of requirements to transform information means that active processing load is relatively low in such tasks.

These tasks therefore do not tap simultaneous visuo-spatial processing and storage, as required for a *working* memory test. In order to overcome this problem, a number of tasks have been proposed in recent literature as measures of VSWM, and some of them are now described and evaluated. It is important to establish that the tasks are tackled using visuo-spatial rather than verbal strategies, and that simultaneous storage and processing are involved.

1. Shah and Miyake (1996) spatial working memory task. In this task subjects are shown a series of letters, varying in terms of orientation to vertical, and whether the letter is "normal" or its mirror image. For each letter, subjects judge whether or not it is mirror-imaged, and at the end of the series recall the orientation of each letter. Both the processing (mental rotation to evaluate whether or not letter is the right way round) and storage (recall of orientation) components of this task appear visuo-spatial in nature, although it is possible that orientation could be memorised using verbal codes. Evidence to support the validity of this task comes from significant correlations with visuo-spatial but not verbal ability measures. However, it would be useful to have further information to validate the task: do the processing and storage components interfere with each other; and is the task selectively disrupted by secondary visuo-spatial tasks? Also, the task is very demanding, and would have to be adapted if used on populations other than undergraduates.

2. Self-ordered pointing tasks: both visual and spatial versions have been used, mainly to assess memory in patient populations. The visual self-ordered pointing task has been claimed to assess visual working memory (Petrides & Milner, 1982). Subjects are presented with a booklet of 12 pages: on each page there are 12 visual patterns, designed to be difficult to label verbally. Each page has the same 12 patterns, but in a different spatial order on the page. The task is to point to a pattern on the first page of the booklet, then a different pattern on the next page of the booklet, and so on, until the final page is reached. Good performance would be indicated by pointing to a different pattern on each page, i.e., selecting each of the 12 patterns only once. An analogous spatial working memory task has been administered as part of the CANTAB battery of neuropsychological tests (see e.g., Owen et al., 1990). Subjects are required to search through a number of boxes presented on a computer screen to find a hidden "token". Once found, another token is hidden in a different box, and the task continues until a token is found in each box. The visuo-spatial *processing* involved in these self-ordered pointing tasks is minimal, the main demands being on storage of patterns or locations. The tasks depend more on effective search strategies than on capacity limitations of VSWM, and there is evidence that many subjects use verbal strategies, at least on the visual self-ordered pointing task (Daigneault & Braun, 1993). More evidence is needed to validate these tasks as measures of VSWM.

3. Corsi distance estimation task (Phillips et al., in prep). In this task, visuo-spatial working memory is assessed by adapting the established Corsi block spatial short-term memory measure to include a processing component. Nine "blocks" are presented on a computer screen and two are then highlighted; subjects must estimate how far apart the blocks are. Another pair of blocks are then highlighted, and distance must again be estimated. Then subjects are asked to recall which blocks were highlighted. The sequence of blocks increases in length, and span is assessed as the maximum length that can be accurately recalled. Validity of the task as a measure of VSWM was shown in terms of

selective correlations with visuo-spatial but not verbal processing, and interference with a spatial secondary task. Also, the requirement to estimate distances reduced Corsi span, indicating a common resource used in both storage and processing components of the task.

4. Jigsaw task (Vecchi & Richardson, 2000). In this task, participants are asked to solve jigsaw puzzles consisting of various numbers of pieces without actually touching or moving the pieces in question. Each piece is numbered, the participants are given a prepared response sheet showing the original outline of the completed puzzle, and they are instructed to write down the numbers corresponding to the pieces in the correct spatial positions. Performance is evaluated in terms of the percentage of correct responses and the time needed to solve each of the puzzles. Several variables can be manipulated for experimental purposes, i.e., the processing load related to the number of pieces, the visual complexity of the pictures, and the rotation of the pieces. In principle, these variables represent three different kinds of complexity with regard to (a) the number of units that the system can process at any one time (number of pieces), (b) the properties of the object (overall visual complexity), and (c) the properties of the pieces (rotation), respectively. This methodology possesses good ecological validity and also appears to be sensitive in identifying individual differences.

5. Mental pathway task (Kerr, 1987; Vecchi et al., 1995). In this task, participants are required mentally to form an image of a two-dimensional or a three-dimensional square matrix and then, from a designated starting point, to follow a series of directions. Directions could be right–left, forward–backward, and up–down (for three-dimensional matrices only). Participants have to form a pathway through the imagined matrix and later to point at the square representing the end of the pathway in a completely blank matrix that is visually presented. This methodology has been one of the first to be used specifically to investigate the active processing component of VSWM.

THE STUDY OF INDIVIDUAL DIFFERENCES IN VSWM

This section will describe differences in VSWM as studied in relation to child development, specific visuo-spatial learning difficulties, or unusually strong visuo-spatial memory, old age, gender, and blind individuals.

Age differences in VSWM: Theoretical issues

It is well established that visuo-spatial memory and cognition change through childhood and late adulthood, although the extent to which the visuo-spatial changes can be differentiated from verbal changes remains a matter of debate. Across childhood there is an increase in the capacity to remember visual and spatial information (e.g., Miles, Morgan, Milne, & Morris, 1996). Also visual and spatial short-term memory declines with age (e.g., in terms of remembering items on a map, locations of objects, routes, or visual patterns, see Hess & Pullen, 1996). There are also age-related changes in visuo-spatial processing (e.g., speed of mental rotation, performance on spatial intelligence tests). Although few studies have explicitly looked at both changes across childhood and in later life, many of the theoretical issues raised in the literature on these two topics overlap. The themes running through such research include: whether age changes are caused by general or specific resources; the distinction between passive and active memory; and whether changes reflect capacity changes or the use of different types of task strategy.

Developmental differences in children

The investigation of developmental differences in VSWM has concentrated on two main theoretical issues: (1) the study of the general or specific cognitive resources related to the development of VSWM; (2) the specific investigation of differential development of separate components of VSWM. In the former case, the study of VSWM in relation to other cognitive systems aims to uncover whether its development is independent of, or related to, more general aspects of cognitive development. In the latter case, the study of VSWM *per se* allows identification of the VSWM components (or functions) that are greatly affected in child development.

General or specific resources.   When studying the development of VSWM, there is variation between children falling within the same age group, as well as developmental changes in the execution of VSWM tasks. In relation to both individual differences and developmental changes, the study of correlations among tasks allows investigation of the general-resources or specific-modality nature of cognitive development.

Swanson (1996) found that verbal WM (e.g., word span, story recall, semantic associations) and visuo-spatial WM (e.g., matrix recall, spatial position recall, memory for abstract scrawls) were generally intercorrelated in children, and predicted performance on a range of ability tests, for example the Detroit Test of Learning Aptitude (Hammill, 1985) or the Kaufman Assessment Battery for Children (Kaufman & Kaufman, 1983). Also, chronological age (range 5–19) correlated at an equivalent level with verbal and visuo-spatial WM measures. Swanson concluded that developmental improvements in WM were largely attributable to general capacity and not to specific verbal or visuo-spatial processes. It was further concluded that the development of WM could be related to the increasing capacity to integrate or coordinate information and processes within the system (Swanson, 1996). Other theories have preferred to focus on the idea that WM limitations in children are related to the inability to inhibit irrelevant information (Brainerd & Reyna, 1993; Dempster, 1992).

Evidence that WM development can be explained by the capacity to integrate information and to coordinate processes comes from a study from Yee, Hunt, and Pellegrino (1991) who argue that developmental changes are more evident in tasks that require extensive coordination between different processes, rather than conditions that simply make high demands on attentional resources.

Development of VSWM.   Although some studies have suggested that aspects of VSWM change little in children (for example, memorising the spatial position of objects, Hasher & Zacks, 1979), recent studies have shown that most VSWM capacities evolve with age (e.g., Conte, Cornoldi, Pazzaglia, & Sanavio, 1995). These authors have shown that children's performance increases significantly from 7 to 11 years old in a series of tasks tapping VSWM, such as recall of spatial positions or solution of a jigsaw puzzle. There have been several attempts to relate the development of VSWM and the use of mental images with intellectual development in children (Piaget & Inhelder, 1966). Despite the fact that imagery abilities develop with age (e.g., Kosslyn et al., 1990) young children tend to use visual representations in processing information more than adults do (Kosslyn, 1980). Mental images created by children under 7 years of age are mostly static, perhaps paralleling the difficulty that children experience in understanding the conservation of quantity when varying the perceptual appearance of the substance (Piaget & Inhelder, 1955).

A key theoretical issue concerning developmental changes in VSWM is whether such changes can best be explained in terms of differences in "capacity" (suggesting a fairly low-level limitation on processing resources) or "strategies" (suggesting relatively high-level variation in the generation and implementation of knowledge). Some authors argue that childhood increases in cognitive performance are best explained in terms of extended capacity (Halford, 1982) or ultimately faster processing speed (Kail, 1993), while others argue that capacity remains constant, but increased knowledge and experience over time allow more efficient use of strategies (Anderson, 1992; Case, 1985).

A study by Kosslyn and colleagues (Kosslyn et al., 1990) found age differences in comparing the performance of 6-, 8-, and 14-year-old children in a battery of tasks tapping VSWM (or visual buffer functioning as the authors described it originally), such as mental rotation or generation, maintenance, and scanning of mental images. Several studies have shown that children are able to perform computationally complex visuo-spatial processing tasks, such as mental rotation (Marmor, 1975, 1977), although requiring a longer time to perform the tasks than adults.

However, young children can show performance similar to adults in tasks requiring only passive storage of visuo-spatial material when specifically trained to use effective strategies (Kosslyn, 1980). The spontaneous use of efficient strategies to integrate and coordinate different information develops in a further stage, after 8 years of age. The capacity to perform complex VSWM tasks (e.g., mental rotation) relates to the ability to use correctly the spatial terms "right" and "left". Benton (1959) and Corballis and Beale (1976) have shown that this ability normally develops in children between 7 and 11 years old. A similar pattern of development is evident when measuring the ability to rotate letters or to recognise mirror images (e.g., Braine, 1978; Vogel, 1980). Furthermore, children's performance in topographical memory tasks is poor before 8 years of age, both in orienting in a real environment and in recognising places; on the contrary 12-year-old children present performance similar to the adults (Cornell, Heth, & Alberts, 1994). The close relation between the use of "left" and "right" and the development of visuo-spatial ability gains support from a study by Roberts and Aman (1993), in which 6- and 8-year-old children were tested in spatial orientation and mental rotation tasks which required imagining rotation of one's own body. Results showed that only the children who were able to use the spatial terms correctly performed well in the rotation tasks, and in only these children was rotation time related to the angle of rotation, as reported in research with adults.

Young children have the capacity to generate mental images and to perform simple visuo-spatial tasks (Hitch, Woodin, & Baker, 1989), but this passive storage capacity later develops into the ability to integrate and manipulate information in parallel with the development of verbal ability. In relation to models of working memory (Baddeley & Hitch, 1974; Logie, 1995) this suggests that development is largely a function of increased knowledge and improved central executive function, rather than changes in subsidiary articulatory or visuo-spatial buffers. In Piagetian terms, the unfolding of the operational stage of thought (Piaget & Inhelder, 1955) will lead to a greater ability to process and transform information, and will result in the development of complex visuo-spatial processes.

Recent studies have suggested the possibility of differentiating more specific components within VSWM in relation to development: visual (related to object recall), sequential spatial (related, for example, to the recall of sequential spatial positions, as in the Corsi test), or simultaneous spatial (e.g., recall of spatial positions in a chess board). Evidence in favour of this distinction has been reported both in analysing the normal pattern of cognitive development (Logie & Pearson, 1997) and considering the performance of single cases with specific visuo-spatial deficits (Cornoldi, Rigoni, Tressoldi, & Vio, 1999).

VSWM in older adults

VSWM appears to be multicomponential, and modifies in function from childhood to adolescence. In this section we will analyse the changes in VSWM functioning that occur at the opposite end of the age spectrum. The ageing process results in poorer performance on at least some aspects of cognitive function (Craik, 1977; Craik & Salthouse, 1992; Poon, 1985), even if the underlying nature and characteristics of the deficits are still unclear.

Central or peripheral deficits?   Welford, in 1958, hypothesised that ageing resulted in reduced capacity to coordinate and organise information in memory. His ideas are clearly consistent with an impairment in the central elaboration components of working memory. Further, other research has shown that age-related memory deficits are dependent on the specific type of task used. There is generally age-stability on tasks of relatively passive short-term memory; but age-related decline on active tasks tapping working memory (for review see Craik & Jennings, 1992). Increasing the executive load of tasks exacerbates age differences, but increasing passive memory load does not (Gick, Craik, & Morris, 1988). This suggests that age changes are linked to tasks that demand active, central processes of cognition.

Older adults have been proposed to show a reduced capacity to inhibit irrelevant information while performing a cognitive task (e.g., Hasher & Zacks, 1988). However, Salthouse and Meinz (1995) showed that the poorer inhibition explained only a very small part of age-related variance in cognition, and that more variance (80%) was explained by a more general factor, speed of information processing. Salthouse and colleagues (e.g., Salthouse, 1994, 1996; Salthouse & Coon, 1993; Salthouse & Meinz, 1995) have repeatedly argued that speed of processing is the main factor affecting older adults' performance on cognitive tasks. Elderly people process information at a slower rate (e.g., Cerella, 1991; Rabbitt, 1981; Salthouse, 1982) and this deficit relates to overall cognitive performance.

Verbal or visuo-spatial deficits?   In relation to adult ageing, it has been argued that age deficits are larger for spatial than verbal tests (e.g., Schaie, 1983). However, it now seems likely that, for example, the differential age deficits on Performance as opposed to Verbal scales of the Wechsler Adult Intelligence Scales reflect the novelty of the tasks rather than the non-verbal nature of the processing involved. Also, verbal and visuo-spatial memory measures do not appear to be distinguishable in terms of their relationship with adult age (Salthouse, 1994; Smith & Earles, 1996). Many authors have reported parallel age-related decline in verbal and visuo-spatial performance (e.g., Shelton, Parsons, & Leber, 1982; Winograd, Smith, & Simon, 1982). Moreover, studies examining the percentage of variance explained by different tasks (e.g., Salthouse, 1994, 1996) suggest a general cognitive deficit and not a modality-specific or specific subsystem one. A problem with such findings is the difficulty of matching verbal and visuo-spatial tasks in terms of complexity. Tubi and Calev (1989) matched the distribution of performance of the elderly on verbal and visuo-spatial tasks, to exclude an overall complexity effect, and found that older adults experienced more difficulty with visuo-spatial tasks. Further, age differences in reasoning tasks such as Raven's Matrices overlap more with visuo-spatial than verbal working memory (Phillips & Forshaw, 1998).

The experimental tasks used to measure verbal abilities are usually more familiar than the tasks used to assess visuo-spatial abilities, and older adults may therefore find the latter more taxing. In fact, although visuo-spatial abilities are largely used in everyday life (e.g., to drive a car, to orient in a city, to remember where an object is), the experimental procedures to assess this ability often require participants to memorise complex matrices, to rotate nonsense figures etc. These are highly non-ecological tasks (in contrast to verbal tasks such as memory for sentences or reading) and could distort the performance of older adults, who appear to be more sensitive to environmental and emotional conditions (Baltes & Baltes, 1990). Moreover, in the last few decades several factors may have improved the visuo-spatial capacity of young adults (the role of television, of video games, or simply the now almost universal capacity to drive vehicles) when compared to older cohorts educated 40 or 50 years ago.

Most visuo-spatial memory tests use abstract stimuli, and therefore adult age-related declines in visuo-spatial memory have been explained in terms of less efficient processing strategies to deal with context-free information (Arbuckle, Cooney, Milne, & Melchior, 1994; Hess & Pullen, 1996). Evidence supports the role of context, familiarity, and knowledge in reducing age deficits in memory for spatial layouts of supermarkets (Kirasic, 1991), visual scenes (Smith, Park, Cherry, & Berkovsky, 1990), location of landmarks (Waddell & Rogoff, 1981), location of household objects (Hess & Slaughter, 1990), spatial layouts of homes (Arbuckle et al., 1994), and memory for routes (Lipman, 1991). In reviewing this literature, Hess and Pullen (1996) conclude that older adults use well developed strategies to remember familiar material, but are poor at formulating strategies for novel visuo-spatial memory tasks. However, some studies have found no evidence for differential improvement for older adults when context information is increased (e.g., Frieske & Park, 1993; Zelinski, 1988).

In conclusion, results do not indicate a clear selective VSWM deficit, although older adults may experience difficulty in the execution of visuo-spatial tasks due to the high processing demands of such tasks, or lack of familiarity with the material.

The role of experience. Visuo-spatial abilities can be greatly influenced by subjective experience, either by the use of specific strategies or simply by more frequent use. While studying the effect of ageing on cognitive performance it is important to evaluate the extent to which experience is related to cognitive change. To this end it is possible to suggest two alternative hypotheses: "preserved differentiation" vs. "differential preservation" (Salthouse, 1991).

• Preserved differentiation: Differences between good and poor visuo-spatial performers are maintained constant across age. There is a decrease in cognitive abilities affecting all individuals to approximately the same extent.

• Differential preservation: Differences between good and poor performers tend to increase with age, such that those with poor VSWM when young will have little practice at VSWM tasks across the lifespan, and therefore will show greater decrements with age. Better strategies and frequent use should reduce the negative effect of age.

To test these hypotheses Salthouse et al. (1990) selected both young and older architects who could be assumed to have high visualisation abilities and frequent practice in the performance of demanding visuo-spatial tasks. Results showed that the architects always had better performance than the control group, but also that age-related cognitive decline was independent of the level of visuo-spatial abilities: both architects and controls showed similarly reduced performance with age. Thus, experience and familiarity improved performance, but did not reduce cognitive decline in VSWM.

One explanation for the differences reported in the ability of older adults to utilise visuo-spatial strategies is the "disuse hypothesis" of ageing, which proposes that age-related deficits reflect increased time elapsed since schooling and/or relevant cognitive activity in the workplace. In order to test this hypothesis, Lindenberger, Kliegl, and Baltes (1992) evaluated performance of younger and older graphic designers on the method of loci mnemonic. Despite the fact that the older graphic designers were still making extensive day-to-day use of visuo-spatial skills, there was still a marked age deficit in performance on the method of loci task. These results therefore support a capacity limitation or "preserved differentiation" view of age differences in visuo-spatial memory.

Active and passive visuo-spatial processes and ageing.   In the initial part of this chapter we described the difference between passive storage and active processing of visuo-spatial material. Older adults seem to be selectively poorer at tasks that require the integration of information or coordination of different processes. Salthouse and Mitchell (1989) differentiate structural and operational capacities in VSWM, a distinction that parallels the passive/active one. In fact, they defined structural capacity as the "amount of information that can be stored while performing the task" (p. 18) and operational capacity as the "amount of processing required to perform the task" (p. 18). Following the results of an experiment by Salthouse (1987), in which elderly people were differentially poor at tasks requiring active processing, Salthouse and Mitchell (1989) devised tasks that discriminate between *passive* recall of segments in a unique stimulus and *active* integration of segments in a 4 × 4 matrix. Older participants did not show any deficit in the passive task, but were significantly poorer at the active task. A similar result was obtained by Morris, Gick, and Craik (1988) in a sentence analysis task: although the oldest participants required longer to perform the task, the presence of a passive interfering task impaired both groups to the same extent. Evidence so far reported suggests a selective deficit in active processing with ageing. However, Salthouse, Babcock, and Shaw (1991) did not replicate the results obtained two years before (Salthouse & Mitchell, 1989), which could be due to variations in the type and presentation of material being used.

A related distinction has been identified by Mayr, Kliegl, and colleagues. They propose that there are two factors underlying age differences in working memory: sequential and coordinative complexity (Mayr & Kliegl, 1993; Mayr,

Kliegl, & Krampe, 1996). Sequential complexity is determined by the number of independent processing components involved in a task, while coordinative complexity is determined by demands for information flow between task components. Sequential complexity is associated with information-processing speed (usually seen as a capacity deficit), while coordinative complexity relates to more "executive" deficits, e.g., task switching, inhibition etc.

Mayr et al. (1996) contrast performance of children, young adults, and older adults on sequential and coordinative dimensions. They provide evidence that children are poorer at dealing with both sequential and coordinative complexity than young adults; however, coordinative function is particularly poor in children. In older adults, both sequential and coordinative functions appear impaired in comparison to the young adults. A distinction can be made in that the age deficits in sequential tasks relate to processing speed, while those in coordinative tasks do not (Mayr & Kliegl, 1993). Mayr et al. (1996) specifically compared the visuo-spatial working memory performance of children, young adults, and older adults in relation to the theory that a single processing parameter could explain developmental changes throughout the age spectrum (Kail & Salthouse, 1994). When older adults and children were compared, the oldest participants were better at sequential processing than 7-year-old children, but worse at coordinative processing. Mayr et al. argued that differences in sequential processing (perhaps dependent on processing speed) may be one factor that is common to cognitive development in childhood and to cognitive ageing; however, an additional factor in ageing is the ability to coordinate multiple task elements.

Deficits and expertise in VSWM

Studies with children presenting specific deficits in visuo-spatial abilities have been very fruitful in understanding the development of VSWM. In particular, children affected by non-verbal learning disability (Rourke, 1989; Rourke & Finlayson, 1978) show normal performance in verbal tasks along with poor scores on visuo-spatial and mathematical tasks, and a large discrepancy between verbal and performance IQ. Cornoldi, Dalla Vecchia, and Tressoldi (1995) analysed the performance of 37 low visuo-spatial intelligence children, ranging from 10 to 14 years old, in a series of tasks designed to assess the ability both to memorise passively and to manipulate visuo-spatial stimuli. The results showed a selective impairment in active processing tasks (e.g., solving jigsaw puzzles or following a pathway in a matrix) when their performance was compared to normal children of the same age. This result parallels the visuo-spatial deficit resulting from the ageing process, and suggests separate development processes for passive and active abilities in VSWM. The latter abilities are greatly affected by the presence of non-verbal learning disabilities and by normal ageing.

There are also some reports of individuals who show extraordinarily good visuo-spatial memory, although there has been little attempt systematically to assess the visuo-spatial nature of such manifestations. For example, Sacks (1985; see also Hermelin & O'Connor, 1990) reports that autistic individuals who can carry out remarkable feats of calendrical calculation (e.g., rapid production of a day of the week in response to a random date) appear to retrieve the numbers from an elaborate stored visual image. Such an image would have to contain a very large amount of visual information, well beyond the normal recognised capacities for VSWM. Also, Luria described a "mnemonist", S, who could retain vast amounts of information, purportedly through visual images. Luria tested the memory of S largely through verbal materials, but argues that "the *visual quality of his recall* was fundamental to his capacity for remembering words" (Luria, 1968/1987, p. 30, original italics). Errors of recall tended to show visual rather than acoustic confusions (e.g., reporting 3 rather than 8). Luria argues that the incredible memory feats shown by S are likely to be the result of innate predisposition to high memory capacity, synaesthesia resulting in multiple coding of stimuli, and repeated practice of visual imagery techniques to aid recall. It would be interesting in future studies to look in detail at the visuo-spatial nature of memory performance in individuals of unusually high memory capacity.

There is also evidence that individuals differ considerably in their ability to use VSWM in everyday situations (Cohen, 1996). Kozlowski and Bryant (1977) found that a constellation of spatial abilities correlated to form a good "sense of direction", such as accuracy of pointing to locations not currently visible, estimating distances, and remembering routes experienced as a car passenger. When taken on an unfamiliar route, those with a good sense of direction were initially no better at locating the start from the end point; however, over repeated trials they learned spatial information more efficiently. This suggests that such individuals differ in their ability or motivation to integrate spatial information and use good visuo-spatial strategies. Thorndyke and Stasz (1980) looked at map learning, and found that those with high visual memory scores learned most information from a map. Good map-learners allocated attention efficiently, used effective encoding strategies, and self-tested their knowledge during trials. Ability to use visuo-spatial information effectively is therefore likely to depend on VSWM capacity, motivation, and aptitude to develop and use effective visuo-spatial strategies.

Gender differences in VSWM

In cognitive psychology many studies have investigated differences between males and females. In particular, differences between the execution of verbal and visuo-spatial tasks have been frequently reported (see Richardson, 1991, for a review). In this section we will review research dealing with this aspect and with the possibility that gender differences are related to the characteristics of the tasks rather than to the characteristics of the material.

Verbal and visuo-spatial tasks.   Studies in this field are extremely numerous. Here, we will briefly consider some studies that have greatly influenced cognitive theories. Females are better at verbal fluency or recalling words (e.g., Cohen, Schaie, & Gribbin, 1977; Hyde, 1981; Maccoby & Jacklin, 1974), even if the result is not always confirmed in developmental studies with children and sometimes differences are not evident until adolescence (e.g., Anastasi, 1981; Kaufman & Doppelt, 1977; Maccoby & Jacklin, 1974). In contrast, visuo-spatial tasks are generally performed better by males (e.g., Cohen et al., 1977; Maccoby & Jacklin, 1974). Males are better in spatial orientation (Oltman, 1968), in mental rotation and transformation tasks (Harshman, Hampson, & Berembaum, 1983; Linn & Petersen, 1985; Newcombe, 1982), and in recognising artificial movements (Price & Goodale, 1988). Several hypotheses have been proposed in order to explain these results: In particular, a biological explanation related to the amount of sex hormones (e.g., Broverman et al., 1981) or to genetic differences (e.g., Dawson, 1972; McGee, 1979), and a socio-cultural explanation (e.g., Baenninger & Newcombe, 1989; Richardson, 1994) have been proposed.

Thus, empirical evidence clearly indicates that gender differences in verbal and visuo-spatial tasks do exist, although recent attempts to investigate this phenomenon emphasise the need to use coherent theoretical frameworks to identify the critical factors (Linn & Petersen, 1985; Voyer, Voyer, & Bryden, 1995). Both Linn and Petersen and Voyer et al. carried out meta-analyses incorporating the results of 50 years of research and found that the magnitude of gender differences varies according to task-specific factors. Gender differences in visuo-spatial skills therefore cannot be considered as a whole, but as a collection of specific abilities which emerge from at least partially independent cognitive processes.

Gender differences and the nature of visuo-spatial processing.   Harshman and Paivio (1987; Paivio & Harshman, 1983) noted that males were better than females in mental rotation and transformation tasks, but that females outperformed males in passive recall and vividness ratings tasks. In particular, females are better than males in recall of judgements of visual characteristics of objects (McKelvie, 1986; Sheehan, 1967). The meta-analysis carried out by Linn and Petersen (1985) again showed a male superiority in manipulation or transformation of mental images. A similar pattern has been reported by Voyer et al. (1995) who showed that male superiority is clear in mental rotation and transformation of images, present but less evident in spatial perception, and rather questionable in spatial visualisation tasks.

This pattern of results is consistent with the findings of Harshman et al. (1983). They looked at male/female differences on 12 spatial ability tests such as surface development folding test, embedded figures tests, rotation and spatial relations tasks, and drawing tasks. They found a male superiority in tasks requiring rotation, transformation, or organisation of spatial information, and a female advantage in figure recognition or size judgement tasks. All subjects performed similarly when required to compare the angles sustained by the hands of analogue clocks. In sum, females performed better than males in tasks that can be defined as static imagery tests, while males showed a superiority in dynamic imagery tests.

A recent study by Vecchi and Girelli (1998) investigated gender differences in passive and active visuo-spatial abilities by using the matrices–mental-pathway tasks described previously. There were no gender differences in recall of spatial positions, but males outperformed females when subjects had to follow a pathway in an imagined matrix. These results support Paivio and Clark's hypothesis (1991) that gender differences in visuo-spatial tasks can be explained in terms of the amount of active processing being required (or in terms of dynamic imagery, using Paivio and Clark's original definition): male advantage in tasks requiring active processing contrasted with a lack of a gender effect (or indeed an inversion of the male advantage) in passive tasks, regardless of their complexity.

Studies with congenitally blind people

In this section we will examine the ability of blind individuals to create and manipulate mental images and the limitations they experience in performing visuo-spatial tasks.

Mental images and blindness.   The fact that congenitally blind people are able to use mental images is counterintuitive if it is assumed that mental images act as a mere buffer for visual perception. On the contrary, if mental images are internal representations (i) generated from information derived from sensory modalities or from long-term memory, and/or (ii) generated from information that is not exclusively coming from visual perception, then there is no contradiction in blind people's use of mental images.

Many studies confirm the similarities between sighted and blind people's use of mental images (e.g., Jonides, Kahn, & Rozin, 1975; Kerr, 1983; Marmor, 1978). Several studies have shown this result and one of the first and most significant investigations was carried out by Marmor and Zaback (1976), later replicated by Carpenter and Eisemberg (1978). The authors adapted the Shepard and Metzler mental rotation task (1971) using tactile presentation and they found that, as in the original condition, the times required to perform the identity judgements are related to the angle of rotation. Recent research has confirmed this result, and also concluded that mental rotation is slower when it is not based on visual perception (Barolo, Masini, & Antonietti, 1990).

Blind people could form visuo-spatial images using haptic, verbal, or motor information. These mental representations can be used to store and maintain visuo-spatial information as well as to orient in space and generate spatial maps (see

Loomis et al., 1993). Despite this apparent efficiency, blind people perform more poorly than sighted individuals (e.g., Rieser et al., 1992), particularly when a task requires updating and transformation of mental representations (Rieser, Guth, & Hill, 1986). Several hypotheses have been suggested to interpret these limitations, either referring to an underlying brain damage (Stuart, 1995) or to a lack of appropriate strategies (Thinus-Blanc & Gaunet, 1997).

VSWM limitations in blind people.   The studies investigating VSWM characteristics and limitations in blind people are very few and this may be due to both the difficulty of recruiting participants and the lack of appropriate experimental procedures to investigate visuo-spatial abilities in blindness. In this section we will focus on studies carried out by Cornoldi and colleagues on congenitally blind individuals, i.e., those who were blind from birth in the absence of neurological damage.

Cornoldi, Cortesi, and Preti (1991) adapted for presentation to blind people the mental pathway methodology used by Kerr (1987) to assess VSWM capacity to process two- and three-dimensional stimuli of different levels of complexity. Kerr (1987) reported that, in a task requiring mental pathways through an imagined matrix, subjects' capacity was defined by the number of units per spatial dimension and not by the overall number of units. She suggested three units per dimension as the capacity limit for visuo-spatial processing (matrix $3 \times 3 = 9$ possible positions; matrix $3 \times 3 \times 3 = 27$ possible positions). It is interesting to note that, in Kerr's study (1987), the number of dimensions did not seem to affect subjects' performance. In contrast, Cornoldi et al. (1991) showed that blind people experienced great difficulty in processing three-dimensional stimuli and their performance was significantly lower than the sighted's in the haptic version of the test. Blind individuals' selective difficulty in using three-dimensional material was confirmed by a study that has highlighted the importance of the rate of presentation of the stimuli (Cornoldi, Bertuccelli, Rocchi, & Sbrana, 1993): When instructions were given at a faster rate (one per second instead of the usual two per second rate) performance of the blind participants was particularly poor.

More recent research has tried to apply the passive store vs. active processing distinction to blind people. Vecchi et al. (1995) used two- and three-dimensional matrices on which subjects had to perform a passive task (memory for spatial positions of target cubes) and an active task (mentally follow a pathway). The results indicated comparable performance of blind and sighted subjects in the passive task while the active task was selectively impaired in the blind subjects. Poor performance in response to three-dimensional stimuli was again replicated. This pattern of results was confirmed by a recent study by Vecchi (1998). Moreover, this study excluded the possibility that blind people were using a verbal strategy to carry out the task, as an articulatory suppression interference task affected both groups to the same extent.

In conclusion, blind people show the capacity to process visuo-spatial information in working memory, although their performance is often lower than that of sighted individuals. Limitations on VSWM in blind individuals are particularly evident when the task requires processing of complex material or dealing with three-dimensional patterns. Blind and sighted subjects seem to rely on similar VSWM strategies, with neither of the groups adopting a verbal strategy to carry out the tasks. Vision could be considered as the "preferred modality" to process visuo-spatial information, even if VSWM is able to process information coming from other sensory modalities, such as tactile experience. The amount of active processing seems to be the variable most affecting performance of blind individuals, while passive storage is less sensitive to visual impairment.

CONCLUSIONS

The present chapter has reviewed a series of important studies on individual differences in VSWM. As VSWM is considered to have an important role in a variety of human behaviours, we can expect that these individual differences affect people's behaviour in a large range of activities (Logie, 1995). For example Conte and Cornoldi (1997) have found that children with higher VSWM were better than other children matched for verbal ability in orienting themselves in an indoor environment, and also in remembering scenes from a movie. Similarly, Pazzaglia and Cornoldi (1999) found that university students with higher VSWM had better memory for a spatial description. This suggests that some visuo-spatial processing difficulties in everyday contexts can be expected in other groups with poor VSWM, such as non-verbal learning-disabled people, blind and elderly individuals.

In reviewing individual differences in VSWM we started with general visuo-spatial ability differences, an issue that has been discussed in the scientific literature for about 50 years, but without a specific reference to an architectural view of mind or to the nature of cognitive activity. The data discussed here suggest that visuo-spatial processes can be differentiated according to the nature of the processes and/or structure of interest. In fact, data showing that single patients or specific groups of subjects are poor in some VSWM tasks but not others offer evidence against the assumption that visuo-spatial ability is globally compromised.

In organising our data, we made reference to three views of VSWM, the working memory model (e.g., Baddeley, 1986), the mental imagery perspective (e.g., Kosslyn, 1994) and the continuum approach (Cornoldi & Vecchi, 2000). In our opinion, the three views are not incompatible, but rather have different emphases. For this reason, it is not easy to evaluate which view fits better with data collected by research in the field, despite the fact that each of them seems particularly adequate for specific subsets of data.

Furthermore the three views all concur with the conclusion that different components and/or processes must be differentiated within VSWM. The evidence presented here supports the distinction between visual and spatial components, which could be interpreted either along a horizontal continuum (Cornoldi, 1995) or with reference to different VSWM components (Logie, 1995). Furthermore, spatial processes seem open to further fractionation, such as that between spatial sequential and spatial simultaneous processes compatible within the horizontal continuum (Pazzaglia & Cornoldi, 1999) or that between spatial categorical and spatial coordinate subsystems proposed within the Kosslyn (1994) framework. Another key issue concerns the degree of active control required by the VSWM task, as it has been shown that some groups of subjects failing in active tasks do not fail in passive/storage VSWM tasks. The theoretical implications of these results can be interpreted within the three frameworks, and in particular the working memory and the continuum models. In the classical working memory framework (e.g., Baddeley, 1986), active tasks can be classified as involving both a modality-specific slave system (the visuo-spatial sketchpad), and the amodal central executive. This suggests that the main locus of deficits is in central executive functioning. This may indeed be an appropriate explanation for the poor performance of older adults on a range of visuo-spatial and verbal active tasks. However, this cannot explain why some individuals show relatively intact performance on passive tasks involving only the visuo-spatial slave system, fail active spatial tasks, yet do well on corresponding active verbal tasks. This is, for example, the case with congenitally blind people and the pattern of performance we have observed while investigating gender differences in verbal and visuo-spatial tasks. Logie's (1995) reorganisation of the working memory perspective proposes, beside a more passive visual cache component, a more active inner scribe component which could be responsible for some active visuo-spatial tasks. The importance of distinguishing between passive and active processes is max-imised in the continuity approach (Cornoldi, 1995; Cornoldi & Vecchi, 2000), and this differentiation is not confined to visuo-spatial processing but rather applies to the whole working memory system. This allows identification of many different points on the vertical continuum and an explanation of the different extent to which people fail in tasks requiring various degrees of active manipulation.

REFERENCES

Anastasi, A. (1981). Sex differences: Historical perspectives and methodological implications. *Developmental Review, 1*, 187–206.

Anderson, M. (1992). *Intelligence and development.* Oxford: Blackwell.

Arbuckle, T.Y., Cooney, R., Milne, J., & Melchior, A. (1994). Memory for spatial layouts in relation to age and schema typicality. *Psychology and Aging, 9*, 467–480.

Baddeley, A.D. (1986). *Working memory.* Oxford: Oxford University Press.

Baddeley, A., Emslie, H., & Nimmo-Smith, I. (1994). *Doors and People Test.* Bury St Edmunds, UK: Thames Valley Test Company.

Baddeley, A.D., & Hitch, G.J. (1974). Working memory. In G. Bower (Ed.), *The psychology of learning and motivation, Vol. VIII* (pp. 47–90). New York: Academic Press.

Baddeley, A.D., & Lewis, V.J. (1981). Inner active processes in reading: The inner voice, the inner ear, and the inner eye. In A.M. Lesgold & C.A. Perfetti (Eds.), *Interactive processes in reading* (pp. 107–129). Hillsdale, NJ: Lawrence Erlbaum Associates Inc.

Baddeley, A.D., Papagno, C., & Vallar, G. (1988). When long-term memory learning depends on short-term storage. *Journal of Memory and Language, 27*, 586–595.

Baenninger, M., & Newcombe, N. (1989). The role of experience in spatial test performance: A meta-analysis. *Sex Roles, 20*, 327–344.

Baltes, P.B., & Baltes, M.M. (Eds.) (1990). *Successful aging.* Cambridge: Cambridge University Press.

Barolo, E., Masini, R., & Antonietti, A. (1990). Mental rotation of solid objects and problem-solving in sighted and blind subjects. *Journal of Mental Imagery, 14*, 65–74.

Benton, A. (1959). *Right–left discrimination and finger localisation.* New York: Hoeber-Harper.

Braine, L.G. (1978). Early stages in the perception of orientation. In M. Bornter (Ed.), *Cognitive growth and development: Essays in memory of Herbert G. Birch* (pp. 105–133). New York: Brunner/Mazel.

Brainerd, C.J., & Reyna, V.F. (1993). Domains of fuzzy trace theory. In M.L. Hove & R. Pasnak (Eds.), *Emerging themes in cognitive development* (pp. 50–93). New York: Springer-Verlag.

Brooks, L.R. (1967). The suppression of visualisation by reading. *Quarterly Journal of Experimental Psychology, 19*, 289–299.

Brooks, L.R. (1968). Spatial and verbal components in the act of recall. *Canadian Journal of Psychology, 22*, 349–368.

Broverman, D.M., Vogel, W., Klaiber, E.L., Majcher, D., Shea, D., & Paul, V. (1981). Changes to cognitive task performance across the menstrual cycle. *Journal of Comparative and Physiological Psychology, 95*, 646–654.

Carpenter, P.A., & Eisemberg, P. (1978). Mental rotation and the frame of reference in blind and sighted individuals. *Perception and Psychophysics, 23*, 117–124.

Case, R. (1985). *Intellectual development: Birth to adulthood.* London: Academic Press.

Cerella, J. (1991). Age effects may be global, not local: Comment on Fisk and Rogers (1991). *Journal of Experimental Psychology: General, 120*, 215–223.

Cohen, D., Schaie, K.W., & Gribbin, K. (1977). The organisation of spatial abilities in older men and women. *Journal of Gerontology, 32*, 578–585.

Cohen, G. (1996). *Memory in the real world* (2nd Ed.) Hove, UK: Psychology Press.

Conte, A., & Cornoldi, C. (1997). Il contributo della memoria visuospaziale alle attività della vita quotidiana. In L. Czerwinsky Domenis (Ed.), *Obiettivo bambino* (pp. 157–166). Milan: Angeli.

Conte, A., Cornoldi, C., Pazzaglia, F., & Sanavio, S. (1995). Lo sviluppo della memoria di lavoro visuospaziale e il suo ruolo nella memoria spaziale. *Ricerche di Psicologia, 19*, 95–114.

Corballis, M.C., & Beale, I.L. (1976). *The psychology of left and right.* Hillsdale, NJ: Lawrence Erlbaum Associates Inc.

Cornell, E.H., Heth, C.D., & Alberts, D.M. (1994). Place recognition and way findings by children and adults. *Memory and Cognition, 22*, 633–643.

Cornoldi, C. (1995). Memoria di lavoro visuospaziale. In F. Marucci (Ed.), *Le immagini mentali* (pp. 145–181). Roma: La Nuova Italia.

Cornoldi, C., Bertuccelli, B., Rocchi, P., & Sbrana, B. (1993). Processing capacity limitations in pictorial and spatial representations in the totally congenitally blind. *Cortex, 29*, 675–689.

Cornoldi, C., Cortesi, A., & Preti, D. (1991). Individual differences in the capacity limitations of visuo-spatial short-term memory: Research on sighted and totally congenitally blind people. *Memory and Cognition, 19*, 459–468.

Cornoldi, C., Dalla Vecchia, R., & Tressoldi, P.E. (1995). Visuo-spatial working memory limitations in low visuo-spatial high verbal intelligence children. *Journal of Child Psychology and Psychiatry, 36*, 1053–1064.

Cornoldi, C., & Rigoni, F. (1999). Spatial working memory deficits in children. *Thalamus, 17*, 60–61.

Cornoldi, C., Rigoni, F., Tressoldi, P.E., & Vio, C. (1999). Imagery deficits in non verbal learning disabilities. *Journal of Learning Disabilities, 32,* 48–57.

Cornoldi, C., & Vecchi, T. (2000). Mental imagery in blind people: The role of passive and active visuo-spatial processes. In M. Heller (Ed.), *Touch, representation, and blindness* (pp. 143–181). Oxford: Oxford University Press.

Craik, F.I.M. (1977). Age differences in human memory. In J.E. Birren & K.W. Schaie (Eds.), *Handbook of the psychology of ageing* (pp. 384–420). New York: Van Nostrand Reinhold.

Craik, F.I.M., & Jennings, J.M. (1992). Human Memory. In F.I.M. Craik & T.A. Salthouse (Eds.), *The handbook of aging and cognition* (pp. 51–110). Hillsdale, NJ: Lawrence Erlbaum Associates Inc.

Craik, F.I.M., & Salthouse, T.A. (1992). *The handbook of aging and cognition.* Hillsdale, NJ: Lawrence Erlbaum Associates Inc.

Daigneault, S., & Braun, C.M.J. (1993). Working memory and the self-ordered pointing task: Further evidence of early prefrontal decline in normal aging. *Journal of Clinical and Experimental Neuropsychology, 15,* 881–895.

Dawson, J.L.M. (1972). Effects of sex hormones on cognitive style in rats and men. *Behavior Genetics, 2,* 21–42.

Della Sala, S., Gray, C., Baddeley, A., & Wilson, L. (1997). *Visual Patterns Test.* Bury St Edmunds, UK: Thames Valley Test Company.

Dempster, F.N. (1992). The rise and fall of inhibiting mechanism: Toward a unified theory of cognitive development and aging. *Developmental Review, 12,* 45–75.

De Renzi, E., Faglioni, P., & Villa, P. (1977). Topographical amnesia. *Journal of Neurology, Neurosurgery and Psychiatry, 40,* 498–505.

Farah, M.J., Hammond, K.M., Levine, D.N., & Calvanio, R. (1988). Visual and spatial mental imagery: Dissociable systems of representation. *Cognitive Psychology, 20,* 439–462.

Frieske, D.A., & Park, D.C. (1993). Effects of organization and working memory on age differences in memory for scene information. *Experimental Aging Research, 19,* 321–332.

Gathercole, S., & Baddeley, A.D. (1989). Evaluation of the role of phonological STM in the development of vocabulary in children. *Journal of Memory and Language, 28,* 200–213.

Gick, M.L., Craik, F.I.M., & Morris, M.G. (1988). Task complexity and age differences in working memory. *Memory and Cognition, 16,* 353–361.

Gilhooly, K.J., Logie, R.H., Wetherick, N.E., & Wynn, V. (1993). Working memory and strategies in syllogistic reasoning task. *Memory and Cognition, 21,* 115–124.

Halford, G.S. (1982). *The development of thought.* Hillsdale, NJ: Lawrence Erlbaum Associates Inc.

Hammill, D.D. (1985). *Detroit tests of learning aptitude – Second edition.* Austin, TX: PRO-ED.

Hanley, J.R., Young, A.W., & Pearson, N.A. (1991). Impairment of the visuo-spatial sketch pad. *Quarterly Journal of Experimental Psychology, 43*A, 101–125.

Harshman, R.A., Hampson, E., & Berembaum, S.A. (1983). Individual differences in cognitive abilities and brain organization, Part 1: Sex and handedness differences in ability. *Canadian Journal of Psychology, 37,* 144–192.

Harshman, R.A., & Paivio, A. (1987). "Paradoxical" sex differences in self-reported imagery. *Canadian Journal of Psychology, 41,* 287–302.

Hasher, L., & Zacks, R.T. (1979). Automatic effortful processes in memory. *Journal of Experimental Psychology: General, 108,* 356–388.

Hasher, L., & Zacks, R.T. (1988). Working memory, comprehension, and aging: A review and a new view. In G.H. Bower (Ed.), *The psychology of learning and motivation* (*Vol. 22*) (pp. 193–225). San Diego, CA: Academic Press.

Hermelin, B., & O'Connor, N. (1990). Factors and primes: A specific numerical ability. *Psychological Medicine, 20,* 163–169.

Hess, T.M., & Pullen, S.M. (1996). Memory in context. In F. Blanchard-Fields & T.M. Hess (Eds.), *Perspectives on cognitive change in adulthood and aging* (pp. 387–427). New York: McGraw-Hill.

Hess, T.M., & Slaughter, S.J. (1990). Schematic knowledge influences on memory for scene information in younger and older adults. *Developmental Psychology*, 26, 855–865.

Hitch, G.J., Woodin, M.E., & Baker, S. (1989). Visual and phonological components of working memory in children. *Memory and Cognition*, 17, 175–185.

Hyde, J.S. (1981). How large are cognitive gender differences? *Developmental Psychology*, 20, 722–736.

Jonides, J., Kahn, R., & Rozin, P. (1975). Imagery instructions improve memory in blind subjects. *Bulletin of the Psychonomic Society*, 5, 424–426.

Just, M., & Carpenter, P.A. (1992). A capacity theory of comprehension: Individual differences in working memory. *Psychological Review*, 99, 122–149.

Kail, R. (1993). Processing time changes globally at an exponential rate during childhood and adolescence. *Journal of Experimental Child Psychology*, 56, 254–265.

Kail, R., & Salthouse, T.A. (1994). Processing speed as a mental capacity. *Acta Psychologica*, 86, 199–225.

Kaufman, A.S., & Doppelt, J.E. (1977). Analysis of WISC-R standardization in terms of the stratifications variables. *Child Development*, 47, 165–171.

Kaufman, A., & Kaufman, N.L. (1983). *Kaufman assessment battery for children*. Circle Pines, MN: American Guidance Service.

Kerr, N.H. (1983). The role of vision in "visual imagery" experiments: Evidence from the congenitally blind. *Journal of Experimental Psychology: General*, 112, 265–277.

Kerr, N.H. (1987). Locational representation in imagery: The third dimension. *Memory and Cognition*, 15, 521–530.

Kirasic, K.C. (1991). Spatial cognition and behaviour in young and elderly adults. *Psychology and Aging*, 6, 10–18.

Kosslyn, S.M. (1980). *Image and mind.* Cambridge, MA: Harvard University Press.

Kosslyn, S.M. (1994). *Image and brain.* Cambridge, MA: MIT Press.

Kosslyn, S.M., Maljkovic, V., Hamilton, S.E., Horvitz, G., & Thompson, W.L. (1995). Two types of image generation: Evidence for left and right hemisphere processes. *Neuropsychologia*, 33, 1485–1510.

Kosslyn, S.M., Margolis, J.A., Barrett, A.M., Goldknopf, E.J., & Caly, P.F. (1990). Age differences in imagery abilities. *Child Development*, 61, 995–1010.

Kozlowski, L.T., & Bryant, K.J. (1977). Sense of direction, spatial orientation and cognitive maps. *Journal of Experimental Psychology: Human Perception and Performance*, 3, 590–598.

Levine, D.N., Warach, J., & Farah, M.J. (1985). Two visual systems in mental imagery: Dissociation of "what" and "where" in imagery disorders due to bilateral posterior cerebral lesions. *Neurology*, 35, 1010–1018.

Lindenberger, U., Kliegl, R., & Baltes, P.B. (1992). Professional expertise does not eliminate age differences in imagery-based memory performance during adulthood. *Psychology and Aging*, 7, 585–593.

Linn, M.C., & Petersen, A.C. (1985). Emergence and characterization of sex differences in spatial ability: A meta-analysis. *Child Development*, 56, 1479–1498.

Lipman, P.D. (1991). Age and exposure differences in acquisition of route information. *Psychology and Aging*, 6, 128–133.

Logie, R.H. (1986). Visuo-spatial processing in working memory. *Quarterly Journal of Experimental Psychology*, 38A, 229–247.

Logie, R.H. (1989). Characteristics of visual short-term memory. *European Journal of Cognitive Psychology*, 1, 275–284.

Logie, R.H. (1995). *Visuo-spatial working memory.* Hove, UK: Lawrence Erlbaum Associates Ltd.

Logie, R.H., & Baddeley, A.D. (1987). Cognitive processes in counting. *Journal of Experimental Psychology: Learning, Memory and Cognition*, 13, 310–326.

Logie, R.H., Gilhooly, K.J., & Wynn, V. (1994). Counting on working memory in arithmetic problem solving. *Memory and Cognition*, 22, 395–410.

Logie, R.H., & Marchetti, C. (1991). Visuo-spatial working memory: Visual, spatial or central executive. In R.H. Logie & M. Denis (Eds.), *Mental images in human cognition* (pp. 105–115). Amsterdam: Elsevier.

Logie, R.H., & Pearson, D. (1997). The inner eye and the inner scribe of visuo-spatial working memory: Evidence from developmental fractioning. *European Journal of Cognitive Psychology*, *9*, 241–257.

Logie, R.H., Zucco, G.M., & Baddeley, A.D. (1990). Interference with visual short-term memory. *Acta Psychologica*, *75*, 55–74.

Loomis, J.M., Klatzky, R.L., Golledge, R.G., Cicinelli, J.G., Pellegrino, J.W., & Fry, P.A. (1993). Nonvisual navigation by blind and sighted: Assessment of path integration ability. *Journal of Experimental Psychology: General*, *122*, 73–91.

Luria, A.R. (1968/1987). *The mind of a mnemonist*. Cambridge, MA: Harvard University Press.

Luzzatti, C., Vecchi, T., Agazzi, D., Cesa-Bianchi, M., & Vergani, G. (1998). A neurological dissociation between preserved visual and impaired spatial processing in mental imagery. *Cortex*, *34*, 461–469.

Maccoby, E.E., & Jacklin, C.N. (1974). *The psychology of sex differences*. Stanford, CA: Stanford University Press.

Marmor, G.S. (1975). Development of kinetic images: When does the child first represent movement in mental images? *Cognitive Psychology*, *7*, 548–559.

Marmor, G.S. (1977). Mental rotation and number conservation: Are they related? *Developmental Psychology*, *13*, 320–325.

Marmor, G.S. (1978). Age at onset of blindness and the development of the semantics of colour names. *Journal of Experimental Child Psychology*, *25*, 267–278.

Marmor, G., & Zaback, L. (1976). Mental rotation by the blind: Does mental rotation depend on visual imagery? *Journal of Experimental Psychology: Human Perception and Performance*, *2*, 515–521.

Mayr, U., & Kliegl, R. (1993). Sequential and coordinative complexity: Age-based processing limitations in figural transformations. *Journal of Experimental Psychology: Learning, Memory, and Cognition*, *19*, 1297–1320.

Mayr, U., Kliegl, R., & Krampe, R.T. (1996). Sequential and coordinative processing dynamics in figural transformations across the life span. *Cognition*, *59*, 61–90.

McGee, M.G. (1979). Human spatial abilities: Psychometric studies and environmental, genetic, hormonal, and neurological influences. *Psychological Bulletin*, *86*, 889–918.

McKelvie, S.J. (1986). Effects of format of the vividness of visual imagery questionnaire on content validity, split-half reliability, and the role of memory in test–retest reliability. *British Journal of Psychology*, *77*, 229–236.

Miles, C., Morgan, M.J., Milne, A.B., & Morris, E.D.M. (1996). Developmental and individual differences in visual memory span. *Current Psychology*, *15*, 53–67.

Morris, R.G., Gick, M.L., & Craik, F.I.M. (1988). Processing resources and age differences in working memory. *Memory and Cognition*, *16*, 362–366.

Morton, N., & Morris, R.G. (1995). Image transformation dissociated from visuo-spatial working memory. *Cognitive Neuropsychology*, *12*, 767–791.

Newcombe, N. (1982). Sex differences in spatial ability: Problems and gaps in current approaches. In M. Potegal (Ed.), *Spatial abilities development and physiological foundations*. New York: Academic Press.

Oltman, P.K. (1968). A portable rod and frame test apparatus. *Perceptual and Motor Skills*, *26*, 503–506.

Owen, A.M., Downes, J.J., Sahakian, B.J., Polkey, C.E., & Robbins, T.W. (1990). Planning and spatial working memory following frontal lobe lesions in man. *Neuropsychologia*, *28*, 1021–1034.

Paivio, A., & Clark, J.M. (1991). Static versus dynamic imagery. In C. Cornoldi & M.A. McDaniel (Eds.), *Imagery and cognition* (pp. 221–245). New York: Springer-Verlag.

Paivio, A., & Harshman, R.A. (1983). Factor analysis of a questionnaire on imagery and verbal habits and skills. *Canadian Journal of Psychology*, *37*, 461–483.

Pazzaglia, F., & Cornoldi, C. (1999). The role of distinct components of visuo-spatial working memory in the processing of texts. *Memory*, *7*, 19–41.

Petrides, M., & Milner, B. (1982). Deficits on subject-ordered tasks after frontal and temporal-lobe lesions in man. *Neuropsychologia*, *20*, 249–262.

Phillips, L.H., & Forshaw, M.J. (1998). The role of working memory in age differences in reasoning. In R.H. Logie & K.J. Gilhooly (Eds.), *Working memory and thinking* (pp. 23–43). Hove, UK: Psychology Press.

Phillips, L.H., Wynn, V., Gilhooly, K.J., Della Sala, S., & Logie, R.H. (1999). The role of memory in the Tower of London task. *Memory*, *7*, 209–231.

Phillips, W.A. (1983). Short-term visual memory. *Philosophical Transactions of the Royal Society of London*, *B302*, 295–309.

Phillips, W.A., & Christie, D.F.M. (1977a). Components of visual memory. *Quarterly Journal of Experimental Psychology*, *29*, 117–133.

Phillips, W.A., & Christie, D.F.M. (1977b). Interference with visualisation. *Quarterly Journal of Experimental Psychology*, *29*, 637–650.

Piaget, J., & Inhelder, B. (1955). *De la logique de l'enfant à la logique de l'adolescent*. Paris: Presses Universitaires de France.

Piaget, J., & Inhelder, B. (1966). *L'image mentale chez l'enfant*. Paris: Presses Universitaires de France.

Poon, L.W. (1985). Differences in human memory with aging: Nature, causes, and clinical implications. In J.E. Birren & K.W. Schaie (Eds.), *Handbook of the psychology of aging* (pp. 427–462). New York: Van Nostrand Reinhold.

Price, B.M., & Goodale, M.A. (1988). *Asymmetries in the perception of biological motion*. Unpublished manuscript, University of Western Ontario, London, Canada.

Rabbitt, P. (1981). Cognitive psychology needs models for changes in performance with old age. In J.B. Long & A.D. Baddeley (Eds.), *Attention and performance*, *IX* (pp. 555–573). Hillsdale, NJ: Lawrence Erlbaum Associates Inc.

Richardson, J.T.E. (1991). Gender differences in imagery, cognition, and memory. In R.H. Logie & M. Denis (Eds.), *Mental images in human cognition* (pp. 271–303). Amsterdam: Elsevier.

Richardson, J.T.E. (1994). Gender differences in mental rotation. *Perceptual and Motor Skills*, *78*, 435–448

Rieser, J.J., Guth, D.A., & Hill, E.W. (1986). Sensitivity to perspective structure while walking without vision. *Perception*, *15*, 173–188.

Rieser, J.J., Hill, E., Talor, C., Bradfield, A., & Rosen, S. (1992). Visual experience, visual field size, and the development of nonvisual sensitivity to the spatial structure of outdoor neighborhoods explored by walking. *Journal of Experimental Psychology: General*, *121*, 210–221.

Roberts, R.J., & Aman, C.J. (1993). Developmental differences in giving directions: Spatial frames of reference and mental rotation. *Child Development*, *64*, 1258–1270.

Rourke, B.P. (1989). *Nonverbal disabilities, the syndrome and the model*. New York: Guilford Press.

Rourke, B.P., & Finlayson, N.A.J. (1978). Neuropsychological significance of variations in patterns of academic performance: Verbal and visuo-spatial abilities. *Journal of Abnormal Child Psychology*, *6*, 121–133.

Saariluoma, P. (1991). Visuo-spatial interference and apperception in chess. In R.H. Logie & M. Denis (Eds.), *Mental images in human cognition* (pp. 83–94). Amsterdam: Elsevier.

Sacks, O. (1985). *The man who mistook his wife for a hat*. London: Duckworth.

Salthouse, T.A. (1982). *Adult cognition*. New York: Springer-Verlag.

Salthouse, T.A. (1987). Adult age differences in integrative spatial ability. *Psychology and Aging*, *2*, 254–260.

Salthouse, T.A. (1991). *Theoretical perspectives on cognitive aging*. Hillsdale, NJ: Lawrence Erlbaum Associates Inc.

Salthouse, T.A. (1994). The nature of the influence of speed on adult age differences in cognition. *Developmental Psychology, 30,* 240–259.

Salthouse, T.A. (1996). General and specific speed mediation of adult age differences in memory. *Journal of Gerontology: Psychological Sciences, 51*B, 30–42.

Salthouse, T.A., Babcock, R.L., & Shaw, R.J. (1991). Effects of adult age on structural and operational capacities in working memory. *Psychology and Aging, 6,* 118–127.

Salthouse, T.A., Babcock, R.L., Skovronek, E., Mitchell, D.R.D., & Palmon R. (1990). Age and experience effect in spatial visualization. *Developmental Psychology, 26,* 128–136.

Salthouse, T.A., & Coon, E.J. (1993). Influence of task-specific processing speed on age differences in memory. *Journal of Gerontology: Psychological Sciences, 48,* 245–255.

Salthouse, T.A., & Meinz, V.E. (1995). Aging, inhibition, working memory, and speed. *Journal of Gerontology: Psychological Sciences, 50,* 297–306.

Salthouse, T.A., & Mitchell, D.R.D. (1989). Structural and operational capacities in integrative spatial ability. *Psychology and Aging, 4,* 18–25.

Schaie, K.W. (1983). The Seattle Longitudinal Study: A twenty-one year exploration of psychometric intelligence in adulthood. In K.W. Schaie (Ed.), *Longitudinal studies of adult psychological development.* New York: Guilford Press.

Shah, P., & Miyake, A. (1996). The separability of working memory resources for spatial thinking and language processing: An individual differences approach. *Journal of Experimental Psychology, 125,* 4–27.

Shallice, T. (1988). *From neuropsychology to mental structure.* Cambridge: Cambridge University Press.

Sheehan, P.W. (1967). A shortened form of Betts' questionnaire upon mental imagery. *Journal of Clinical Psychology, 23,* 386–389.

Shelton, M.D., Parsons, O.A., & Leber, W.R. (1982). Verbal and visuo-spatial performance and aging: A neuropsychological approach. *Journal of Gerontology, 37,* 336–341.

Shepard, R.N., & Metzler, J. (1971). Mental rotation of three-dimensional objects. *Science, 171,* 701–703.

Smith, A.D., & Earles, J.L. (1996). Memory changes in normal aging. In F. Blanchard-Fields & T.M. Hess (Eds.), *Perspectives on cognitive change in adulthood and aging.* New York: McGraw Hill.

Smith, A.D., Park, D.C., Cherry, K., & Berkovsky, K. (1990). Age differences in memory for concrete and abstract pictures. *Journal of Gerontology, 45,* 205–209.

Stuart, I. (1995). Spatial orientation and congenital blindness: A neuropsychological approach. *Journal of Visual Impairment and Blindness, 89,* 129–141.

Swanson, H.L. (1996). Individual and age related differences in children's working memory. *Memory and Cognition, 24,* 70–82.

Thinus-Blanc, C., & Gaunet, F. (1997). Representation of space in blind people: Vision as a spatial sense? *Psychological Bulletin, 121,* 20–42.

Thorndyke, P.W., & Stasz, C. (1980). Individual differences in procedures for knowledge acquisition from maps. *Cognitive Psychology, 12,* 137–175.

Tubi, N., & Calev, A. (1989). Verbal and visuo-spatial recall by younger and older subjects: Use of matched tasks. *Psychology and Aging, 4,* 493–495.

Ungerleider, L.G., & Mishkin, M. (1982). Two cortical visual systems. In D.J. Engle, M.A. Goodale, & R.J.W. Mansfield (Eds.), *Analysis of visual behavior* (pp. 549–568). Cambridge, MA: MIT Press.

Vallar, G., & Baddeley, A.D. (1984). Fractionation of working memory: Neuropsychological evidence for a phonological short-term store. *Journal of Verbal Learning and Verbal Behavior, 23,* 151–161.

Vecchi, T. (1998). Visuo-spatial limitations in congenitally totally blind people. *Memory, 6,* 91–102.

Vecchi, T., & Girelli, L. (1998). Gender differences in visuo-spatial processing: The importance of distinguishing between passive storage and active manipulation. *Acta Psychologica, 99,* 1–16.

Vecchi, T., Monticelli, M.L., & Cornoldi, C. (1995). Visuo-spatial working memory: Structures and variables affecting a capacity measure. *Neuropsychologia*, *33*, 1549–1564.

Vecchi, T., & Richardson, J.T.E. (2000). Active processing in visuo-spatial working memory. *Cahiers de Psychologie Cognitive*, *19*, 3–32.

Vogel, J.M. (1980). Limitations on children's short-term memory for left–right orientation. *Journal of Experimental Child Psychology*, *30*, 473–495.

Voyer, D., Voyer, S., & Bryden, M.P. (1995). Magnitude of sex differences in spatial abilities: A meta-analysis and consideration of critical variables. *Psychological Bulletin*, *117*, 250–270.

Waddell, K.J., & Rogoff, B. (1981). Effects of contextual organization on spatial memory of middle-aged and older women. *Developmental Psychology*, *23*, 514–520.

Welford, A.T. (1958). *Ageing and human skill*. London: Oxford University Press.

Winograd, E., Smith, A.D., & Simon, E.W. (1982). Aging and the picture superiority effect in recall. *Journal of Gerontology*, *37*, 70–75.

Yee, P.L., Hunt, E., & Pellegrino, J.W. (1991). Coordinating cognitive information: Task effects and individual difference in integrating information from several sources. *Cognitive Psychology*, *23*, 615–680.

Zelinski, E.M. (1988). Integrating information from discourse: Do older adults show deficits? In L.L. Light & D.M. Burke (Eds.), *Language, memory and aging* (pp. 117–132). Cambridge, UK: Cambridge University Press.

CHAPTER THREE

Pictures in memory: The role of visual-imaginal information

Johannes Engelkamp and Hubert D. Zimmer
Universität des Saarlandes, Germany

Manuel de Vega
Universidad de La Laguna, Tenerife, Canary Islands

INTRODUCTION

In the late 1970s, there was the so-called imagery debate. The core of the debate was the question of whether a unitary (conceptual) system was sufficient to explain all cognitive performance. The debate ended with the conclusion that a clear decision cannot be reached, because any pattern of performance can be explained by any appropriate mixture of structural and process assumptions (e.g., Anderson, 1978).

In spite of this open end to the debate, in other fields of psychology the assumption of a visual-imaginal system in addition to a conceptual knowledge system was widely accepted (e.g., Ellis & Young, 1989; Humphreys & Bruce, 1989). Surprisingly, the field of episodic memory lagged behind, although the idea of dual codes was initiated in this field as early as in the late 1960s by Paivio (e.g., 1969, 1971). It is our goal in this chapter to demonstrate that, besides conceptual information, a visual-imaginal system, or more generally sensory systems, contribute to episodic remembering.

As mentioned, one of the early proposals of a dual code in the field of episodic memory stemmed from Paivio (1969, 1971). The background for his theory was, among other things, (a) the excellent recognition memory for pictures (e.g., Shepard, 1967; Standing, 1973), (b) the picture-superiority effect in memory (e.g., Madigan, 1983), and (c) the imagery effect, i.e., the enhancement of memory for concrete words when their referents are imagined (see Denis, 1975; Engelkamp, 1998, for a review). Whereas Paivio explained these phenomena by the assumption of the involvement of two different codes, a non-verbal, primarily visual one and a verbal one, proponents of a unitary code suggested only a propositional code for all mental entries (e.g., Anderson & Bower, 1973; Roediger & Weldon, 1987). However, none of these explanations can be upheld in their original forms. The dual-code theory was demonstrated to be wrong in one of its central assumptions, namely that pictures are spontaneously dually encoded (e.g., Intraub, 1979); the unitary conceptual position was confronted with findings that were difficult to reconcile without taking into account the contribution of visual-imaginal information to memory, such as the visual similarity effect (e.g., Nelson, Reed, & Walling, 1976). However, whereas interest in the dual-code model declined, surprisingly the unitary conceptual system assumption is still widely accepted. One reason for sticking with a unitary system was that incompatible results were "explained" by postulating different processes which could be more or less arbitrarily combined with tasks.

In this chapter, we aim to convince the reader that both system and process assumptions are necessary to explain the findings. Thereby we define systems by the information that is represented. We assume that systems are specialised in handling specific *types* of information, which again require specific processes. Furthermore, we want to convince the reader that visual-imaginal information has to be taken into account in order to explain the findings in the field of memory for pictures.

A BRIEF REVIEW OF DEVELOPMENTS
UNTIL 1990

Until about 1985, memory research was confined to explicit memory. Typical memory tests for explicit memory were free recall, cued recall, and recognition memory. In order to explain the patterns of performance in these tests, only conceptual information was considered. The important distinction made hereby was the one between item-specific and relational information (e.g., Hunt & Einstein, 1981). Relational information (that is, associations among items) served above all to generate items in recall. Item-specific information determined whether a presented or generated item belonged to the requested episode in recognition memory and recall, respectively. The excellent recognition memory for pictures was attributed to the rich item-specific information provided by pictures. The picture superiority effect and the visual imagery effect with concrete words were explained analogously. The good item-specific information provided by pictures was thereby considered as conceptual (e.g., Marschark, Richman, Yuille, & Hunt, 1987; Ritchey, 1980; Roediger & Weldon, 1987).

In the mid 1980s, the focus shifted to implicit memory testing. Implicit memory effects are influences of earlier study episodes on actual test performance. Subjects have no retrieval intention because they are not informed about the memory test. Typical tests are word stem completion, i.e., naming the first word that comes to

mind on reading the word stem, or fragment completion, i.e., identifying fragments of words or pictures (for reviews see Richardson-Klavehn & Bjork, 1988;
Schacter, Delaney, & Merikle, 1990). It soon became clear that implicit memory
tests were sensitive to changes in physical stimulus properties between study
and test, and insensitive to variations in conceptual encoding at study. This
pattern appeared to be just the opposite of that for explicit memory tests. In
typical explicit memory tests, levels of processing or conceptual elaboration
instructions at study were highly influential, whereas change of physical stimulus
properties at test seemed to be non-critical (for review see Moscovitch, Goshen-
Gottstein & Vriezen, 1994).

The dissociation between type of test and memory variables was explained
by assuming either different sets of processes or different memory systems. The
system approach equated implicit memory performance with an underlying procedural memory system and explicit memory performance with an underlying
declarative (or episodic) memory system (e.g., Squire, 1987). All performance
patterns with regard to pictorial stimuli in explicit memory tests were attributed
to the declarative system, and it was assumed that in amnesics this system
was impaired. The effects of physical item properties on implicit memory were
attributed to the procedural system.

The process approach, also called the transfer-appropriate processing approach,
essentially explained the explicit memory effects by resorting to conceptual
processes, and the implicit memory effects by resorting to perceptual processes.
Therefore, changing the surface of pictures from study to test (but not the kind
of conceptual encoding) influenced implicit memory testing, and variations of
conceptual encoding (but not surface variations from study to test) influenced
explicit memory tests.

This kind of process theory was widely accepted until Roediger (1990) suggested a modification. Roediger proposed that the distinction of perceptual and
conceptual processes was sufficient, and that both kinds of processes could occur
in implicit as well as in explicit tests. Effects of conceptual information were
also observed in implicit tests when these were conceptual tests (e.g., a category
production test) and non-conceptual, perceptual information also influenced
explicit tests when these were perceptual (e.g., a rhyme cue) (Blaxton, 1989).

The implications of this modified process theory for the picture-related memory
effects were scarcely discussed. For instance, one implication is that if the picture superiority effect is a conceptual effect, there should also be a pictorial
superiority effect in conceptual implicit tests. However, Weldon and Coyote
(1996) did not find any picture superiority effect in conceptual implicit memory
tests. In the logic of the transfer-appropriate processing approach, the result
forces the conclusion that the picture superiority effect is a perceptual effect. The
problem is that this assumption causes another conflict. For free recall a strong
picture advantage is reported, and this advantage must be caused by perceptual
information if the picture superiority effect is perceptual and not conceptual. This

conclusion contradicts the assumptions of the transfer-appropriate processing approach, in which free recall is considered as a conceptual test.

However, these were not the only findings that were inconsistent with the transfer-appropriate processing assumption, which is based on the dichotomy of perceptual and conceptual processes. A number of further conflicting results exist, which were widely ignored.

NEGLECTED FINDINGS SUPPORTING
THE SENSORY–CONCEPTUAL DISTINCTION

Visual-imaginal information in explicit memory tests

The influence of surface features on recall and recognition

It was repeatedly observed that free recall of pictures varied with physical complexity although the meaning, i.e., conceptual information, was kept constant. For example, identical objects (such as an apple or a house) were presented as line drawings, as black and white photographs, and as coloured photographs, and their memory performance in verbal free recall was measured. It was generally observed that coloured photographs were better recalled than photographs in black and white, and these photographs were better recalled than line drawings (e.g., Bousfield, Esterson, & Whitmarsh, 1957; Gollin & Sharps, 1988; Madigan & Lawrence, 1980; Ritchey, 1982).

Other widely ignored findings stem from studies by Douglas Nelson in which he investigated paired-associate learning (see Nelson, 1979, for a review). He presented his subjects with either word–word or picture–word pairs. Stimulus and response items were unrelated. The stimulus items could be pictures or their labels, and the similarity among the stimulus items was varied: (a) they were phonetically similar if they were words; (b) the pictures or the words' referents were visually similar; (c) stimulus items were conceptually similar (e.g., they came from the same semantic category); or (d) they were dissimilar (on all three dimensions). Upon cue presentation a verbal response was always requested. The essential findings of these experiments were: (1) word–word learning was influenced by phonemic similarity but not by visual similarity; (2) picture–word learning was influenced by visual similarity but not by phonemic similarity; (3) word–word and picture–word learning were equally influenced by conceptual similarity (Nelson & Brooks, 1973; Nelson et al., 1976).

The situation in recognition memory is more complex than that in free recall because the effects of sensory features of stimuli depend on the kind of distractors used. When the distractors were conceptually different from the to-be-learned items, stimulus complexity did not influence the accuracy of recognition (Madigan, 1983; Nelson, Metzler & Reed, 1974). This finding was considered to support the assumption that explicit memory is based only on conceptual information (e.g., Anderson, 1985; Klatzky, 1980). However, this interpretation was too hasty.

In studies in which distractors were conceptually similar to the targets, recognition memory was influenced by surface qualities of the stimulus. Bahrick and Boucher (1968), for instance, used intra-categorial distractors. They showed their subjects pictures of objects and presented at test several variants of the objects (e.g., several cups). Subjects had to decide whether a picture (e.g., a cup) that they saw was old or new. Under these conditions, recognition memory was clearly dependent on the physical similarity between the distractor and the original stimulus. The number of false alarms increased with increasing visual similarity between the distractor and the studied item. Corresponding effects were reported by Homa and Viera (1988).

The negative effect of changed surface features on old–new discrimination

Whereas in the previously mentioned recognition studies the task of the subjects was to discriminate between different physical appearances of the stimuli, in other experiments surface effects were obtained although the surface form of the stimulus was irrelevant. In these studies subjects had only to decide whether a stimulus was old or new independent of surface variations. The effect observed in these experiments is called the sensory incongruency effect in recognition memory.

To our knowledge, the first systematic experiments were run by Jolicoeur (1987). He presented his subjects with sticks and blobs as stimuli, and from study to test the size of the stimuli was varied. The "old" stimuli were either of the same size as at study or of a different size. Subjects were required to recognise whether a stimulus at test was old or new, whereby variations in size should be ignored. The important result was that subjects recognised old stimuli faster and more accurately as old when they were size-congruent than when they were size-incongruent. Several replications of this size congruency effect in recognition memory have been reported (e.g., Cooper, Schacter, Ballesteros, & Moore, 1992; Zimmer, 1995).

However, such congruency effects of physical features on recognition memory were not only found for size. In other experiments a number of different surface features were manipulated from study to test, and usually recognition memory was impaired. For example, the orientation of objects was changed from study to test by rotating the items or mirror-reversing them. This variation dramatically reduced recognition performance (Srinivas, 1995; Zimmer, 1995). Similarly, the colour of the stimuli was changed. If only the lines of the drawings were in colour, the congruency effects were very small (Cave, Bost, & Cobb, 1996; Zimmer, 1993); however, if the stimuli had multiple colours, strong effects were obtained (Zimmer & Engelkamp, 1996; Zimmer & Steiner, 2000). Additionally, strong effects were always observed if the shape of a stimulus was varied from

TABLE 3.1
Effects of changing surface features in old–new recognition

Sensory feature	Source	Study condition	Proportion correct/congruent	Congruency effect accuracy	reaction time
Size	Jolicoeur (1987) 1a	Subjects studied 20 closed curves, intentional – size was irrelevant	.85	.12*	300*
	1c	20 line drawings, intentional learning	.97	.06*	98*
	3	identical learning	.92	.12*	261*
	Biederman & Cooper (1992)	48 line drawings, incidental learning by naming	.86	.11*	40*
	Zimmer (1993)	intentional learning, 80 items	.92	.06	46*
	Zimmer (1995)	incidental learning, 144 items – learning by naming	.98	.02	41*
		intentional learning, 144 items	.92	.05	56*
	Groninger (1974) 5, 200%	incidental learning, 64 items	.94	.03	23*
	6, 300%	96 items (48 pairs), incidental learning by naming	.94	.05	42*
Orientation	Srinivas (1995)	42 black-and-white photographs, incidental learning by naming	.95	ns	158*
Colour	Cave, Bost, & Cobb (1996)	64 silhouettes, incidental learning by naming, 1h delay	.92	0	24*
		64 silhouettes, incidental learning by naming, 48 h delay	.82	.03*	–
		64 silhouettes, incidental learning by a colour word–picture match	.42	.04*	21

(continued)

TABLE 3.1
(continued)

Sensory feature	Source	Study condition	Proportion correct/congruent	Congruency effect	
				accuracy	reaction time
	Zimmer & Engelkamp (1996)	48 multicoloured line drawings, intentional learning	.98	.03	41*
		80 multicoloured line drawings, intentional learning	.87	.05*	56*
		80 multicoloured line drawings, intentional learning	.92	.08*	55*

An overview of effects of changing surface features from study to test in old–new recognition. The match of the surface feature was explicitly explained as irrelevant and to be ignored.
* means that this effect was significant.

study to test. For this purpose the line drawings were embedded in different randomly shaped envelopes which distorted them in different ways (e.g., Zimmer, 1995, Exp. 7).

An overview of recent results of some relevant studies including those that were conducted in our laboratory is given in Table 3.1. The general results of these experiments can be summarised as follows:

- Incongruent stimuli were recognised less well and more slowly than congruent stimuli.
- This effect increased with the number of changed features.
- Even within one dimension the size of the effect was a positive function over the extent of the change. For example, the size incongruency effect was more pronounced for stronger changes in size than for smaller ones.

Interestingly, these effects were even found with very brief exposure times of a few hundred milliseconds, as was demonstrated in a recent study conducted at the Saarland University (Zimmer, 2000). In these experiments, subjects studied lists of pictures, with instructions to remember them. Each picture was seen for three seconds. During testing, old and new pictures were presented, and subjects had to decide whether the object was old or new. Old objects could either be identical or their colours were changed; this change, however, was to be ignored. Unlike other experiments on the influence of sensory features on recognition, in these studies a response signal procedure was adopted (for more details of this method, see Hintzman & Curran, 1997). During testing, the pictures were presented

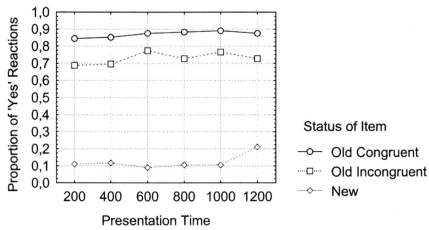

Recognition Performances Dependent on
Type of Item and Presentation Time during Testing
Changed Feature: Shape of Object

Figure 3.1.   The dependence of object recognition performances on changed outlines in a response signal procedure.

again by a computer. After a variable time, the picture was removed and an acoustic stimulus indicated that the subjects were to respond. The time interval for process- ing of the stimulus and for memory retrieval ranged from 200 ms to 1200 ms. The data from one experiment with shape variations are reported in Figure 3.1.

The figure gives the proportion of yes answers dependent on the type of stimuli: old congruent, old incongruent, and new pictures. As one can see, even with very brief exposure duration incongruent stimuli were less well recognised than congruent ones. This result not only demonstrates the robustness of the effect, but also suggests that these effects were caused by early processes of visual encoding or memory retrieval and not by late post-retrieval checks.

The visual imagery effect

We have already mentioned that instructions to form images with concrete words enhance memory compared to a control condition (standard learning instruction). These effects are explained by an enrichment of memory. Pictorial information enriches the otherwise abstract memory trace of an item. We will discuss this effect here in more detail.

A closer look at the literature reveals that the findings are inconsistent (see Paivio, 1976, p. 108). In comparison with standard learning instructions, posit- ive memory effects of imagery instructions are often reported, especially when learning is incidental (e.g., Denis, 1975, Ch. 3; Kirkpatrick, 1894; Paivio &

Csapo, 1973), but sometimes no effects were found (e.g., Groninger, 1974; Zimmer & Mohr, 1986). All these studies have the problem that it is difficult to attribute the findings to the experimental manipulation. First, it is difficult to decide whether subjects used imagery or not when they were instructed to do so. However, it is also possible that subjects did so spontaneously in the control condition because they believed that imagery improves memory (e.g., Denis & Carfantan, 1985a, b). Second, specific encoding strategies in the non-imagery control condition might be used, which enhance memory under standard learning instructions, and could also mask possible effects of imagery (see Jones, 1988). Hence, in order to demonstrate an imagery effect, these aspects have to be controlled. If such controls are in place, an imagery effect can be consistently observed (e.g., Denis, 1975, p. 57; Paivio, Smythe, & Yuille, 1968; Richardson, 1978). Particularly instructive is an experiment by Richardson (1985). He observed better recall under imagery than under standard learning instructions. Moreover, he observed that his subjects reported more often having formed images after an imagery instruction than after a standard learning instruction. Finally, he observed that the recall depended on the use of imagery strategies. Subjects who reported having formed images showed an imagery effect; subjects who reported not having formed images did not show an imagery effect (see also Ritchey & Beal, 1980).

Visual-imaginal information in implicit memory tests

Pictures and words in perceptual implicit tests

Implicit perceptual tests are assumed to rely on surface repetition of stimuli. Identical repetition of a stimulus from study to test improves the processing of this stimulus at test. This repetition effect can also be observed when during test only a fragment of the study stimulus is presented, in so-called fragment completion tests (for review see Roediger & Srinivas, 1993).

When pictorial stimuli are used, fragments of these pictures should be better recognised at test than when fragments of "new" pictures are used. In order to demonstrate that such repetition effects are based on the repetition of surface information and not on the repetition of conceptual information, a control condition is needed in which the concept is repeated but the surface is not. In such a condition, word fragments (the labels of the pictures) are presented at test instead of picture fragments.

Such an experiment was conducted by Roediger and Weldon (1987). They used pictures and their labels as study stimuli and tested them with either picture fragments or word fragments. The fragments were based half on the presented pictures and words at study, and half on new pictures and words. The subjects' task at test was to recognise the presented fragment. What Roediger and Weldon (1987) observed was a modality-specific repetition effect. There was a repetition priming effect for pictures when picture fragments were used at test, but not when word fragments were used, and vice versa. Similar results were reported by Watkins, Peynircioglu, and Brems (1984).

This finding has two important theoretical implications. First, it demonstrated again that perceptual implicit tests do not use conceptual information. Otherwise, there should have been cross-modal repetition priming, which was not observed. Second, and more important, the finding demonstrates that pictures and words provide different types of surface information.

The lack of picture superiority effects in conceptual tasks

In this part we want to show that conceptual effects that are expected from a unitary memory view have not been observed. A first result which demonstrated that conceptual processing of pictures and words is similar did not come from implicit memory experiments but from a semantic priming study conducted by Bajo (1988). Subjects had to assess whether prime and target were from the same conceptual category (e.g., "wild animal"). Bajo observed cross-modal priming (i.e., picture–word and word–picture priming) in a conceptual test. Additionally, she observed that for the conceptual-categorisation task the priming effects were of comparable size (about 100 ms) in all types of prime–target combination (word–word, word–picture, picture–picture, picture–word). Thus, there was no picture superiority effect in conceptual priming.

Corresponding results were reported more recently for conceptual repetition priming. Weldon and Coyote (1996) presented pictures and words to their subjects. The implicit tests were conceptual (category production and word association) and the explicit test was free recall. As usual, in free recall, a consistent picture superiority effect was observed. However, there was *no* picture superiority effect in priming, although for pictures as well as for words a conceptual priming effect was observed. From these findings, Weldon and Coyote (1996) concluded that conceptual information plays no critical role in the picture superiority effect.

The absence of physical congruency effects in implicit memory tests

As mentioned earlier, physical congruency is an important factor in explicit recognition memory. When a surface feature of an item was changed from study to test, recognition memory was impaired although the physical feature was defined as irrelevant for the decision. The old/new decision was slowed down and often accuracy was impaired (in comparison with the identical presentation). This indicates that the match of the physical features is automatically processed during a recognition memory test.

However, when the same congruency variations were applied in perceptual implicit tests, a surprising result was observed. From the sensory specificity of implicit tests one should expect that the negative effects of these changes would be even stronger in perceptual implicit tests than in explicit tests. In fact, the result was the opposite. The implicit tests were identification tasks, word–picture matching tasks, or object decision tasks (is the depicted object real or fantasy?). In all these tasks a clear repetition effect was observed, i.e., the performance for old objects was better than for new objects, but the repetition effect was uninfluenced by most of the congruency variations.

One of the first results of that type was the observation that the repetition effect was equally good independent of whether the stimulus at test was presented in the same or in a different size than at study (e.g., Biederman & Cooper, 1992; Cooper, Biederman, & Hummel, 1992; Fiser & Biederman, 1995; Zimmer, 1993, 1995). These results were not unique. Invariance of implicit memory was also reported for changes of orientation (Biederman & Cooper, 1991a; Zimmer, 1993, 1995), for specifically filtered spatial frequency complements (Biederman & Kalocsai, 1997), and for colour (Cave et al., 1996; Zimmer, 1993). However, this lack of sensory congruency effects does not mean that only conceptual information influences identification. Changes to the shape of objects (Zimmer, 1995, Exp. 7) or to the specific token that was shown (Biederman & Cooper, 1992; see also Table 3.2) reduced the repetition effect. Similar results were observed when complements of line drawings were presented during testing which showed different parts of objects (e.g., Biederman & Cooper, 1991b), and also if spatial frequency complements were presented which depicted different sectors of the visual field (Fiser & Biederman, 1996). These effects are important to note because they demonstrate that specific surface features are represented in memory and used in identification, too.

Recently, Zimmer and Steiner (2000) investigated these sensory effects more closely in a series of experiments. An objection against the general acceptance of these invariance effects is the relative size of possible effects. One could imagine that physical congruency effects are not observed because perceptual processing during identification is so fast that changes in the efficacy of this process are too small to be detected. To exclude this possibility Zimmer and Steiner made perceptual processing more difficult by blurring pictures or hiding coloured objects behind black and white masks. In doing so, the contribution of data-driven processes to the observed performance was enhanced, as the prolonged identification times proved. In spite of this effect, the congruence of surface features (the colours of the objects) did not matter. Only in one condition were effects of manipulating the physical aspects of objects observed. A change of colour from study to test reduced the repetition effect if the task was identification at a specific level in contrast to a basic level, e.g., ladybird instead of bug, and if the objects had prototypical colours (Zimmer & Steiner, 2000). In this case two aspects of the sensory features influenced processing. First, the appropriateness of colour, i.e., the match to pre-experimental knowledge; and second, the repetition of actual colour of the stimulus within the experiment.

TABLE 3.2
Effects of changing surface features in implicit testing

Sensory feature	Source	Study Condition	Testing	Object Priming (in ms)	Congruency Effect on Priming (in ms)
Shape	Biederman & Cooper (1992)	48 line drawings (24 pairs: same name, different shape)	continuous naming		
		incidental learning by naming	same token	95*	4
			same concept	62*	10
Size		72 line drawings (36 pairs: same name, different shape)	continuous naming		
		incidental learning by naming	same size	91*	2
			different size	89*	
Size	Zimmer (1995)	64 line drawings, intentional learning	word–picture matching	104*	−11
Colour	Cave, Bost, & Cobb (1996)	64 silhouettes, incidental learning by naming	object naming	86*	−2
	Zimmer (1993)	64 silhouettes, intentional learning	object decision	107*	1
	Zimmer & Engelkamp (1996)	80 multicoloured drawings, intentional learning	word–picture matching	43*	19

An overview of the effects of changing surface features from study to test in implicit testing. Only the reaction time data are given because the proportion correct were usually at the ceiling.
* means that this effect was significant.

In Table 3.2 the repetition effects of a number of studies are summarised. In the table the object repetition effects, i.e., the difference between old and new objects, and the surface feature effect, i.e., the difference between congruent and incongruent old stimuli, are reported. Positive values represent a repetition effect, i.e., faster or better decisions, and negative values mean a reduction of this effect. Although an object repetition effect was usually observed, which was reduced if the shape or token was changed, in general, the congruency of surface features was not relevant. This stands in contrast to explicit recognition memory, in which corresponding congruency effects have consistently been observed.

Summary of relevant findings

In addition to the typical memory effects—excellent recognition memory, picture superiority effect, visual imagery effect for concrete nouns—which often featured in the context of the question of whether we need a visual-imaginal system besides a conceptual system, we have presented a great number of findings from memory research which were widely ignored in this discussion. Among these findings are:

- Free recall of pictures depends on the complexity of the pictorial surface with the meaning of the pictures held constant.
- Cued recall in paired-associate learning depends on phonemic similarity with word cues and on visual similarity with picture cues, and the influence of conceptual similarity is independent of modality cued.
- Recognition memory depends on physical congruency (e.g., size congruency) of old stimuli between study and test, and the size of the effect varies with the extent of the change of the surface feature.
- This congruency is even observed when physical congruency is irrelevant for the old–new decision.
- In perceptual implicit memory tests, a repetition effect for the physical stimuli is generally observed.
- The repetition effect is modality-specific in the sense that it disappears in the cross-modal condition, i.e., switching from pictures to words and vice versa.
- In these perceptual implicit memory tests, the physical congruency of the same surface features that influenced recognition memory is not relevant.
- However, other stimulus changes from study to test such as fragment presentations, token changes, or changes in shape (outline of the figure) strongly influence repetition priming.
- There is also conceptual repetition priming, and this repetition priming can be cross-modal, for instance, from word to picture and the other way round.
- A picture superiority effect does not show up in conceptual repetition priming.

THEORETICAL INTEGRATION: THE CASE FOR A MULTI-SYSTEM MULTI-PROCESS APPROACH

We will now present the multi-system multi-process approach and show that the assumptions of different systems, together with assumptions of different processes which can be applied to the systems, allow for explanations of the phenomena reported.

Multiple systems and multiple processes

As mentioned in the introduction, in several fields of cognitive psychology it is assumed that non-conceptual entry systems are connected with the conceptual system (e.g., Ellis & Young, 1989; Engelkamp & Rummer, 1998). In our context, three systems are relevant: a verbal entry system, a non-verbal visual entry system, and a conceptual system (for more details see Engelkamp & Zimmer, 1994). This system approach differs from Paivio's (1971, 1986) dual-code theory in that the verbal and the visual systems are non-conceptual (presemantic) and allow access to the conceptual (semantic) system. An early proposal along these lines in the psychology of memory stems from D. Nelson (1979).

As to the stimuli, it is assumed that verbal stimuli necessarily activate their representations in the verbal entry system, and pictures activate their representations in the visual non-verbal entry system. Both kinds of stimuli also lead spontaneously to the activation of their concepts in the conceptual system except when specific orienting tasks keep processing on the physical level (see later).

Beyond these obligatory activation processes, there are strategic possibilities to trigger processes. Strategic processes can be induced by the experimenter through specific instructions. For instance, it is assumed that pictorial stimuli automatically activate their pictorial representations (sometimes called images or imagens) and their concepts (meanings), but that they do not automatically activate their corresponding verbal representations (or logogens). In order to activate logogens with pictures, a naming instruction would be appropriate. According to the theory, pictures can only be named via their concepts (e.g., Humphreys & Bruce, 1989). That is, logogens with pictures are activated top down from the conceptual to the entry system. Analogously, words do not automatically activate the images of their referents. Typical instructions to activate images in the context of words are imagery instructions. The formation of images usually goes along with a specific subjective experience of visualisation. However, this subjective experience can vary strongly, and it is an open question whether the subjective experience of visualisation is a necessary condition accompanying image activation. It is also undecided up to which sensory level visual representations are activated during imaging (see Logie, Engelkamp, Dehn, & Rudkin, Chapter 7, this volume; Turnbull, Denis, Mellet, Ghaëm, & Carey, Chapter 4, this volume).

Conceptual activation beyond the activation of the core concepts can be induced by instructions to elaborate on meanings (e.g., form a sentence containing a word or assess the emotional value of a picture).

In order to explain memory performance for episodes, the encoding phase and the retrieval phase must be distinguished. With regard to the encoding phase, it must be considered whether the stimuli are automatically or strategically processed. With regard to the retrieval phase, it must first of all be determined whether or not the episode is retrieved intentionally as in explicit memory testing. In this case, subjects consciously try to recollect the learning episode or parts thereof. In contrast, in implicit memory tests subjects have no retrieval intention, but they just process the stimuli according to the tasks given. In the latter case, it must be carefully considered what kinds of processes are required by the task. The task can focus more on the surface of the stimuli. Then primarily specific entry systems are involved (verbal with verbal or visual with pictorial stimuli). Or the task can focus more on meaning. In this case, conceptual processes are triggered (e.g., in a conceptual categorisation task).

In the case of explicit memory tests, it is crucial to distinguish between free recall and recognition memory tests. In free recall, the whole study episode must be reconstructed, and generation and discrimination processes are demanded equally. Processes are largely top down. In recognition memory, test performance is based on an interaction of bottom up processes triggered by the stimuli presented at test and by top down processes when it is assessed whether the stimulus was part of the learning episode or not.

In the next section, these theoretical considerations will be applied in explaining the observed findings and, where necessary, further theoretical distinctions will be added.

Explaining findings from implicit memory tests

In the field of implicit memory, perceptual and conceptual tests are distinguished. Perceptual tests focus on processes of the entry systems. Conceptual tests focus on semantic processes. Typical perceptual tests such as word and object identification tests require the identification of representations that correspond to the stimuli presented; that is, logogens with words and imagens with pictures. Conceptual processing is not central for these tasks. In our model, identification is realised when the stimulus has accessed its entry node and via this node has activated the corresponding concept. Further conceptual processing does not necessarily take place.

These assumptions explain why implicit memory effects in word identification are confined to words as stimuli and do not generalise to pictures as stimuli, and why implicit memory effects in picture identification are confined to pictures as stimuli and do not generalise to verbal stimuli. What causes the implicit memory effect is the automatic (re)activation of a memory token of the surface of the stimulus which was generated by the processes during study (see also Moscovitch et al., 1994).

These modality-specific implicit memory effects support the distinction of a verbal and a visual-imaginal system. The fact that these implicit memory effects decrease when the physical appearance of the study stimulus is modified at test, as with fragments or a changed token, fits into the theoretical considerations. However, the observation that changes of size, orientation, colour, etc., from study to test do not influence implicit memory effects offers a theoretical challenge. Different suggestions have been made to resolve this contradiction.

A first position suggests that perceptual features such as shape, colour, or size are independently processed and, in implicit memory, it strictly depends on the overlap of the processes whether or not a stimulus variation influences test performance. When the goal at test is to identify the stimulus, then the task is to match the stimulus to its internal representation (imagen or logogen). That requires the identification of the shape of the stimulus. Those stimulus aspects that are shape-irrelevant (i.e., which do not change the shape), do not change the identification process, and therefore do not change the implicit memory effects. This can easily explain why size changes do not influence identification. In order to explain the insensitivity to changes in orientation it is additionally necessary to assume that the representation used in identification is object-centred and therefore does not represent orientation. With this assumption the explanation moves closer to the second suggestion.

In this model it is suggested that (at least) two different memory tokens exist: one is an object-centred representation, which represents the viewpoint-invariant features of a stimulus, and the other one is a viewpoint-specific representation, which integrates all features of a stimulus including those that are viewpoint-specific, such as size and orientation (e.g., Biederman & Cooper, 1992; Cooper et al., 1992). The viewpoint-invariant representation is a description of the object parts and their interrelations, and possibly is based on abstractions of geometrical shapes (e.g., Hummel & Biederman, 1992). However, the colour effects on identification that we observed make it necessary also to modify these assumptions. It is not only geometrical information that is represented in these prototypes, but also colour information, given that the object is associated with specific colours, for example in the case of living objects.

Conceptual implicit tests are different from perceptual ones. Conceptual tests require assessment of meaning information. A central aspect of conceptual information processing is categorical identification, for example to recognise that an apple is a fruit. It has been assumed, as mentioned earlier, that conceptual categorisation is not modality-specific and that conceptual information, at its core, does not differ essentially for pictures and their labels. The word "apple" and a real apple should trigger more or less the same categorical information. Therefore, when just this categorisation is required in a conceptual implicit test (as when a categorical judgement is required), there should be a cross-modal priming effect. This conceptual implicit memory effect should occur not only when words are tested with pictures and vice versa, but also when the language is changed from study to test (e.g., "Hund" – "dog"). Because this conceptual repetition effect is based on the repeated categorisation that does not differ for words and pictures, there should be no picture superiority effect in conceptual repetition priming.

Explaining findings from explicit memory tests

The main theoretical assumption for free recall is that subjects are requested to recollect the whole study episode. Although this process starts from the conceptual system, it continues, to end with the entry systems. In the case of pictures, this means activating the imagens of the episode. This fact explains why the physical stimulus properties at study influence recall performance. The richer the pictures of the study episode, the more readily they are recollected. More complex pictures are therefore more easily recalled than less complex ones.

For the same reason, we expect a picture superiority effect in free recall because the imagens of the visual-imaginal system are richer on average than their corresponding logogens in the verbal system. That pictorial surface information is indeed critical in explicit memory performance is underlined by D. Nelson's findings (e.g., 1979) in paired-associate learning experiments. Visual similarity among stimulus elements impaired cued recall, but only when the stimulus elements were pictures, not when they were words.

The theory assumes that imagens can also be activated top down. This activation can be induced by imagery instructions with words. According to the theoretical assumptions, this top down activation should provide visual-imaginal information, and this information should produce the imagery effect. We have seen that this imagery effect cannot be observed consistently. There are three conditions that must be fulfilled for the effect to occur. First, subjects instructed to form images must follow these instructions; second, subjects in the control condition must not spontaneously use imagery encoding (at least not to the same degree as the imagery subjects); and third, subjects in the control conditions must not use efficient alternative encoding strategies such as conceptual elaboration.

The multi-system multi-process approach makes it obvious that the three conditions must be controlled for. The theory assumes that image activation with words must be triggered strategically. It recognises that such an activation can be induced by experimenter instructions, but also—although this is less likely— by self-instructions. Further, the theory does see the option of conceptual elaboration. Such elaborative processes can also be self-induced. Image activation as well as conceptual elaboration is assumed to improve memory.

In recognition memory for pictures, there are two remarkable effects. First is the finding that more complex pictures such as scenes are recognised extremely well. This phenomenon, according to our theoretical position, arises for two reasons: first, complex pictures have complex pictorial memory representations; second, complex pictures offer substantial scope for conceptual interpretation. Unlike a simple object such as an apple or a cup, which has essentially one dominant categorical status, complex pictures offer multiple categorisations. A landscape picture may induce categorisations such as "spring", "mountain region", "forest", etc. Hence, the excellent memory for complex pictures might be due to very rich images and multiple conceptual encoding. These alternative explanations are difficult to disentangle experimentally.

The other remarkable finding is the physical congruency effect. This effect demonstrates (a) that picture memory always includes surface information, and (b) that recognition resorts to a viewer-centred visual representation. The latter aspect means that in recognition memory subjects not only retrieve an abstract memory entry, but they also retrieve a specific visual token which represents the shape of the stimulus as seen from the specific perspective at study. In addition to this specific token, an object-centred visual representation might exist, which is relevant in implicit memory. This fact emphasises that the visual-imaginal system is itself complex and encompasses representations of several types.

Comparing implicit and explicit memory

There are three critical differences between implicit and explicit retention. The first concerns the use of the visual-imaginal system. In explicit memory, visual representations are always used as part of a specific, visually experienced episode which integrates all aspects of the episode into a whole. Therefore, the images used in explicit retrieval are viewer-centred and also include invariant aspects of object representations such as size. In contrast, implicit perceptual memory tests do not refer to past episodes, but focus on the processing of a specific stimulus under a specific task. Most of the perceptual implicit tests basically request the identification of the stimulus form, be it in a tachistoscopic presentation condition, as in the fragment presentation condition, or in a masked condition. It is generally agreed that for identification the shape of an object plays the major role. Therefore, repetition of the same shape from study to test is critical; variations of shape (as when fragments are used in tests or the pictures are distorted) are important and such changes reduce repetition priming. On the other hand, shape-irrelevant stimulus aspects such as size do not influence repetition priming in these tests.

The second difference concerns the conceptual system and its use. Again, the critical aspect of conceptual implicit tests is that they usually demand conceptual categorisation without regard to the specific learning episode, that is, without context. Stimuli are assessed as living/non-living, as belonging to animals, vehicles, furniture etc. In any case, the episode-specific aspects are not critical. Because these processes that categorise the stimuli conceptually do not differ between pictures and words—or are differently formulated, because the specific physical appearances of pictures and words are irrelevant for their conceptual categorisation—there is no picture superiority effect in conceptual implicit tests of this type. Taken together, what makes an episode an episode for the subject— namely that he/she integrates all specific physical and conceptual aspects of it— is critical in explicit but not in implicit memory tests. In implicit tests, subjects process a stimulus as an event in the present.

This leads to the third difference. Only explicit tests require intentional retrieval of the study episodes. That is, subjects have to focus their attention voluntarily on the study episodes. This focusing on the study episodes is by definition not required in implicit tests, in which the stimuli are processed as in a neutral situation when no study episodes are experienced. It is well known that it is difficult to exclude such an intentional retrieval of the study episodes in implicit memory testing.

CONCLUSION

Taken together, the findings discussed in this chapter suggest that it was an important step forward to formulate the transfer-appropriate processing principle and to consider within this approach perceptual and conceptual processes as memory-relevant. However, the findings suggest (a) that domains of knowledge have to be distinguished which represent and process specific types of information and which are necessarily accessed if this information is needed; (b) that, in particular, perceptual processes have to be further differentiated; and moreover (c) that it has to be taken into account whether processes are automatic or controlled.

The differentiation of perceptual processes concerns the distinction of verbal and non-verbal perceptual processes and the consideration of different levels of perceptual processing. Object-centred representations of invariant features have to be distinguished from viewer-centred representations including the viewpoint-specific and arbitrary features that are unique for the specific episode.

The additional processes are particularly important to explain differences between explicit and implicit memory tests. In this context, it is an essential question whether retrieval takes place intentionally or not. Intentional retrieval is by definition involved in explicit tests and means that whole episodes are recollected—including conceptual and perceptual information and including the specific features unique for the episode. The tasks of implicit memory testing by definition exclude such intentional retrieval. Here, processes at test focus on task-specific aspects. In order to cause an implicit memory effect, processes at test have to be related to the information processed at study. In addition, processes at study as well as at test have to be differentiated as to whether they are obligatory (or automatic), and they have to be differentiated as to what systems are involved (verbal, visual-imaginal, and conceptual).

In the context of memory for pictures, it turns out that visual-imaginal processes play a central role. Stimulus complexity effects in recall as well as in recognition are attributed to visual-imaginal processes, as well as visual similarity effects in paired-associate learning when pictures are used as stimuli and cues. Physical congruency effects of pictures are also due to visual-imaginal processes, as are effects of imagery instructions with concrete nouns and modality-specific perceptual priming effects in implicit memory tests. Hence, it is more than surprising that picture memory has been so long and exclusively ascribed to rich conceptual encoding processes. The memory traces of pictures include surface information, not just conceptual information.

ACKNOWLEDGEMENTS

We thank the Deutsche Forschungsgemeinschaft (DFG) for supporting our research (Zi 308–2), and we thank Astrid Steiner, Lars Kaboth, and our student assistants for their support in running the experiments.

REFERENCES

Anderson, J.R. (1978). Arguments concerning representations for mental imagery. *Psychological Review*, 85, 249–277.

Anderson, J.R. (1985). *Cognitive psychology and its implications.* New York: Freeman.

Anderson, J.R., & Bower, G.H. (1973). *Human associative memory*. Washington, DC: Winston & Sons.

Bahrick, H.P., & Boucher, B. (1968). Retention of visual and verbal codes of the same stimuli. *Journal of Experimental Psychology, 78*, 417–422.

Bajo, M.T. (1988). Semantic facilitation with pictures and words. *Journal of Experimental Psychology: Learning, Memory, and Cognition, 14*, 579–589.

Biederman, I., & Cooper, E.E. (1991a). Evidence for complete translational and reflexional invariance in visual object priming. *Perception, 20*, 585–593.

Biederman, I., & Cooper, E.E. (1991b). Priming contour-deleted images: Evidence for intermediate representations in visual object recognition. *Cognitive Psychology, 23*, 393–419.

Biederman, I., & Cooper, E.E. (1992). Size invariance in visual object priming. *Journal of Experimental Psychology: Human Perception and Performance, 18*, 121–133.

Biederman, I., & Kalocsai, P. (1997). Neurocomputational bases of object and face recognition. *Philosophical Transactions of the Royal Society of London B, 352*, 1203–1219.

Blaxton, T. (1989). Investigating dissociations among memory measures: Support for a transfer-appropriate processing framework. *Journal of Experimental Psychology: Learning, Memory, and Cognition, 15*, 657–668.

Bousfield, W., Esterson, J., & Whitmarsh, G.A. (1957). The effects of concomitant colored and uncolored pictorial representations on the learning of stimulus words. *Journal of Applied Psychology, 41*, 165–168.

Cave, C.B., Bost, P.R., & Cobb, R.E. (1996). Effects of color and pattern on implicit and explicit picture memory. *Journal of Experimental Psychology: Learning, Memory, and Cognition, 22*, 639–653.

Cooper, E.E., Biederman, I., & Hummel, J.E. (1992). Metric invariance in object recognition: A review and further evidence. *Canadian Journal of Psychology, 46*, 191–214.

Cooper, L.A., Schacter, D.L., Ballesteros, S., & Moore, C. (1992). Priming and recognition of transformed three-dimensional objects: Effects of size and reflection. *Journal of Experimental Psychology: Learning, Memory, and Cognition, 18*, 43–58.

Denis, M. (1975). *Représentation imagée et activité de mémorisation*. Paris: Centre National.

Denis, M., & Carfantan, M. (1985a). People's knowledge about images. *Cognition, 20*, 49–60.

Denis, M., & Carfantan, M. (1985b). What people know about visual images: A metacognitive approach to imagery. In D.G. Russell & D.F. Marks (Eds.), *Imagery 2* (pp. 27–32). Dunedin, New Zealand: Human Performance Associates.

Ellis, A., & Young, A.W. (1989). *Human cognitive neuropsychology*. Hillsdale, NJ: Lawrence Erlbaum Associates MC.

Engelkamp, J. (1998). Gedächtnis für Bilder. In K. Sachs-Hombach & K. Rehkämper (Eds.), *Bild, Bildwahrnehmung, Bildverarbeitung* (pp. 227–242). Wiesbaden: Deutscher Universitätsverlag.

Engelkamp, J., & Rummer, R. (1998). The architecture of the mental lexicon. In A. Friederici (Ed.), *Language comprehension: A biological perspective* (pp. 133–175). Berlin: Springer.

Engelkamp, J., & Zimmer, H.D. (1994). *The human memory: A multimodal approach*. Seattle: Hogrefe.

Fiser, J., & Biederman, I. (1995). Size invariance in visual object priming of gray-scale images. *Perception, 24*, 741–748.

Fiser, J., & Biederman, I. (1996, Nov). *Do spatial frequency and orientation information contribute similarly to visual object priming?* Paper presented at the OPAM meeting of the Psychonomic Society at Los Angeles, California.

Gollin, E.S., & Sharps, M.J. (1988). Facilitation of free recall by categorical blocking depends on stimulus type. *Memory & Cognition, 16*, 539–544.

Groninger, L.D. (1974). The role of images within the memory system: Storage or retrieval? *Journal of Experimental Psychology, 103*, 178–180.

Hintzman, D.L., & Curran, T. (1997). Comparing retrieval dynamics in recognition memory and lexical decision. *Journal of Experimental Psychology: General, 126*, 228–247.

Homa, D., & Viera, C. (1988). Long-term memory for pictures under conditions of thematically related foils. *Memory & Cognition*, *16*, 411–421.

Hummel, J.E., & Biederman, I. (1992). Dynamic binding in a neural network for shape recognition. *Psychological Review*, *99*, 480–517.

Humphreys, G., & Bruce, V. (1989). *Visual cognition*. Hove, UK: Lawrence Erlbaum Associates Ltd.

Hunt, R.R., & Einstein, G.O. (1981). Relational and item-specific information in memory. *Journal of Verbal Learning and Verbal Behavior*, *20*, 497–514.

Intraub, H. (1979). The role of implicit naming in pictorial encoding. *Journal of Experimental Psychology: Human Learning and Memory*, *5*, 78–87.

Jolicoeur, P. (1987). A size-congruency effect in memory for visual shape. *Memory & Cognition*, *15*, 531–543.

Jones, G.V. (1988). Images, predicates, and retrieval cues. In M. Denis, J. Engelkamp, & J.T.E. Richardson (Eds.), *Cognitive and neuropsychological approaches to mental imagery* (pp. 89–98). Dordrecht: Nijhoff.

Kirkpatrick, E.A. (1894). An experimental study of memory. *Psychological Review*, *1*, 602–609.

Klatzky, R.L. (1980). *Human memory*. San Francisco: Freeman.

Madigan, S. (1983). Picture memory. In J.C. Yuille (Ed.), *Imagery, memory and cognition* (pp. 65–89). Hillsdale, NJ: Lawrence Erlbaum Associates Inc.

Madigan, S., & Lawrence, V. (1980). Factors effecting item recovery and reminiscence in free recall. *American Journal of Psychology*, *93*, 489–504.

Marschark, M., Richman, C.L., Yuille, J.C., & Hunt, R.R. (1987). The role of imagery in memory: On shared and distinctive information. *Psychological Bulletin*, *102*, 28–41.

Moscovitch, M., Goshen-Gottstein, Y., & Vriezen, E. (1994). Memory without conscious recollection: A tutorial review from a neuropsychological perspective. In C. Umilta & M. Moscovitch (Eds.), *Attention and Performance 15* (pp. 619–660). Cambridge, MA: MIT Press.

Nelson, D.L. (1979). Remembering pictures and words: Appearance, significance and name. In L. Cermak & F.I.M. Craik (Eds.), *Levels of processing in human memory* (pp. 45–76). Hillsdale, NJ: Lawrence Erlbaum Associates Inc.

Nelson, D.L., & Brooks, D.H. (1973). Independence of phonetic and imaginal features. *Journal of Experimental Psychology*, *97*, 1–7.

Nelson, D.L., Reed, D.A., & Walling, J.R. (1976). Pictorial superiority effect. *Journal of Experimental Psychology: Human Learning and Memory*, *2*, 523–528.

Nelson, T.O., Metzler, J., & Reed, D.A. (1974). Role of details in the long-term recognition of pictures and verbal descriptions. *Journal of Experimental Psychology*, *102*, 184–186.

Paivio, A. (1969). Mental imagery in associative learning and memory. *Psychological Review*, *76*, 241–263.

Paivio, A. (1971). *Imagery and verbal processes*. New York: Holt, Rinehart & Winston.

Paivio, A. (1976). Imagery in recall and recognition. In J. Brown (Ed.), *Recall and recognition* (pp. 103–129). New York: Wiley.

Paivio, A. (1986). *Mental representations: A dual coding approach*. New York: Oxford University Press.

Paivio, A., & Csapo, K. (1973). Picture superiority in free recall: Imagery or dual coding? *Cognitive Psychology*, *80*, 279–285.

Paivio, A., Smythe, P., & Yuille, J.C. (1968). Imagery versus meaningfulness of nouns in paired-associate learning. *Canadian Journal of Psychology*, *22*, 427–441.

Richardson, J.T.E. (1978). Reported mediators and individual differences in mental imagery. *Memory & Cognition*, *6*, 376–378.

Richardson, J.T.E. (1985). Converging operations and reported mediators in the investigation of mental imagery. *British Journal of Psychology*, *76*, 205–214.

Richardson-Klavehn, A., & Bjork, R.A. (1988). Measures of memory. *Annual Review of Psychology*, *39*, 475–543.

Ritchey, G.H. (1980). Picture superiority in free recall: The effects of organization and elaboration. *Journal of Experimental Child Psychology*, *29*, 460–474.

Ritchey, G.H. (1982). Pictorial detail and recall in adults and children. *Journal of Experimental Psychology: Learning, Memory, and Cognition*, *8*, 139–141.

Ritchey, G.H., & Beal, R.C. (1980). Image detail and recall: Evidence for within-item elaboration. *Journal of Experimental Psychology: Human Learning and Memory*, *6*, 66–76.

Roediger, H.L. (1990). Implicit memory. *American Psychologist*, *45*, 1045–1056.

Roediger, H.L., & Srinivas, K. (1993). Specificity of operations in perceptual priming. In P. Graf & M.E. Masson (Eds.), *Implicit memory and new directions in cognition, development, and neuropsychology* (pp. 17–48). Hillsdale, NJ: Lawrence Erlbaum Associates Inc.

Roediger, H.L., & Weldon, M.S. (1987). Reversing the picture superiority effect. In M. McDaniel & M. Pressley (Eds.), *Imagery and related mnemonic processes* (pp. 151–174). New York: Springer.

Schacter, D.L., Delaney, S.M., & Merikle, E.P. (1990). Priming of nonverbal information and the nature of implicit memory. In G.H. Bower (Ed.), *The psychology of learning and motivation* (pp. 83–123). San Diego: Academic Press.

Shepard, R.N. (1967). Recognition memory for words, sentences and pictures. *Journal of Verbal Learning and Verbal Behavior*, *6*, 156–163.

Squire, L.R. (1987). *Memory and brain*. New York: Oxford University Press.

Srinivas, K. (1995). Representation of rotated objects in explicit and implicit memory. *Journal of Experimental Psychology: Learning, Memory, and Cognition*, *21*, 1019–1036.

Standing, L. (1973). Learning 10,000 pictures. *Quarterly Journal of Experimental Psychology*, *25*, 207–222.

Watkins, M.J., Peynircioglu, Z.F., & Brems, D.J. (1984). Pictorial rehearsal. *Memory & Cognition*, *12*, 553–557.

Weldon, M.S., & Coyote, K.C. (1996). Failure to find the picture superiority effect in implicit conceptual memory tests. *Journal of Experimental Psychology: Learning, Memory, and Cognition*, *22*, 670–686.

Zimmer, H.D. (1993). Sensorische Bildmerkmale im expliziten und impliziten Gedächtnis. In L. Montada (Ed.), *Bericht über den 38. Kongreß der Deutschen Gesellschaft für Psychologie in Trier* (Vol. 2, pp. 458–465). Göttingen: Hogrefe.

Zimmer, H.D. (1995). Size and orientation of objects in explicit and implicit memory: A reversal of the dissociation between perceptual similarity and type of test. *Psychological Research*, *57*, 260–273.

Zimmer, H.D. (2000). *The time course of sensory feature match in episodic object recognition*. Unpublished manuscript. Saarbrücken: Saarland University.

Zimmer, H.D., & Engelkamp, J. (1996, Sept.). *Size and color of objects in implicit memory tasks and in recognition*. Paper presented at the IX Conference of the European Society for Cognitive Psychology, Würzburg, Germany.

Zimmer, H.D., & Mohr, M. (1986). *Organisation und Organisierbarkeit von Verben und Substantiven bei einer verbal-semantischen bzw. "modalitätsspezifischen" Lernweise*. Arbeiten der Fachrichtung Psychologie Nr. 100. Saarbrücken: Universität des Saarlandes.

Zimmer, H.D., & Steiner, A. (2000). *Is color an element of the structural description of objects?* Manuscript submitted for publication.

CHAPTER FOUR

The processing of visuo-spatial information: Neuropsychological and neuroimaging investigations

Oliver H. Turnbull
University of Bangor, UK

Michel Denis
LIMSI-CNRS, Université de Paris-Sud, Orsay, France

Emmanuel Mellet
GIN-CYCERON, Caen, France

Olivier Ghaëm
LIMSI-CNRS, Université de Paris-Sud, Orsay, France

David P. Carey
University of Aberdeen, UK

The traditional neuropsychological understanding of the breakdown of disorders of vision and more broadly visuo-spatial cognition has been one of a bewildering variety of disorders. There are "visual" components to disorders as diverse as agnosia, alexia, apraxia, and topographical disorientation—as well as more esoteric disorders such as optic aphasia and simultanagnosia. This traditional pattern of classification has, by and large, involved discussing this range of disorders independently, in terms of disorders of visual and spatial ability. This classification system has also involved identifying the lesion site typically associated with each disorder. The rationale for identifying these disorders as being independent, or unrelated to each other, is partly undermined by the fact that, in many cases, the lesion sites for different disorders largely overlap. Thus, there

81

has been debate on the necessity of a bilateral lesion in prosopagnosia, of a lesion involving the splenium of the corpus callosum in optic aphasia, and of the possibility of "dorsal" and "ventral" simultanagnosia (De Renzi, 1982; Farah, 1990; Grusser & Landis, 1991). This approach has served the diagnostic needs of clinical work very well, and it has offered a body of sound and replicable observational findings that form the basis of any science. However, the very complexity, and diversity, of the clinical disorders have made it difficult to conceptualise their relationship to the overall manner in which the visual system operates. Certainly, there are many disorders of vision, but are there any under-lying trends or patterns that might help us to understand the general landscape of the visual system? Thus, in order to move from observation to theory, it might be useful to suggest a parsimonious unifying principle which simplifies this world of complex clinical descriptions, and may also provide a framework for a cognitive neuroscience of high-level vision.

In the domain of visual perception, one such useful distinction would be to differentiate between the tasks of object recognition and spatial abilities. There is some intuitive appeal in contrasting these two "visual" tasks, partly because changing one dimension has so little effect on the other. Thus, a "dog" remains a dog independent of its spatial location. Similarly, different objects, like dogs and cats, can occupy the same spatial location (at different times) without changing its spatial properties. The same is true of visual *images* of objects and of their location in *imagined* configurations. Another intuitive reason for promoting this distinction is the fact that the tasks of object recognition and spatial knowledge seem to demand the use of rather different properties from vision. Object recognition relies on knowing about object shape and colour, and this information remains relatively stable across time (chameleons aside). Spatial abilities rely on knowledge of precise retinally based co-ordinates, and frequently the use of motion information. The spatial domain is also one where moment-by-moment changes in the position of either object or observer are critical.

What are we to gain, then, from viewing the domains of object recognition and spatial abilities as possibly being independent, and what might it require in terms of a re-consideration of classical neuropsychology? It requires that we might loosely lump together the many visual object agnosias, including perhaps some of the specialised losses of face recognition (prosopagnosia) and word recognition (alexia), and consider their independence from spatial abilities. Clear support for the claim of independence comes from the fact that spatial abilities (as defined by tasks of orientation, size, location, and distance judgements) have been tested in many patients with visual agnosia—and these abilities appear to be relatively intact, in spite of the deficits of object recognition (Damasio, Tranel, & Damasio, 1989; De Haan & Newcombe, 1992; Farah & Ratcliff, 1994; Humphreys & Riddoch, 1993; McCarthy & Warrington, 1990). The "spatial" category would also include a variety of neuropsychological disorders: loss of topographical orientation, and impairments in domains such as attention, reaching, and voluntary gaze. In many patients with such disorders, object recognition (at least as assessed clinically) seems relatively intact (De Renzi, 1982; Ellis & Young, 1993; Halligan & Marshall, 1993; McCarthy & Warrington, 1990; Newcombe & Ratcliff, 1989). Thus, there is clinical precedent for considering object recognition and spatial abilities as operating relatively independently—although the classical literature in neuropsychology made little more of this distinction than of many other ways in which the visual system might be organised.

An influential attempt to unify perceptual and spatial abilities in a model that might account for the neuropsychological findings (as well as findings with normal subjects), has grown out of the idea that there are two "cortical visual systems". These are proposed to be specialised, as suggested earlier, for spatial and object perception, and this specialisation, as will be seen later, also extends to spatial and object imagination. The original formulation was presented by Ungerleider and Mishkin (1982), based on work in monkeys (although see Grusser & Landis, 1991, for some precursors in the German neurological literature), and was more-or-less unrelated to the work on cognitive models of the recognition process in normal humans that the growing disciplines of cognitive psychology and neuropsychology were developing. More recently, the two visual systems account has been highly influential in relating work on the neural substrate of recognition to issues of object representation and visual imagery, and will be discussed later (Biederman & Cooper, 1992; Farah, 1992; Haxby et al., 1994; Kosslyn, 1994; Logothetis & Sheinberg, 1996; McCarthy, 1993; Milner & Goodale, 1993).

TWO CORTICAL VISUAL SYSTEMS

The key hypothesis of the Ungerleider and Mishkin (1982) account can be summarised by the simple idea that the many areas of extrastriate cortex are organised into two relatively independent pathways. One system (the so-called "dorsal stream") runs from the occipital to the parietal cortex, and is primarily concerned with the perception of spatial information, in particular the spatial location of the object. The second ("ventral stream") system runs from occipital to infero-temporal cortex, and is concerned with the recognition of objects as members of a familiar class.

One problem with Ungerleider and Mishkin's (1982) scheme is the fact that the two visual systems hypothesis is a generalisation about the monkey visual system, which cannot be applied indiscriminately to human vision. This seems particularly germane because it is claimed that the human homologue of several key areas of the ventral and dorsal systems has yet to be identified or clearly specified (Eidelberg & Galaburda, 1984; Ungerleider & Haxby, 1994; see also Courtney, Ungerleider, Keil, & Haxby, 1996). The most problematic claim would be that there is no monkey homologue for the regions of recent evolutionary development of great importance to human visual cognition, in particular the human inferior parietal lobule. However, it has recently been suggested that STP (in the monkey superior temporal cortex) may be the monkey homologue of the human inferior parietal lobule (Milner, 1995; Morel & Bullier, 1990; Watson, Valenstein, Day, & Heilman, 1994). It has also been suggested that, in humans, the inferior parietal lobule is involved in the "binding" of information from the two visual systems (Watson et al., 1994; see Boussaoud, Ungerleider, & Desimone, 1990, and Morel & Bullier, 1990, for similar suggestions about macaque visual cortex).

Evidence from human neuropsychology

In spite of these concerns about generalising from monkeys to humans, the two visual systems approach appears to be consistent with the large body of know-ledge acquired in human neuropsychology. Lesions of the temporal cortex, par-ticularly on the ventral surface of the temporal lobe, produce disorders of object recognition (Damasio et al., 1989; Kertesz, 1983) which (arguably) are similar to the deficits seen after experimental lesions of infero-temporal cortex in the monkey (Dean, 1982; Gross, 1973; Walsh & Butler, 1996). While the issue of the laterality of lesion necessary to produce such disorders remains contentious (see Farah, 1990), there is a great deal of converging evidence for an occipito-temporal lesion site in prosopagnosia, and in some cases of visual agnosia (Damasio et al., 1989; Grossman et al., 1996; Kertesz, 1983). Similarly, parietal lesions result in disorders that may be broadly characterised as "spatial". These include visuo-spatial neglect, the spatial aspects of drawing and constructional tasks, peri-personal spatial disorders such as left–right orientation and ideo-motor apraxia, disorders of reaching (optic ataxia) and of voluntary gaze (ocular apraxia) (De Renzi, 1982; Kertesz, 1983; Newcombe & Ratcliff, 1989; Perenin & Vighetto, 1988; Rondot, De Recondo, & Ribadeau-Dumas, 1977). Thus, to a first approximation, the Ungerleider and Mishkin (1982) model seems an accurate account of the gross differences between occipito-parietal and occipito-temporal neuropsychological syndromes.

More recent work has suggested some areas of common interest between the two cortical visual systems model and work within cognitive psychology. Within the object recognition domain itself, Kosslyn (1994; Kosslyn et al., 1994) has argued that there are two separate mechanisms by which object recognition can be achieved within the ventral stream. The most important of these is a system that is viewpoint-independent, and perhaps operating along the lines suggested by Lowe (1985) and Biederman (1987), which involve the development of a viewpoint-invariant structural description of the object. Biederman's (1987) scheme proposes such a description of an object based on object primitives known as "geons", which are simple (typically symmetrical) geometric object compon-ents such as cylinders and blocks. Kosslyn (1994) does not commit himself to the "geon" concept, which might well be replaced with another viewpoint-independent account, such as Marr (1982). Nevertheless, Kosslyn's (1994) scheme suggests that the primary mechanism by which the ventral stream achieves object recognition is viewpoint-independent. It is notable that Kosslyn (1994) offers the alternative of feature-based recognition, also carried out within the ventral stream, which may be sufficient for recognition under certain circumstances. Again, such a feature-based system might be presumed to operate by viewpoint-independent means. (See Biederman & Gerhardstein, 1993, for similar proposals and a review.)

Kosslyn's (1994) argument clearly offers a great deal more of relevance to the present discussion than a simple version of the two visual systems theory of Ungerleider and Mishkin (1982), offering a point of contact between cognitive accounts of the recognition process and their neural basis, as will be discussed later. Another line of research has also reached similar conclusions.

A reinterpretation of the two visual systems account

In an influential series of papers, Milner and Goodale (1993, 1995; Goodale, 1993; Goodale et al., 1994; Goodale & Milner, 1992; Goodale et al., 1992) have suggested a substantial reinterpretation of the Ungerleider and Mishkin (1982) two visual systems account. Milner and Goodale (1993) agree that there is strong evidence for separate "dorsal" and "ventral" systems of processing in the monkey and human visual systems. However, they suggest that the Ungerleider and Mishkin (1982) description of the properties of the two systems (i.e., between the process of the recognition and spatial location of the object) does not appropriately describe the differences in function between these systems. Specifically, they claim that, although the ventral stream appears to be involved in object recognition, the dorsal stream appears to be more directly tied to the visuo-motor processes than to characterising the spatial location of an object. Milner and Goodale also acknowledge the possibility that inferior parietal regions in humans may play a role in many visuo-spatial cognitive tasks, which could require the use of information from both streams.

Much of their evidence in support of this position comes from a review of the human neuropsychology literature (Goodale et al., 1994; Goodale & Milner, 1992; Milner & Goodale, 1993) and some more recent evidence from patients whom they have investigated. For example, a visual form agnosic (DF) was unable to describe the size, shape, and orientation of visual targets, yet was able to use the same types of visual information to guide her motor responses. The opposite pattern has been demonstrated in a patient with optic ataxia (RV) who could describe the shape of objects but could not accurately reach for them (Goodale et al., 1994). This dissociation cannot be easily accommodated within the Ungerleider and Mishkin (1982) account. In the Milner and Goodale (1993; Goodale & Milner, 1992) theory, different forms of representation are employed by the visuo-motor and object recognition systems, with the ventral (object recognition) stream utilising "object-centred" (i.e., viewpoint-independent) codes, and the visuomotor systems of the dorsal stream employing viewer-centred codes.

The argument proposed by Milner and Goodale (1993; Goodale & Milner, 1992) offers some predictions about the types of neuropsychological disorder that might be seen in circumstances where patients have access only to a single form of representation. Milner and Goodale (1993) have suggested that patients with isolated viewer-centred coding might perform poorly on tasks that required knowledge of an object's three-dimensional structure, or involved manipulation of images in a third (depth) dimension. Alternatively, in the case of isolated access to the object-centred code, object recognition would be intact, but the patient would be particularly challenged on tasks that required the discrimination of attributes which cannot be coded in this type of structural description, namely mirror-images and orientation.

The proposals of Milner and Goodale (1993; Goodale & Milner, 1992), relating to the anatomical basis of viewer and object-centred representations, link directly to theories of object recognition. As discussed earlier, viewpoint-independent recognition requires an object-centred code, meaning that the Milner and Goodale (1993; Goodale & Milner, 1992) argument relating object-centred representations to the ventral stream is effectively the same argument proposed by Kosslyn (1994) that viewpoint-independent object recognition is achieved by the ventral stream.

The claim that object recognition is achieved by viewpoint-independent means within the structures of the occipito-temporal region has a strong bearing on the importance of the various cognitive accounts of the recognition process reviewed earlier. Although neither Kosslyn (1994), nor Milner and Goodale (1995), explicitly discuss this issue, this position appears to imply a minor, or non-existent, role for the viewpoint-dependent accounts such as those of Jolicoeur (1985, 1990) and Tarr and Pinker (1989) within the recognition process of the ventral stream. This position is surprising, given extensive evidence that the recognition process, at least under certain circumstances, appears to employ such viewpoint-dependent mechanisms (Bulthoff, Edelman, & Tarr, 1995; Jolicoeur, 1990; Tarr & Pinker, 1989). The situation might be clarified when consensus has been reached regarding specific neural correlates for object recognition using a viewpoint-dependent mechanism.

In relation to this point, there is other evidence in human neuropsychology that bears on the issue of the neural correlates of viewer and object-centred representations which has not previously been directly discussed in relation to the two visual systems account. These data relate to the difficult issue of the role of parietal cortex in object recognition (Carey, Harvey, & Milner, 1996; Jeannerod, Arbib, Rizzolatti, & Sakata, 1995; Warrington & James, 1967; Warrington & Taylor, 1973).

The only possible role identified by Kosslyn (1994) for viewpoint-dependent recognition is in circumstances in which the primary routes to recognition (by a viewpoint-independent description or feature-based analysis) fail strongly to implicate a single object. Under these circumstances, Kosslyn (1994) suggests, the orientation information associated with the image (as well as other classes of information, such as scale and position) might be "adjusted" in the dorsal stream until a better match is found between the image and existing memory representations. Kosslyn (1994) is not clear about the nature of dorsal stream involvement under such circumstances. He stresses the importance of top-down activation, and alteration of the position and resolution of an "attention window" under these circumstances, although he does not directly deal with the issue of mental rotation. However, taken together with the Milner and Goodale (1993) argument that viewer-centred descriptions are coded in the dorsal system, this explanation might offer a role for viewpoint-dependent process in the recognition of objects. The arguments imply that the dorsal stream might be used as an optional resource under circumstances where recognition is not immediately successful. This sort of evidence may explain why the effects of picture-plane misorientation on object recognition are greatest under non-optimal circumstances, such as the initial exposure to a novel exemplar of a known object (Jolicoeur, 1985).

OBJECT RECOGNITION

Several classes of neuropsychological evidence will be reviewed to support the position that parietal cortex may have a role in object recognition. Some of these data relate to the possibility that viewpoint-dependent recognition processes are associated with parietal cortex—in the case of the "unusual views" deficit, and in patients with disorders of mental rotation. These possibilities are of interest because they are associated with (right) parietal lesion sites. This would represent an instance of a lesion of the parietal cortex resulting in a recognition disorder. This would be a challenge to the strong version of the two visual systems account, as it would involve a parietal lobe component to object recognition. Finally, some unusual cases (after parietal lobe lesions) of loss of knowledge of object orientation and mirror-image discrimination are reviewed, which may be evidence for isolated access to viewpoint-independent image representations in the ventral stream.

The "unusual views" deficit

Patients with the "unusual views" deficit can successfully identify objects when they are presented from conventional viewpoints, but fail to recognise objects when viewed from perspectives classified as "unusual" (Landis, Regard, Bliestle, & Kleihues, 1988; Warrington & James, 1986; Warrington & Taylor, 1973, 1978). Such views of objects may be relatively common (e.g., a bucket viewed from above), but generally do not offer adequate views of many important aspects of object structure, and all such views are non-canonical (Palmer, Rosch, & Chase, 1981). Several hypotheses have been proposed to explain this deficit. The first is that these patients have a difficulty in establishing the principal axis of an object when it is foreshortened (Marr, 1982; Marr & Nishihara, 1978). A second suggestion is that the deficit is due to a difficulty in identifying the critical features of the object, which become occluded when an object is seen from an unusual perspective (Warrington & James, 1986). A role for both of these accounts has been suggested by the finding that, in a small group of visually agnosic patients, either class of disorder may be the cause of the object recognition deficit (Humphreys & Riddoch, 1984). Four of these five patients performed poorly when the principal axis was foreshortened, although recognition was not affected by the occlusion of features. In a final patient, performance was poor when the critical features could not be seen, but recognition was unaffected by manipulations of the principal axis. Thus, Humphreys and Riddoch (1984) suggest that there are two "routes" to object constancy: via "axes" or "features".

As discussed earlier, both the "axis-based" and "feature-based" accounts of recognition have been associated with the viewpoint-independent recognition systems of the ventral stream (Kosslyn, 1994; Milner & Goodale, 1993). On such accounts, the ability to derive "axis" or "feature" information should be lost after lesion to the occipito-temporal lobes. However, the "unusual views" deficit appears to occur after an inferior parietal lobe lesion (usually on the right, Warrington & James, 1986; Warrington & Taylor, 1973, 1978). Why should a lesion to a brain region that subserves visuo-spatial abilities have such an effect on object recognition, when viewer-centred spatial information is generally unimportant to recognition? Paradoxically, information about the precise location of object components relative to the observer might be extremely useful under "unusual view" circumstances, perhaps to allow the observer to establish that the principal axis of the object has been foreshortened—and such information is carried in the dorsal system. Notably, however, it has been argued that the inferior parietal cortex should not be considered part of the "dorsal" stream, on anatomical and neuropsychological grounds (e.g., Milner, 1995). This paradox might be resolved given the suggestion that the inferior parietal lobule (the lesion site in the "unusual views" deficit) might be involved in binding the viewer-centred and viewpoint-independent information derived from the dorsal and ventral systems respectively (McCarthy, 1993; Milner, 1995; Morel & Bullier, 1990; Watson et al., 1994).

Thus, the viewpoint-independent (ventral) system might be successful in recognising objects under optimal viewing circumstances, although it might require further viewer-centred information under non-optimal conditions. In this account, the inferior parietal lobule, which may have access to both classes of information, would be well placed to provide such data to ventral structures, and a lesion to this region would result in an "unusual views" deficit. This argument implies that the parietal lobe, in isolation, is not capable of recognising objects. However, it can play a role in object recognition in circumstances where information about the position of the observer in relation to object components is crucial.

This argument does not explain the fact that such patients also have difficulty with stimuli involving overlapping drawings, employing unusual lighting, involving fragmentation of the stimulus, or restricting the stimulus to a silhouette (see Warrington & James, 1986, for a review). The effects of such manipulations on the performance of these neurological patients suggest some role for the right parietal lobe in a wider variety of image manipulation and re-organisation strategies. These might, for example, be used to "clean up" a degraded image during object recognition (McCarthy, 1993) as part of a process of visual "problem-solving" (Farah, 1990). This process presumably relies on visuo-spatial cognitive abilities, which (as noted earlier) may be more closely associated with the structures of the inferior parietal lobe than the visuo-motor systems of the classical "dorsal" stream (Milner & Goodale, 1995).

Another explanation of the "unusual views" deficit is that of Layman and Greene (1988), who suggested that these patients had lost their ability to rotate images mentally. This argument was based on the gross anatomical association between loss of mental rotation and the "unusual views" deficit—as both tend to follow from right posterior brain lesions (Layman & Greene, 1988). This suggestion is somewhat at variance with a single-case dissociation found by Farah and Hammond (1988), whose patient was able to perform orientation-invariant object recognition, but failed a number of tasks of mental rotation. Turnbull and McCarthy (1996b) have also investigated a patient (AS) who shows the reverse dissociation—impaired performance in the recognition of misoriented objects with good performance on mental rotation tasks.

Although the patient of Farah and Hammond (1988) appears to show that mental rotation is not the only means by which a misoriented object is recognised, this does not imply that mental rotation has no role in the recognition process. Mental rotation may be another optional resource, to be used when more direct viewpoint-independent mechanisms fail. As discussed earlier, the cognitive psychology literature on mental rotation (Jolicoeur, 1985, 1990; Tarr & Pinker, 1989) suggests that viewpoint-dependent recognition would be based on a viewer-centred representation. Thus, in the account of Milner and Goodale (1993) it might be expected that such a system would operate in the parietal lobe. This possibility is investigated later.

Loss of mental rotation after brain injury

The vast majority of neuropsychological work on mental rotation has been in the comparison of the performance of groups of brain-damaged patients. These studies have generally involved comparing the deficits of patients with lesions in large anatomical regions, in particular the left/right or anterior/posterior dimensions (Butters & Barton, 1970; Butters, Barton, & Brody, 1970; De Renzi & Faglioni, 1967; Ditunno & Mann, 1990; Kim, Morrow, Passafiume, & Boller, 1984; Mehta, Newcombe, & Damasio, 1987; Ratcliff, 1979). Unfortunately, such group studies have not compared mental rotation abilities after lesion to parietal or temporal lobe structures.

Some more pertinent anatomical data come from case studies. LH, the patient of Farah, Hammond, Levine and Calvanio (1988a), had bilateral occipito-temporal lesions, leaving the parietal lobes intact. Consistent with this lesion site the patient had a profound visual recognition deficit, for both faces and common objects. LH's deficit extended into the domain of visual imagery (Farah et al., 1988a), where he was impaired at providing information about object properties such as colour, shape, and relative size. However, he had above average mental rotation abilities, as assessed on letter and Shepard and Metzler (1971) type figure-rotation tasks (Farah et al., 1988a).

A second patient, RT (Farah & Hammond, 1988), had extensive fronto-parietal lesions in the right hemisphere, partly extending into the lateral surface of the right temporal lobe. Consistent with a more parietal site of pathology, RT had poor constructional abilities, and had recovered from a severe hemi-spatial neglect. He performed below control levels on three tasks of mental rotation, including the Ratcliff (1979) Manikin task (although not including the Shepard and Metzler, 1971, tasks administered to LH). In contrast, RT showed no disturbances in reading, or in recognising people or real objects (although he was mildly impaired at recognising line drawings). He also showed no decrement in performance when he was required to recognise inverted objects, or read inverted words. Thus, RT had the obverse pattern of dissociation to that seen in LH (Farah et al., 1988a), showing normal visual imagery for object properties, but having a profound impairment on several tasks of mental rotation (Farah & Hammond, 1988). More recently, Morton and Morris (1995) described a patient (MG) with poor mental rotation ability (as assessed by Shepard and Metzler's task, Ratcliff's Manikin test, and the Flags test) with intact object recognition (including unusual views). MG had a left occipito-parietal lesion after a cerebro-vascular accident in her left hemisphere.

These investigations into the neuropsychology of mental rotation suggest that a profound loss of object recognition after temporal lobe lesions can co-exist with intact mental rotation abilities. Further, a parietal lobe lesion can severely disrupt the ability to perform mental rotation while sparing the ability to recognise objects, even when they are inverted (a simplified case of recognition across multiple viewpoints). This is consistent with the claim that the viewer-centred representations required for the performance of mental rotation are not coded in the ventral stream (Goodale & Milner, 1992; Milner & Goodale, 1993) and that such a strategy is used in the recognition process only when viewer-centred information is required because the more "direct" route of viewpoint-independent recognition has insufficient information for its usual processes (Kosslyn et al., 1990, 1994). Thus, mental rotation would be employed as an optional resource, which would occur under circumstances where recognition was not immediately successful—perhaps on the first exposure to a new exemplar (Jolicoeur, 1985) or under "unusual views" conditions. Given the available lesion evidence and recent theories regarding inferior parietal cortex, it seems plausible that this region plays a major role in visuo-spatial cognitive operations including mental rotation.

However, a recent report by Cohen et al. (1996) is at odds with this suggestion: they found evidence for superior parietal activation in subjects performing mental rotation. Bonda, Petrides, Frey, and Evans (1995) and Parsons et al. (1995) report superior and inferior parietal activation using tasks that included a mental rotation component. Clearly additional experiments may be required to disentangle some of these discrepancies. As noted by Milner and Goodale (1995), it is fairly crucial to ensure that differential eye movement patterns do not occur in experimental and control conditions in imaging studies, if the claim is that superior parietal activation is a consequence of visuo-spatial processing *per se*.

Spontaneous rotation and mirror-image discrimination

There are other neuropsychological disorders that are not generally cited in the debate on viewpoint-independent object recognition. The first relates to a neuropsychological sign, previously referred to as "spontaneous" rotation (see Royer & Holland, 1975, for review). An example was reported by Solms, Kaplan-Solms, Saling, and Miller (1988) whose patient, WB, made substantial errors of orientation on a number of tasks. He frequently copied drawings accurately but rotated them relative to the original (the Rey Complex Figure was usually rotated through 90° onto its base, or through 180°). He also failed orientation-dependent letter identification tasks (e.g., discriminating "p" from "d"), and made structurally correct, but orthogonally rotated, responses on a number of other tests.

We have recently described similar patients, LG (Turnbull, Laws, & McCarthy, 1995), NL and SC (Turnbull, Beschin, & Della Sala, 1997a), who also appeared to lack knowledge of the upright canonical orientation of objects. For example, in a series of experiments it was possible to show that LG's deficit also involved loss of the knowledge of the orientation of known objects, such as a chair and a bicycle (Turnbull et al., 1995)—a disorder that might be described as an "agnosia for object orientation". Critically, LG was able to name objects for which she could not provide the correct upright canonical orientation, suggesting that she had some form of viewpoint-independent object recognition. It is also notable that WB was also reported to have had clinically intact object recognition. This apparent dissociation between the ability to recognise objects and knowledge of their upright canonical orientation would be consistent with an argument in which such patients had lost the viewer-centred descriptions necessary accurately to judge object orientation (as a result of parietal lobe lesions), although they retained access to viewpoint-independent descriptions of the object necessary for recognition.

Another neuropsychological deficit that may well be related to the issue of viewpoint-independent object recognition is the inability of some patients to discriminate between mirror-image objects (Gold, Adair, Jacobs, & Heilman, 1995; Riddoch & Humphreys, 1988; Turnbull & McCarthy, 1996a; for a review of the relevant animal lesion literature, see Walsh & Butler, 1996). These patients failed on a number of tasks that required the discrimination of objects which differ in the left–right dimension (although RJ, the patient reported by Turnbull & McCarthy, 1996a, *could* perform mirror-image word discriminations, while failing to distinguish between mirror-image drawings of objects). However, the patients could perform tasks on which the stimuli differed on the up–down dimension.

Based on the argument presented earlier, patients showing spontaneous rotation and mirror-image discrimination deficits should have occipito-parietal lesion sites, leaving the occipito-temporal structures (subserving viewpoint-independent recognition) intact. Some of the cases have clear-cut parietal lesions (e.g., Turnbull & McCarthy, 1996a). However, the lesion sites in these cases are not always easy to interpret in terms of the two visual systems account (Milner & Goodale, 1995). For example, several cases (Turnbull et al., 1995; Riddoch & Humphreys, 1988) had largely parietal lesions that also involved the temporal lobe and some (Turnbull et al., 1997a) involved large middle cerebral artery lesions with similar problems of localisation. In such instances, involvement of the ventral stream cannot be excluded (although the structures of the inferior temporal lobe were clearly quite distant from the main focus of the lesion, and the patients invariably showed a number of visuo-spatial deficits, rather than disorders of object recognition). Finally, WB's lesion (Solms et al., 1988) was restricted to the frontal lobes, rather than involving the posterior brain regions which have been the focus of interest in the two visual systems account. Note, however, that the dorso-lateral aspect of the frontal lobes has been considered an extension of the dorsal system into the frontal lobe for the purposes of action (Milner & Goodale, 1995).

Thus, there appears to be support for the claim that a viewpoint-independent mechanism is the primary means by which object recognition is achieved. There is some debate about which precise account of the recognition process produces such viewpoint-independent recognition (Biederman, 1987; Marr, 1982; Poggio & Edelman, 1990). However, regardless of the debate, such a system (or systems) might be found in the structures of the occipito-temporal region (i.e., the ventral stream). There appears to be further support for a second mechanism by which the recognition process may be assisted, which operates along viewpoint-dependent lines, and involves the structures of the occipito-parietal region (i.e., the dorsal stream, or perhaps a "third" stream; see Milner, 1995). It would appear that this is not the primary route to recognition, but operates in non-optimal circumstances, serving perhaps to re-organise and normalise an otherwise "noisy" visual image in order for another attempt to be made at object recognition (presumably by the ventral system). Thus, the "two streams" model offers a neurobiological basis for both viewpoint-dependent and independent accounts of the recognition process, and suggests the participation of diverse areas of visual cortex in the complex process of object recognition.

VISUO-SPATIAL IMAGERY

We now turn to the examination of the studies, mainly neuroimaging studies, that were aimed at assessing the brain structures responsible for the processing of visual images. A number of behavioural studies have suggested that visual mental images are internal representations whose structure reflects the structure of the corresponding perceived objects (see Denis, 1991; Denis & Kosslyn, 1999; Kosslyn, 1994). In Kosslyn's theory the "visual buffer", on which images are inscribed, is claimed to possess functional characteristics that are similar to those of visual perception. Furthermore, the existence of functional interactions between images and percepts has led the researchers to consider that imagery and perception may share common mechanisms. Starting from the similarities of images and percepts as regards their processing mechanisms, it comes as a natural hypothesis to consider that perceptual and imaginal processing share at least some brain structures.

The investigations conducted in this domain also have the opportunity of assessing the respective roles of the dorsal and the ventral stream, depending on the visual and/or spatial content of the tasks under examination. In this domain, neuroimaging, mainly positron emission tomography (PET) and functional magnetic resonance imaging (fMRI), has provided invaluable information for the last 10 years. The main results are reviewed in the present section. This review is introduced by a summary of some relevant neuropsychological data. This summary is especially useful because the neuroimaging studies that have been conducted in recent years elaborate on the assumptions tested in the context of neuropsychological studies and the studies based on event-related potentials (ERPs).

Data from neuropsychological studies

Two major classes of neuropsychological studies are relevant for the domain at issue. The first one concerns the deficits that affect perception and mental imagery in similar ways. The second is related to the deficits in the generation of visual images not associated with visual recognition deficits. The most remarkable and extensively documented phenomenon of the first type is spatial neglect, a syndrome generally associated with a lesion of the right parietal lobe, in which patients tend to "ignore" the left half of the visual scenes in front of them. Bisiach and Luzzatti (1978) seem to have been the first to report evidence that unilateral neglect patients could show the same deficit in a mental imagery condition. When invited to visualise even a very familiar spatial environment, the patients do not "see" the left half of the scene. This finding is generally taken as reflecting the fact that some central mechanisms subserving mental imagery may be similar to those involved in visual processing. One should note, however, that some patients with unilateral neglect have deficits that are purely confined to visual imagery, without any neglect of visual objects available to perception (Beschin, Cocchini, Della Sala, & Logie, 1997; Cantagallo & Della Sala, 1998; Guaraglia, Padovani, Pantano, & Pizzamiglio, 1993).

Another class of informative neuropsychological studies are those reporting cases of "imagery loss" or "imagery deficit" (Basso, Bisiach, & Luzzatti, 1980; Grossi, Orsini, Modafferi, & Liotti, 1986). Such deficits may occur without being accompanied by deficits in perceptual recognition. Farah (1984) proposed a distinction between the deficits affecting the process of image generation itself and those resulting from the fact that the long-term memory representations that are normally used to construct visual images have been damaged. Although the deficits of the latter type do not seem to be associated with specific cortical lesions, the deficits of image generation occur in patients whose cortical lesions are consistently located in the occipital regions, mainly in the left hemisphere. Farah, Levine, and Calvanio (1988b) reported the case of RM, a patient who suffered left occipital and medio-parietal lesions. All RM's perceptual capacities and object recognition were preserved. Although he was capable of copying drawings correctly, he was unable to draw familiar objects from memory or even recently perceived figures. RM was required to verify sentences, some that had been rated previously as calling on visual imagery for verification (e.g., "*A grapefruit is larger than an orange*") and others that did not elicit imagery (e.g., "*The US government functions under a two party system*"). Although RM responded correctly to the latter type of sentences, his performance was severely diminished for sentences requiring visualisation.

Georg Goldenberg's (1989, 1992) studies have documented the various types of imagery deficit in patients with unilateral cortical lesions. In particular, all the tested patients with left temporo-occipital lesions were unable to take advantage of imagery instructions in verbal learning tasks. Goldenberg and Artner (1991) investigated patients with either left or right posterior cerebral artery lesions. Patients with left lesions showed especially low performance when they were invited to verify sentences calling on visual imagery (e.g., "*The ears of a bear are rounded*"). They also showed special difficulty when asked to produce the same type of judgements based on drawings (select one of two drawings, one of a bear with rounded ears, the other with pointed ears). A reasonable account of these two joint deficits should stress that the patients with left lesions have lost long-term visuo-spatial knowledge rather than being simply deficient at converting this knowledge into the form of visual images.

Neuropsychological studies have also contributed to documenting the issue of the cerebral lateralisation of mental imagery. The first trend of research in this domain tended to favour data suggesting the role of the right hemisphere in the generation and use of images (Jones-Gotman, 1979; Jones-Gotman & Milner,

1978; Sergent, 1989). The more recent lines of research (mainly inspired by computational approaches) are more likely to consider the involvement of the left hemisphere. Note also that arguments have been presented against the notion that the left hemisphere alone is in charge of image generation, and favouring the view of a joint contribution of the two hemispheres to the generation process (Sergent, 1990). It remains the case, however, that neuropsychological studies, taken as a whole, have repeatedly suggested that when image generation is perturbed, the probability is high that the patients have left posterior lesions. The reverse is not true, in that left temporo-occipital lesions do not systematically entail imagery deficits. However, the studies conducted with extended groups of patients attest to overall decrease of performance in imagery tasks when lesions are assessed in these cortical regions (Farah, 1988, 1995; Tippett, 1992).

Data from ERP studies

The hypothesis that occipital regions are involved in the generation of visual images is supported by studies based on electrophysiological techniques. It has long been established that the alpha rhythm is attenuated in visual areas when subjects are constructing images, more markedly in the left hemisphere (Davidson & Schwartz, 1977; Marks, 1990). Strong arguments have been consistently provided by researchers using ERPs. Farah, Weisberg, Monheit, and Péronnet (1989) reported a study in which concrete words were visually presented to subjects, each for 200 milliseconds. In the control condition, the subjects were invited simply to read the words. In the experimental condition, they had to read the words and form a visual image of the objects to which the words referred. The results show that during the first 450 milliseconds, the evoked potentials exhibit the same pattern in the two conditions. Thereafter, the patterns of the two conditions diverge. The main difference resides in increased positivity in the imagery condition as compared to the control condition, mainly at the occipital and posterior temporal regions of the scalp. Although the effect is bilateral, it is of greater magnitude on the left than on the right side. Converging ERP data were also reported on the role of the posterior brain regions in mental rotation (Péronnet & Farah, 1989). Thus, a number of data converge onto the notion that cortical areas involved in the processing of visual information, mainly the occipital and occipito-temporal regions, are also involved in the generation and manipulation of mental images. Actually, the fact that common areas are shared by visual and imaginal processing is not a definite argument for the identity of the mechanisms implemented in these areas in both cases. The issue is not only that perception and imagery share common sites of the nervous architecture, but that the same processing mechanisms are actually implemented in those sites in both conditions.

The assumption that perception and imagery use the same processing mechanisms has long been supported by the behavioural data reflecting the interactions (facilitation or interference) between both sets of representations (Farah, 1985;

Freyd & Finke, 1984; Segal, 1972). Here the ERP approach also provided strong arguments. Farah, Péronnet, Gonon, and Giard (1988c) recorded ERPs in a task that Farah (1985) had previously shown as reflecting the interactions between percepts and images. In this task, the subjects were invited to form the visual image of a capital letter, say letter H. Simultaneously with the formation of this image, the subjects had to detect letters in difficult perceptual conditions (with low figure/background contrast). In some cases, the letter to be detected was the letter that the subject was imagining at that moment (in this example, H), whereas in other cases it was a different letter (for instance, T). The results showed that the probability of correctly detecting the letter was affected by the currently imagined letter. When the imagined letter matched the to-be-detected letter, detection was better than when the two letters were different. Farah et al. (1988c) recorded ERPs during the two conditions of detection. The results showed that evoked potentials had greater amplitude when detection occurred for the letter that the subject was currently imagining, and were of lesser amplitude when the two letters were different. The occipital topography of the phenomenon clearly suggested that the cortical areas involved by the interaction between images and percepts are modality-specific, as in this case they concern the visual modality. To conclude, the effects of visual imagery on the pattern of evoked potentials provide a strong suggestion of a common cerebral localisation, where image and perceptual processing entertain close functional interactions.

It is of interest to note that studies involving the measurement of cortical potentials during visual imagery revealed negative shifts in the same regions as those identified by Farah et al. (1989), but the topography was modulated by the type of image generated. During the generation of images with a strong spatial component, a parietal maximum was observed, whereas the temporal and occipital regions were more active when the images reflected mainly visual qualities, this being more marked in the left hemisphere (see Uhl et al., 1990).

Neuroimaging assessments of visuo-spatial imagery

The objective of the neuroimaging studies conducted since the mid-1980s was to establish whether the metabolism of specific neuronal populations is modified by specific forms of cognitive activity. In the domain of mental imagery, the first research consisted of measuring variations in the cerebral blood flow while subjects reconstructed a visuo-spatial experience. The technique used in this research was single photon emission computerised tomography (SPECT). Roland and Friberg (1985) asked subjects to perform several cognitive tasks, among which one consisted of visualising the successive views encountered along a route in a familiar environment. The subjects were required to imagine that they were leaving their home and then proceeding, turning alternately left and right at each new intersection. This task, like the other tasks, induced blood flow increase in the superior prefrontal cortex, which probably reflected the high-level organising processes controlling cognitive activity. Specific to this task was blood flow increase in the superior occipital cortex, the postero-inferior temporal cortex, and the postero-superior parietal cortex. These are associative regions, which are known to be active in the processing of visual information. In the absence of any perceptual input, it is of interest to note that the primary visual cortex was not activated. In a further PET study, Roland, Eriksson, Stone-Elander, and Widen (1987) obtained confirmation of the involvement of the postero-superior parietal cortex in the same visualisation task, suggesting that the neuronal populations of this associative region have specific functional significance in the reconstruction of visual experience with a strong spatial component.

The brain activity accompanying visual imagery was extensively investigated by Goldenberg and his associates, using the SPECT technique. Goldenberg, Podreka, Steiner, and Willmes (1987) designed a task in which subjects were presented with a list of meaningless words, abstract nouns, or concrete nouns, the last case being given either with or without instructions to visualise the objects to which the nouns referred. After a short interval, a recognition test was presented. In the condition where subjects visualised the objects designated by the concrete nouns, blood flow measures showed a significant increase in the occipital cortex, mainly the left inferior occipital cortex. The activation of the parietal cortex, which was assessed in the Roland studies, was not confirmed here, which may be accounted for by the fact that Goldenberg's task essentially concentrated on the reconstruction of visual aspects of objects, whereas Roland's task included a strong spatial component.

In a further study (Goldenberg et al., 1989a), subjects participated in a sentence verification task. There were no imagery instructions, but some sentences were selected in such a way that it was highly likely that they would elicit a visual image in order to be verified (e.g., "*The green of fir trees is darker than that of grass*"). In contrast, some sentences referred to more abstract information and were unlikely to require visual imagery to be verified (e.g., "*The intensity of electrical current is measured in amperes*"). It turned out that verification of high-imagery sentences was accompanied by greater activation of the left inferior occipital cortex than verification of the other sentences. The same cortical region was again found activated in the visualisation of faces (Goldenberg et al., 1989b), in a task where subjects generated spontaneous visual images in association with acoustic images (Goldenberg et al., 1991), and in the verification of sentences requiring the inspection of a visual image (Goldenberg, Steiner, Podreka, & Deecke, 1992).

The SPECT technique was also used in a study that attempted to establish whether cerebral blood flow variations may be correlated with individual imagery differences. Charlot et al. (1992) selected two groups of subjects, who scored respectively in the upper and lower thirds of scores at two visuo-spatial tests (the Minnesota Paper Form Board and the Mental Rotations Test). Brain activity was measured in a rest condition, in a verbal task (mental conjugation of abstract verbs), and in a visual imagery task (mental exploration of a previously memorised spatial configuration). High imagers showed selective activation of the left sensory-motor cortex in the verbal task, and of the left temporo-occipital cortex in the visual imagery task (without any activation of the primary visual cortex). Low imagers, on the other hand, showed overall less differentiated increase of their cerebral activity.

An important set of PET experiments were conducted by Kosslyn et al. (1993), with the aim of assessing the role of the primary visual cortex in the generation of visual images. This investigation was in line with the theoretical framework claiming that the primary visual cortex is the anatomical substrate of the "visual buffer" (e.g., Kosslyn, 1994). Subjects were presented with a grid of 5×5 cells, one of the cells being occupied by an X. Two conditions were contrasted. In the imagery condition, the subjects were to visualise an uppercase block letter and "project" that image onto the grid. Their task consisted of reporting whether the cell marked with an X was one of the cells occupied by the imagined letter. In the perceptual condition, the letter actually appeared on the grid, and the subjects had to respond as in the imagery condition. In both conditions, the task resulted in significant activation of the primary visual cortex. This was suggestive of the fact that imagery and perception call on common cerebral mechanisms. In addition, the activation was even more marked during the imagery than the perception condition, indicating that generating the image of a visual pattern is a more costly cognitive task than simply seeing the pattern.

In the last experiment of the series, Kosslyn et al. (1993) asked the subjects to generate images of letters at a small size or large size. Visualising small letters engendered greater activation in the posterior part of the visual cortex, whereas large images activated more the anterior part. These data suggest that the cortical regions involved in mental imagery are topographically organised. As the posterior part of Area 17 is known to represent the foveal region, it is not surprising that the generation of a smaller image produces more activation in this part, whereas a larger image engenders greater activation farther ahead in the medial occipital cortex. Other PET studies reported similar blood flow increase in primary visual areas when subjects visualise specific places or familiar people (see Damasio et al., 1993; see also Kosslyn, Thompson, Kim, & Alpert, 1995). In addition, fMRI studies have provided support to the assumption that the visual cortex is the neuroanatomical substrate of both visual perception and imagery, as it is similarly activated in both conditions (cf. Le Bihan et al., 1993; see also Ogawa et al., 1993).

The issue of the involvement of the primary visual areas in the generation of visual imagery was the starting point of a theoretical debate in which Roland and Gulyas (1994) defended the idea that the cortical areas subserving mental imagery are a subset of the areas involved in visual perception, but that this subset does not include primary visual areas (see Mellet et al., 1998a, for a review). Actually, these areas are not activated in all subjects during imagery tasks, and it is likely that their activation is mostly detectable when the images generated have a high degree of resolution (see Sakai & Miyashita, 1994). Based on further PET recordings during the visualisation of complex geometric forms, Roland and Gulyas (1995) proposed the hypothesis that the neuronal populations of the temporo-occipital and parieto-occipital regions are mainly responsible for visual imagery.

Further PET data were reported by Mellet, Tzourio, Denis, and Mazoyer (1995) on the brain activity associated with mental scanning. In this experiment, subjects were first involved in a learning phase, in which they were asked to inspect and memorise a spatial configuration (the map of an island with six landmarks located on the periphery). Regional cerebral blood flow was then recorded as the subjects performed either perceptual or imaginal scanning of the map. In the perceptual condition, the subjects were shown the map and asked to scan visually from landmark to landmark. In the imagery condition, the subjects were placed in total darkness and were instructed to recreate a vivid image of the map, then perform mental scanning from landmark to landmark. The results showed that scanning in both conditions involved a common network of cerebral structures, including a bilateral superior external occipital region and a left internal parietal region (precuneus). The occipital region was interpreted as reflecting the processes involved in the generation and maintenance of the visual image, whereas the parietal region was thought to reflect more specifically the scanning component of the process. Other PET studies also indicated that memory-related imagery is associated with precuneus activation (e.g., Fletcher et al., 1995). Another finding of the Mellet et al. (1995) data was that bilateral activation of the primary visual areas occurred in the perceptual condition, but these areas were not activated during mental scanning in the imagery condition.

In the Mellet et al. (1995) study, it is relevant to stress that parietal regions were involved in an imagery process with a spatial component. The fact that regions of the dorsal stream were activated during the mental exploration of a previously learned visual configuration is consistent with conceptions reviewed earlier of the role of the parieto-occipital cortex. In a further study, where subjects were trained to construct mental images of novel objects from verbal instructions, PET recordings provided evidence that the dorsal pathway was recruited in the absence of any visual input (Mellet et al., 1996). This finding indicates that the role of the dorsal route in spatial processing is not linked to the modality in which information is presented. The same network is apparently engaged in both mental scanning of visual images and the creative construction of purely mental objects (see Denis & Kosslyn, 1999).

Several further studies confirmed the lack of any detectable activation in the primary visual cortex when people generate visual images in response to concrete nouns. This was found using fMRI (D'Esposito et al., 1997) and PET (Mellet, Tzourio, Denis, & Mazoyer, 1998b). D'Esposito et al. (1997) found activation in the left inferior temporal cortex, which confirms the involvement of the ventral stream in the reconstruction of the visual aspects of objects. The Mellet et al. (1998b) study showed that a network including part of the bilateral ventral stream and the frontal working memory areas was recruited when subjects listened to the definition of concrete words and were asked to generate images of corresponding objects.

The controversy about the involvement of the primary visual areas in mental imagery tasks has recently been addressed by the review and meta-analysis of the neuroimaging literature provided by Thompson and Kosslyn (2000). The review established that the activation of the primary visual areas during visual imagery tasks depends mainly on whether high resolution is required in the tasks. When high-resolution images are required, not only is the primary visual cortex activated, but activation of the inferior temporal cortex takes place as well. If only low resolution is required (for instance, when only a general shape is necessary for achieving the task), the inferior temporal regions are activated, but not the primary visual cortex. When the imagery task mainly requires the visualisation of spatial relations and high resolution is not necessary, then the inferior parietal regions are activated, but not the occipital cortex.

Visuo-spatial imagery and spatial knowledge

Another domain of interest is the brain activity involved in the mental exploration of geographical entities. Learning an environment may involve several types of experience. Two types of learning may be contrasted, one based on actual navigational experience of an environment, and the other on learning a map of this environment (Ghaëm et al., 1997; Ghaëm et al., 1998). Navigation involves a composite sensory experience, including visual and kinaesthetic aspects, organised according to a route perspective. The subject must process a sequence of frontal views of the traversed environment, connected by a sequence of segments. On the other hand, map learning essentially involves the visual experience of two-dimensional configurations. The subject takes a survey perspective on the environment, which provides a bird's-eye view of the whole environment and makes all landmarks and distances simultaneously available to inspection. Although being essentially different from each other, these two learning conditions generate representations that are supposed to serve similar orienting behaviour. The Ghaëm et al. (1997, 1998) studies did not test any navigational behaviour, but considered a form of mental activity accomplished after each type of learning, that is, the mental reconstruction of the experience associated with route segments. For instance, after navigational experience, a subject may be asked to reconstruct mentally the sequence of events he or she experienced along a segment of the environment. After map learning, the subject may be asked to perform mental scanning along a route segment present on the map. Because the two forms of learning differ radically from each other, it is of interest to establish if the neural substrate of the mental navigation would reflect this difference.

In the Ghaëm et al. (1997) study, subjects learned a real urban environment by actual navigation. During the PET session, the subjects were given the names of two landmarks that limited a route segment. They were asked mentally to reconstruct the sequential visual and kinaesthetic experience of walking along this segment. The subjects pressed a button when they got to the end of the segment so that the time of the simulated progression was recorded. A strong positive correlation was found between the time taken to reconstruct mentally the progression along a segment and the length of the segment, indicating that the subjects had encoded an accurate representation of the distances from their navigational experience. In the map learning condition (Ghaëm et al., 1998), subjects learned a map of the same urban environment by repeated inspection of the map. Learning ended when the subjects were capable of locating accurately the seven landmarks in the street network of the map. Then, during the PET session, the subjects performed mental scanning between all possible pairs of landmarks. They were asked to scan mentally along the streets by taking the shortest street route in all cases. A highly significant positive correlation coefficient was calculated between scanning time and distance, reflecting the fact that the visual image of the map reconstructed from memory contained accurate metric information.

The PET recordings evidenced similarities in the two experiments. When the recordings in the mental navigation task were compared to those obtained in a resting state in darkness, significant blood flow increases were found in the precuneus on the internal side part of the parietal lobe and in the frontal cortex, at the intersection of the precentral and the superior frontal sulcus. Interestingly, this fronto-parietal network is involved in spatial mental imagery (see Mellet et al., 1998b, for a review) and in spatial working memory (see Courtney, Petit, Haxby, & Ungerleider, 1998, for a review). This result gave a neural substrate to the cognitive proximity among mental navigation, spatial mental imagery, and spatial working memory. An additional activation was bilaterally detected in the hippocampal regions, which are known to play a key role in navigation (see Aguirre & D'Esposito, 1997; Maguire, Frackowiak, & Frith, 1996). The recordings in the mental scanning task following map learning were compared to recordings during rest. The task involved a fronto-parietal network similar to the one involved in mental navigation. Although of weaker amplitude than in the previous protocol, an activation of the right hippocampal gyrus was also detected during mental scanning. These anatomofunctional similarities between navigation and mental scanning fit well with the common properties shared by the two types of representations (Taylor & Tversky, 1992).

A further point of interest is that the chronometric data reflect the fact that in two contrasted learning conditions, the mental reconstruction of a visuo-spatial representation contains accurate metric information, whether this has been acquired through physical displacement or from visual inspection of a two-dimensional spatial configuration.

CONCLUSIONS

The work reviewed in this chapter clearly demonstrates a number of principles of modern cognitive neuroscience, which may rightly be interpreted as inspiring a certain amount of confidence in the future of this relatively new discipline. First, cognitive neuroscience, and especially work in the area broadly defined as "vision", appears to be highly productive. As the foregoing review demonstrates, vision research involves a remarkably broad range of issues, and it appears that, in the best scientific tradition, new issues instigate a burst of empirical research on the novel topic. In almost every case, these findings move the field forward, and in most cases the issues are *much* better understood after this process. This is a field with few "blind alleys", which is always a healthy sign for a science.

Second, cognitive neuroscience also appears to be generating some sound theoretical advances on the back of the empirical work, with the "two visual systems" account forming the basis for organising the present review. Such accounts are perhaps always destined to be over-simplifications of complex issues. Nevertheless, generating simple models that explain a wide range of phenomena has been the cornerstone of work in the natural sciences, and advances in this area are welcome.

Third, it is gratifying to see the extent to which multiple techniques are being employed to investigate a single issue. This chapter has focused largely on the investigation of patients with neurological lesions, and on functional imaging studies in neurologically normal subjects, together with some mention of a range of other methods. One of the most rewarding features of the use of such multiple techniques is the fact that it so frequently generates converging evidence. We now have a substantial body of evidence relating to the neural substrate of a wide range of visual and spatial abilities, and the evidence from diverse investigative techniques appears to point in the same direction in so many instances. This suggests that the discoveries in visual neuroscience represent reliable findings, rather than "slippery" experimental findings that might well be an artefact of a particular method of data collection. Taking the evidence of this chapter as a sample of the wider field of cognitive neuroscience, it appears that the discipline has a bright future.

REFERENCES

Aguirre, G.K., & D'Esposito, M. (1997). Environmental knowledge is subserved by separable dorsal/ventral neural areas. *Journal of Neuroscience, 17*, 2512–2518.

Basso, A., Bisiach, E., & Luzzatti, C. (1980). Loss of mental imagery: A case study. *Neuropsychologia, 18*, 435–442.

Beschin, N., Cocchini, G., Della Sala, S., & Logie, R.H. (1997). What the eyes perceive, the brain ignores: A case of pure unilateral representational neglect. *Cortex, 33*, 3–26.

Biederman, I. (1987). Recognition-by-components: A theory of human image understanding. *Psychological Review, 94*, 115–147.

Biederman, I., & Cooper, E.E. (1992). Size invariance in visual object priming. *Journal of Experimental Psychology: Human Perception and Performance, 18*, 121–133.

Biederman, I., & Gerhardstein, P.C. (1993). Recognizing depth-rotated objects: Evidence and conditions for three-dimensional invariance. *Journal of Experimental Psychology, 19*, 1162–1182.

Bisiach, E., & Luzzatti, C. (1978). Unilateral neglect of representational space. *Cortex, 14*, 129–133.

Bonda, E., Petrides, M., Frey, S., & Evans, A. (1995). Neural correlates of mental transformations of the body-in-space. *Proceedings of the National Academy of Sciences of the United States of America, 92*, 11180–11184.

Boussaoud, D., Ungerleider, L.G., & Desimone, R. (1990). Pathways for motion analysis: Cortical connections of the medial superior temporal and fundus of the superior temporal visual areas in the macaque. *Journal of Comparative Neurology, 296*, 462–495.

Bulthoff, H.H., Edelman, S., & Tarr, M.J. (1995). How are three-dimensional objects represented in the brain? *Cerebral Cortex, 3*, 247–260.

Butters, N., & Barton, M. (1970). Effect of parietal lobe damage on the performance of reversible operations in space. *Neuropsychologia, 8*, 205–214.

Butters, N., Barton, M., & Brody, B.A. (1970). Role of the right parietal lobe in the mediation of cross-modal associations and reversible operations in space. *Neuropsychologia, 6*, 174–190.

Cantagallo, A., & Della Sala, S. (1998). Preserved insight in an artist with extrapersonal spatial neglect. *Cortex, 34*, 163–189.

Carey, D.P., Harvey, M., & Milner, A.D. (1996). Visuomotor sensitivity for shape and orientation in a patient with visual form agnosia. *Neuropsychologia, 34*, 329–339.

Charlot, V., Tzourio, N., Zilbovicius, M., Mazoyer, B., & Denis, M. (1992). Different mental imagery abilities result in different regional cerebral blood flow activation patterns during cognitive tasks. *Neuropsychologia, 30*, 565–580.

Cohen, M.S., Kosslyn, S.M., Breiter, H.C., DiGirolamo, G.J., Thompson, W.L., Anderson, A.K., Bookheimer, S.Y., Rosen, B.R., & Belliveau, J.W. (1996). Changes in cortical activity during mental rotation: A mapping study using functional MRI. *Brain, 119*, 89–100.

Courtney, S.M., Petit, L., Haxby, J.V., & Ungerleider, L.G. (1998). The role of prefrontal cortex in working memory: Examining the contents of consciousness. *Philosophical Transactions of the Royal Society of London (Biol.), 353*, 1819–1828.

Courtney, S.M., Ungerleider, L.G., Keil, K., & Haxby, J.V. (1996). Object and spatial visual working memory activate separate neural systems in human cortex. *Cerebral Cortex, 6*, 39–49.

Damasio, A.R., Tranel, D., & Damasio, H. (1989). Disorders of visual recognition. In F. Boller & J. Grafman (Eds.), *Handbook of neuropsychology (Vol. 2)*. Amsterdam: Elsevier.

Damasio, H., Grabowski, T.J., Damasio, A., Tranel, D., Boles-Ponto, L., Watkins, G.L., & Hichwa, R.D. (1993). Visual recall with eyes closed and covered activates early visual cortices. *Society for Neuroscience Abstracts, 19*, 1603.

Davidson, R.J., & Schwartz, G.E. (1977). Brain mechanisms subserving self-generated imagery: Electrophysiological specificity and patterning. *Psychophysiology, 14*, 129–133.

Dean, P. (1982). Visual behavior of monkeys with inferotemporal lesions. In D.J. Ingle, M.A. Goodale, & R.J.W. Mansfield (Eds.), *Analysis of visual behavior*. Cambridge, MA: The MIT Press.

De Haan, E.H.F., & Newcombe, F. (1992). Neuropsychology of vision. *Current Opinion in Neurology and Neurosurgery, 5*, 65–70.

Denis, M. (1991). *Image and cognition*. New York: Harvester Wheatsheaf.

Denis, M., & Kosslyn, S.M. (1999). Scanning visual mental images: A window on the mind. *Current Psychology of Cognition, 18*, 409–465.

De Renzi, E. (1982). *Disorders of space exploration and cognition*. Chichester, UK: Wiley.

De Renzi, E., & Faglioni, P. (1967). The relationship between visuo-spatial impairment and constructional apraxia. *Cortex, 3*, 327–342.

D'Esposito, M., Detre, J.A., Aguirre, G.K., Stallcup, M., Alsop, D.C., Tippett, L.J., & Farah, M.J. (1997). A functional MRI study of mental image generation. *Neuropsychologia, 35*, 725–730.

Ditunno, P.L., & Mann, V.A. (1990). Right hemisphere specialisation for mental rotation in normals and brain damaged subjects. *Cortex, 26*, 177–188.

Eidelberg, D., & Galaburda, A.M. (1984). Inferior parietal lobule: Divergent architectonic asymmetries in the human brain. *Archives of Neurology, 41*, 843–852.

Ellis, A.W., & Young, A.W. (1993). *Human cognitive neuropsychology*. Hove, UK: Lawrence Erlbaum Associates Ltd.

Farah, M.J. (1984). The neurological basis of mental imagery: A componential analysis. *Cognition, 18*, 245–272.

Farah, M.J. (1985). Psychophysical evidence for a shared representational medium for mental images and percepts. *Journal of Experimental Psychology: General, 114*, 91–103.

Farah, M.J. (1988). Is visual imagery really visual? Overlooked evidence from neuropsychology. *Psychological Review, 95*, 307–317.

Farah, M.J. (1990). *Visual agnosia*. Cambridge, MA: The MIT Press.

Farah, M.J. (1992). Agnosia. *Current Opinion in Neurobiology, 2*, 162–164.

Farah, M.J. (1995). The neural bases of mental imagery. In M.S. Gazzaniga (Ed.), *The cognitive neurosciences* (pp. 963–975). Cambridge, MA: The MIT Press.

Farah, M.J., & Hammond, K.M. (1988). Mental rotation and orientation-invariant object recognition: Dissociable processes. *Cognition, 29*, 29–46.

Farah, M.J., Hammond, K.M., Levine, D.N., & Calvanio, R. (1988a). Visual and spatial mental imagery: Dissociable systems of representation. *Cognitive Psychology, 20*, 439–462.

Farah, M.J., Levine, D.N., & Calvanio, R. (1988b). A case study of mental imagery deficit. *Brain and Cognition, 8*, 147–164.

Farah, M.J., Péronnet, F., Gonon, M.-A., & Giard, M.-H. (1988c). Electrophysiological evidence for a shared representational medium for visual images and visual percepts. *Journal of Experimental Psychology: General, 117*, 248–257.

Farah, M.J., & Ratcliff, G. (1994). *Neuropsychology of high-level vision*. Hillsdale, NJ: Lawrence Erlbaum Associates Inc.

Farah, M.J., Weisberg, L.L., Monheit, M., & Péronnet, F. (1989). Brain activity underlying mental imagery: Event-related potentials during mental image generation. *Journal of Cognitive Neuroscience, 1*, 302–316.

Fletcher, P.C., Frith, C.D., Baker, S.C., Shallice, T., Frackowiak, R.S.J., & Dolan, R.J. (1995). The mind's eye—Precuneus activation in memory-related imagery. *NeuroImage, 2*, 195–200.

Freyd, J.J., & Finke, R.A. (1984). Facilitation of length discrimination using real and imaged context frames. *American Journal of Psychology, 97*, 323–341.

Ghaëm, O., Mellet, E., Crivello, F., Tzourio, N., Mazoyer, B., Berthoz, A., & Denis, M. (1997). Mental navigation along memorized routes activates the hippocampus, precuneus, and insula. *NeuroReport, 8*, 739–744.

Ghaëm, O., Mellet, E., Tzourio, N., Bricogne, S., Etard, O., Tirel, O., Beaudouin, V., Mazoyer, B., Berthoz, A., & Denis, M. (1998). *Mental exploration of an environment learned from a map: A PET study*. Fourth International Conference on Functional Mapping of the Human Brain, Montréal, Canada, 7–12 June.

Gold, M., Adair, J.C., Jacobs, D.H., & Heilman, K.M. (1995). Right–left confusion in Gerstmann's syndrome: A model of body centred spatial orientation. *Cortex, 31*, 267–283.

Goldenberg, G. (1989). The ability of patients with brain damage to generate mental visual images. *Brain, 112*, 305–325.

Goldenberg, G. (1992). Loss of visual imagery and loss of visual knowledge—A case study. *Neuropsychologia, 30*, 1081–1099.

Goldenberg, G., & Artner, C. (1991). Visual imagery and knowledge about the visual appearance of objects in patients with posterior cerebral artery lesions. *Brain and Cognition, 15*, 160–186.

Goldenberg, G., Podreka, I., Steiner, M., Franzen, P., & Deecke, L. (1991). Contributions of occipital and temporal brain regions to visual and acoustic imagery—A SPECT study. *Neuropsychologia, 29*, 695–702.

Goldenberg, G., Podreka, I., Steiner, M., & Willmes, K. (1987). Patterns of regional cerebral blood flow related to memorizing of high and low imagery words—An emission computer tomography study. *Neuropsychologia, 25,* 473–485.

Goldenberg, G., Podreka, I., Steiner, M., Willmes, K., Suess, E., & Deecke, L. (1989a). Regional cerebral blood flow patterns in visual imagery. *Neuropsychologia, 27,* 641–664.

Goldenberg, G., Podreka, I., Uhl, F., Steiner, M., Willmes, K. & Deecke, L. (1989b). Cerebral correlates of imagining colours, faces and a map—I. SPECT of regional cerebral blood flow. *Neuropsychologia, 27,* 1315–1328.

Goldenberg, G., Steiner, M., Podreka, I., & Deecke, L. (1992). Regional cerebral blood flow patterns related to verification of low- and high-imagery sentences. *Neuropsychologia, 30,* 581–586.

Goodale, M.A. (1993). Visual pathways supporting perception and action in the primate cerebral cortex. *Current Opinion in Neurobiology, 3,* 578–585.

Goodale, M.A., Meenan, J.P., Bulthoff, H.H., Nicolle, D.A., Murphy, K.J., & Racicot, C.I. (1994). Separate neural pathways for the visual analysis of object shape in perception and prehension. *Current Biology, 4,* 604–610.

Goodale, M.A., & Milner, A.D. (1992). Separate visual pathways for perception and action. *Trends in Neuroscience, 15,* 20–25.

Goodale, M.A., Milner, A.D., Jakobson, L.S., & Carey, D.P. (1992). A neurological dissociation between perceiving objects and grasping them. *Nature, 349,* 154–156.

Gross, C.G. (1973). Visual functions of inferotemporal cortex. In R. Jung (Ed.), *Handbook of sensory physiology (Vol. VII/3),* (pp. 451–482). Berlin: Springer-Verlag.

Grossi, D., Orsini, A., Modafferi, A., & Liotti, M. (1986). Visuoimaginal constructional apraxia: On a case of selective deficit of imagery. *Brain and Cognition, 5,* 255–267.

Grossman, M., Galetta, S., Ding, X.S., Morrison, D., D'Esposito, M., Robinson, K., Jaggi, J., Alavi, A., & Reivich, M. (1996). Clinical and positron emission tomography studies of visual apperceptive agnosia. *Neuropsychiatry, Neuropsychology and Behavioural Neurology, 9,* 70–77.

Grusser, O.-J., & Landis, T. (1991). Visual agnosias and other disturbances of visual perception and cognition. In J.R. Cronly-Dillon (Ed.), *Vision and visual dysfunction, Vol. 12.* London: Macmillan.

Guaraglia, C., Padovani, A., Pantano, P., & Pizzamiglio, L. (1993). Unilateral neglect restricted to visual imagery. *Nature, 364,* 235–237.

Halligan, P.W., & Marshall, J.C. (1993). The history and clinical presentation of neglect. In I.H. Robertson & J.C. Marshall (Eds.), *Unilateral neglect: Clinical and experimental studies.* Hove, UK: Lawrence Erlbaum Associates Ltd.

Haxby, J.V., Horwitz, B., Ungerleider, L.G., Maisog, J.M., Pietrini, P., & Grady, C.L. (1994). The functional organisation of human extrastriate cortex: A PET-rCBF study of selective attention to faces and locations. *Journal of Neuroscience, 14,* 6336–6353.

Humphreys, G.W., & Riddoch, M.J. (1984). Routes to object constancy: Implications from neurological impairments of object constancy. *Quarterly Journal of Experimental Psychology, 36*A, 385–418.

Humphreys, G.W., & Riddoch, M.J. (1993). Object agnosias. *Baillière's Clinical Neurology, 2,* 339–359.

Jeannerod, M., Arbib, M.A., Rizzolatti, G., & Sakata, H. (1995). Grasping objects: The cortical mechanisms of visuomotor transformation. *Trends in Neuroscience, 18,* 314–320.

Jolicoeur, P. (1985). Time to name disoriented natural objects. *Memory and Cognition, 13,* 289–303.

Jolicoeur, P. (1990). Identification of disoriented objects: A dual systems theory. *Mind and Language, 5,* 387–410.

Jones-Gotman, M. (1979). Incidental learning of image-mediated or pronounced words after right temporal lobectomy. *Cortex, 15,* 187–197.

Jones-Gotman, M., & Milner, B. (1978). Right temporal-lobe contribution to image-mediated verbal learning. *Neuropsychologia, 16,* 61–71.

Kertesz, A. (1983). *Localisation in neuropsychology.* New York: Academic Press.

Kim, Y., Morrow, L., Passafiume, D., & Boller, F. (1984). Visuoperceptual and visuomotor abilities and locus of lesion. *Neuropsychologia*, *22*, 177–185.

Kosslyn, S.M. (1994). *Image and brain: The resolution of the imagery debate*. Cambridge, MA: The MIT Press.

Kosslyn, S.M., Alpert, N.M., Thompson, W.L., Chabris, C.F., Rauch, S.L., & Anderson, A.K. (1994). Identifying objects seen from different viewpoints: A PET investigation. *Brain*, *117*, 1055–1071.

Kosslyn, S.M., Alpert, N.M., Thompson, W.L., Maljkovic, V., Weise, S.B., Chabris, C.F., Hamilton, S.E., Rauch, S.L., & Buonanno, F.S. (1993). Visual mental imagery activates topographically organized visual cortex: PET investigations. *Journal of Cognitive Neuroscience*, *5*, 263–287.

Kosslyn, S.M., Flynn, R.A., Amsterdam, J.B., & Wang, G. (1990). Components of high-level vision: A cognitive neuroscience analysis and accounts of neurological syndromes. *Cognition*, *34*, 203–277.

Kosslyn, S.M., Thompson, W.L., Kim, I.J., & Alpert, N.M. (1995). Topographical representations of mental images in primary visual cortex. *Nature*, *378*, 496–498.

Landis, T., Regard, M., Bliestle, A., & Kleihues, P. (1988). Prosopagnosia and agnosia for noncanonical views–An autopsied case. *Brain*, *111*, 1287–1297.

Layman, S., & Greene, E. (1988). The effect of stroke on object recognition. *Brain and Cognition*, *7*, 87–114.

Le Bihan, D., Turner, R., Zeffiro, T.A., Cuénod, C.A., Jezzard, P., & Bonnerot, V. (1993). Activation of human primary visual cortex during visual recall: A magnetic resonance imaging study. *Proceedings of the National Academy of Sciences of the United States of America*, *90*, 11802–11805.

Logothetis, N.K., & Sheinberg, D.L. (1996). Visual object recognition. *Annual Review of Neuroscience*, *19*, 577–621.

Lowe, D.G. (1985). *Perceptual organisation and visual recognition*. Boston: Kluwer.

Maguire, E.A., Frackowiak, R.S.J., & Frith, C.D. (1996). Learning to find your way: A role for the human hippocampal formation. *Proceedings of the Royal Society of London, Series B*, *263*, 1745–1750.

Marks, D.F. (1990). On the relationship between imagery, body, and mind. In P.J. Hampson, D.F. Marks, & J.T.E. Richardson (Eds.), *Imagery: Current developments* (pp. 1–38). London: Routledge.

Marr, D. (1982). *Vision*. San Francisco: Freeman.

Marr, D., & Nishihara, H.K. (1978). Representation and recognition of the spatial organisation of three-dimensional shapes. *Proceedings of the Royal Society of London, Series B*, *200*, 269–294.

McCarthy, R.A. (1993). Assembling routines and addressing representations: An alternative conceptualisation of "what" and "where" in the human brain. In N. Elian, R.A. McCarthy, & B. Brewer (Eds.), *Spatial representation: Problems in philosophy and psychology*. Oxford: Blackwell.

McCarthy, R.A., & Warrington, E.K. (1990). *Cognitive neuropsychology: A clinical approach*. San Diego: Academic Press.

Mehta, Z., Newcombe, F. & Damasio, H. (1987). A left hemisphere contribution to visuospatial processing. *Cortex*, *23*, 447–461.

Mellet, E., Petit, L., Mazoyer, B., Denis, M., & Tzourio, N. (1998a). Reopening the imagery debate: Lessons from functional anatomy. *NeuroImage*, *8*, 129–139.

Mellet, E., Tzourio, N., Crivello, F., Joliot, M., Denis, M., & Mazoyer, B. (1996). Functional anatomy of spatial mental imagery generated from verbal instructions. *Journal of Neuroscience*, *16*, 6504–6512.

Mellet, E., Tzourio, N., Denis, M., & Mazoyer, B. (1995). A positron emission tomography study of visual and mental spatial exploration. *Journal of Cognitive Neuroscience*, *7*, 433–445.

Mellet, E., Tzourio, N., Denis, M., & Mazoyer, B. (1998b). Cortical anatomy of mental imagery of concrete nouns based on their dictionary definition. *NeuroReport*, *9*, 803–808.

Milner, A.D. (1995). Cerebral correlates of visual awareness. *Neuropsychologia, 33,* 1117–1130.

Milner, A.D., & Goodale, M.A. (1993). Visual pathways to perception and action. *Progress in Brain Research, 95,* 317–337.

Milner, A.D., & Goodale, M.A. (1995). *The visual brain in action.* Oxford: Oxford University Press.

Morel, A., & Bullier, J. (1990). Anatomical segregation of two cortical visual pathways in the macaque monkey. *Visual Neuroscience, 4,* 555–578.

Morton, N., & Morris, R.G. (1995). Image transformation dissociated from visuo-spatial working memory. *Cognitive Neuropsychology, 12,* 767–791.

Newcombe, F., & Ratcliff, G. (1989) Disorders of visuospatial analysis. In F. Boller & J. Grafman (Eds.), *Handbook of Neuropsychology (Vol. 2).* Amsterdam: Elsevier.

Ogawa, S., Tank, D.W., Menon, R., Ellermann, J.M., Merkle, H., & Ugurbil, K. (1993). Functional brain MRI of cortical areas activated by visual mental imagery. *Society for Neuroscience Abstracts, 19,* 976.

Palmer, S.E., Rosch, E., & Chase, P. (1981). Canonical perspective and the perception of objects. In J. Long & A. Baddeley (Eds.), *Attention and performance IX.* Hillsdale, NJ: Lawrence Erlbaum Associates Luc.

Parsons, L.M., Fox, P.T., Hunter Downs, J., Glass, T., Hirsch, T.B., Martin, C.C., Jerabek, P.A., & Lancaster, J.L. (1995). Use of implicit motor imagery for visual shape discrimination as revealed by PET. *Nature, 375,* 54–58.

Perenin, M.-T., & Vighetto, A. (1988). Optic ataxia: A specific disruption in visuomotor mechanisms: Different aspects of the deficit in reaching for objects. *Brain, 111,* 643–474.

Péronnet, F., & Farah, M.J. (1989). Mental rotation: An event-related potential study with a validated mental rotation task. *Brain and Cognition, 9,* 279–288.

Poggio, T., & Edelman, S. (1990). A network that learns to recognise three-dimensional objects. *Nature, 343,* 263–266.

Ratcliff, G. (1979). Spatial thought, mental rotation and the right cerebral hemisphere. *Neuropsychologia, 17,* 49–54.

Riddoch, M.J., & Humphreys, G.W. (1988). Description of a left–right coding deficit in a case of constructional apraxia. *Cognitive Neuropsychology, 5,* 289–315.

Roland, P.E., Eriksson, L., Stone-Elander, S., & Widen, L. (1987). Does mental activity change the oxidative metabolism of the brain? *Journal of Neuroscience, 7,* 2373–2389.

Roland, P.E., & Friberg, L. (1985). Localization of cortical areas activated by thinking. *Journal of Neurophysiology, 53,* 1219–1243.

Roland, P.E., & Gulyas, B. (1994). Visual imagery and visual representation. *Trends in Neurosciences, 17,* 281–287.

Roland, P.E., & Gulyas, B. (1995). Visual memory, visual imagery, and visual recognition of large field patterns by the human brain: Functional anatomy by positron emission tomography. *Cerebral Cortex, 1,* 79–93.

Rondot, P., De Recondo, J., & Ribadeau-Dumas, J.-L. (1977). Visuomotor ataxia. *Brain, 100,* 355–376.

Royer, F.L., & Holland, T.R. (1975). Rotational transformation of visual figures as a clinical phenomenon. *Psychological Bulletin, 82,* 843–868.

Sakai, K., & Miyashita, Y. (1994). Visual imagery: An interaction between memory retrieval and focal attention. *Trends in Neurosciences, 17,* 287–289.

Segal, S.J. (1972). Assimilation of a stimulus in the construction of an image: The Perky effect revisited. In P.W. Sheehan (Ed.), *The function and nature of imagery* (pp. 203–230). New York: Academic Press.

Sergent, J. (1989). Image generation and processing of generated images in the cerebral hemispheres. *Journal of Experimental Psychology: Human Perception and Performance, 15,* 170–178.

Sergent, J. (1990). The neuropsychology of visual image generation: Data, method, and theory. *Brain and Cognition, 13,* 98–129.

Shepard, R.N., & Metzler, J. (1971). Mental rotation of three-dimensional objects. *Science, 171,* 701–703.

Solms, M., Kaplan-Solms, K., Saling, M., & Miller, P. (1988). Inverted vision after frontal lobe disease. *Cortex, 24,* 499–509.

Tarr, M.J., & Pinker, S. (1989). Mental rotation and orientation-dependence in shape recognition. *Cognitive Psychology, 21,* 233–282.

Taylor, H.A., & Tversky, B. (1992). Spatial mental models derived from survey and route descriptions. *Journal of Memory and Language, 31,* 261–292.

Thompson, W.L. & Kosslyn, S.M. (2000). Neural systems activated during visual mental imagery: A review and meta-analyses. In J.C. Mazziotta & A.W. Toga (Eds.), *Brain mapping: The Systems* (pp. 535–560). San Diego, CA: Academic Press.

Tippett, L.J. (1992). The generation of visual images: A review of neuropsychological research and theory. *Psychological Bulletin, 112,* 415–432.

Turnbull, O.H., Beschin, N., & Della Sala, S. (1997a). Agnosia for object orientation: Implications for theories of object recognition. *Neuropsychologia, 35,* 153–163.

Turnbull, O.H., Carey, D.P., & McCarthy, R.A. (1997b). The neuropsychology of object constancy. *Journal of the International Neuropsychology Society, 3,* 288–298.

Turnbull, O.H., Della Sala, S., & Beschin, N. (1997c). Rotated drawing: An MMSE performance with strong lateralising significance. *Journal of Neurology, Neurosurgery and Psychiatry, 62,* 419–420.

Turnbull, O.H., Laws, K.R., & McCarthy, R.A. (1995). Object recognition without knowledge of object orientation. *Cortex, 31,* 387–395.

Turnbull, O.H., & McCarthy, R.A. (1996a). Failure to discriminate between mirror-image objects: A case of viewpoint-independent object recognition? *NeuroCase, 2,* 63–72.

Turnbull, O.H., & McCarthy, R.A. (1996b). When is a view unusual? A single case study of orientation-dependent visual agnosia. *Brain Research Bulletin, 40,* 497–503.

Uhl, F., Goldenberg, G., Lang, W., Lindinger, G., Steiner, M., & Deecke, L. (1990). Cerebral correlates of imagining colours, faces and a map—II. Negative cortical DC potentials. *Neuropsychologia, 28,* 81–93.

Ungerleider, L.G., & Haxby, J.V. (1994). "What" and "where" in the human brain. *Current Opinion in Neurobiology, 4,* 157–165.

Ungerleider, L.G., & Mishkin, M. (1982). Two cortical visual systems. In D.J. Ingle, M.A. Goodale, & R.J.W. Mansfield (Eds.), *Analysis of visual behavior.* Cambridge, MA: The MIT Press.

Walsh, V., & Butler, S.R. (1996). The effects of visual cortex lesions on the perception of rotated shapes. *Behavioural Brain Research, 76,* 127–142.

Warrington, E.K., & James, M. (1967). Disorders of visual perception in patients with localised cerebral lesions. *Neuropsychologia, 5,* 253–266.

Warrington, E.K., & James, M. (1986). Visual object recognition in patients with right-hemisphere lesions: Axes or features? *Perception, 15,* 355–366.

Warrington, E.K., & Taylor, A.M. (1973). The contribution of the right parietal lobe to object recognition. *Cortex, 9,* 152–164.

Warrington, E.K., & Taylor, A.M. (1978). Two categorical stages of object recognition. *Perception, 7,* 695–705.

Watson, R.T., Valenstein, E., Day, A., & Heilman, K.M. (1994). Posterior neocortical systems subserving awareness and neglect. *Archives of Neurology, 51,* 1014–1021.

CHAPTER FIVE

The interface between language and visuo-spatial representations

Manuel de Vega
Universidad de La Laguna, Tenerife, Canary Islands

Marguerite Cocude and Michel Denis
LIMSI-CNRS, Université de Paris-Sud, Orsay, France

Maria José Rodrigo
Universidad de La Laguna, Tenerife, Canary Islands

Hubert D. Zimmer
Universität des Saarlandes, Saarbrücken, Germany

INTRODUCTION

Some animals develop a sophisticated spatial knowledge necessary for way-finding, migrating, establishing the boundaries of their territory, nesting and so on. However, only humans are able to share their spatial knowledge by using language to communicate. This chapter addresses the issue of spatial communication with a focus on the mental representations that underlie our locative expressions and, more generally, spatial discourse. All languages have a rich vocabulary of locative terms that cover several linguistic categories. For instance, in English and in most Indo-European languages there are spatial adverbials (e.g., "here", "there", "behind", "below"), prepositions (e.g., "in", "on", "from", "near"), adjectives (e.g., "big", "short", "large"), pronouns (e.g., "this", "that"), nouns (e.g., "circle", "square", "triangle"), and verbs (e.g., "to enter", "to leave", "to jump", "to cross", "to support", "to contain"). Some of these locatives are particularly important because they are closed-class words (e.g., prepositions) or, in some languages like German, morphological flexions (case affixes) that convey spatial meaning. Closed-class words and morphological flexions

109

correspond to concepts incorporated into the grammar of a language, and their use is frequently mandatory in sentences. Only a few concepts enter the closed-class category of words or become grammaticalised. Thus, in many languages, time, person, quantity, or gender are incorporated into the grammar. Some spatial concepts also belong to this privileged "club" although their use in each sentence is generally optional rather than mandatory (unlike other concepts such as time incorporated in verb tenses, or quantity implicit in number morphemes).

The semantics of visuo-spatial vocabulary are also rich in most languages. In English, locatives refer to axial relations (e.g., "front", "back", "right", "left", "north", "south"), distance (e.g., "close to", "nearby", "away from"), containment (e.g., "inside", "outside", "into"), support and contact (e.g., "in", "on"), configurations (e.g., "between", "among", "around"), places (e.g., "here", "there"), size (e.g., "big", "small", "short", "large"), motion (e.g., "fast", "slow", "to speed", "to stop"), pathway direction (e.g., "from", "towards", "ahead"), and pathway stage (e.g., "beginning", "start", "pathway", "goal"). The salience of spatial communication is not restricted to spoken communication. Thus, deaf people who use American Sign Language or any other sign language have a variety of gestures to describe visuo-spatial relations (Emmorey, 1996; Klima & Bellugi, 1979). Furthermore, gestural communication with a spatial content (e.g., pointing) is used by very young children and by most adult speakers as complementary to their verbal utterances (Petitto, 1993).

How do we understand spatial utterances? There are various approaches to this question, on which it is worth commenting briefly, namely the formal semantics and the quantitative theories of meaning. We will argue that these approaches run into serious difficulties when attempting to convey the referential nature of meaning. Consequently, we will propose that the comprehension of spatial utterances requires exploration of the interface between language and spatial representations.

Formal semantics of spatial vocabulary

Linguists have devoted considerable effort to analysing the semantic properties of spatial vocabulary in terms of predicate logic (e.g., Bierwisch, 1996; Herskovits, 1985; Miller & Johnson-Laird, 1976; Talmy, 1983). For instance, Miller and Johnson-Laird (1976, p. 385) analysed the meaning of the English preposition "in" by means of a rule or meaning postulate:

(R1)   IN (x, y): A target x is "in" a frame y if: [PART (x, z) and INCL (z, y)]

In other words, the utterance "x is in y" is appropriate if some *part* of x (z) is *included* in y. The frame y must have the property of "enclosure" or "containment", or must be a kind of thing that has an "interior". According to Miller and Johnson-Laird (1976), rule R1 is appropriate to explain the meaning of utterances that are quite different such as:

(1) A city in Sweden.
(2) John in a city.
(3) The coffee in the cup.
(4) The spoon in the cup.

However, this formalisation leaves some problems unsolved. First, polysemy is neglected by a free-content rule such as R1. Thus, in English (and probably in most languages) there are no different prepositions to denote the multiple ways in which containers and contents interact depending on their size, form, substance, and the like. For instance, the "containers" in these sentences differ considerably. A "cup" is a typical container but "Sweden" can be considered a container only metaphorically and, consequently, the relation conveyed by "in" in (1) and (3) also differs. Even if we keep constant the container "cup", the instantiation of "in" is rather different for (3) and (4): the coffee "fills" the interior surface of the cup whereas the spoon leans against specific points on the interior surface of the cup. The problem, as Landau and Jackendoff (1993) formulated it, is that prepositions provide a very coarse meaning and do not incorporate any constraint about the geometric properties of the target and the frame objects.

Second, the rule R1 does not deal with the predicative asymmetry of a spatial relation between two entities (Landau & Jackendoff, 1993). Thus, (5) is semantically correct but (6) is not (unless it is understood in some metaphorical non-spatial sense):

(5) John in a city.
(6) A city in John.

Third, the primitive operator INCL (includes) is exactly the core meaning of "in" and remains undefined; therefore the rule becomes tautological. Finally, despite being formulated as a procedural "if-then" rule, (R1) is not an effective procedure that can be implemented in any computer, because the rule is referentially "blind"; it cannot be applied to the real world unless the system has the appropriate perceptual system, the appropriate world knowledge, and so on. This is related to the well-known problem of symbolic circularity or the ground problem (de Vega, 1981; Glenberg, 1997; Harnad, 1990; Johnson-Laird, Herrmann, & Chaffin, 1984). In a propositional system, symbols refer just to other symbols within a semantic network but they never connect with the world.

Quantitative approaches to semantic knowledge representations

Some recent approaches to studying the semantics of words and sentences (including spatial utterances) apparently overcome some of these problems. A new generation of powerful quantitative tools, such as Hyperspace Analog to Language

(HAL) or the Latent Semantic Analysis (LSA) reduce the problem of meaning to a simple matter of computing word co-occurrence (e.g., Burgess, Livesay, & Lund, 1998; Landauer & Dumais, 1997). Using very large corpora of natural texts, these authors derive vector representations of sets of words based on their co-occurrence. The resulting high-dimensional semantic spaces of words can be used to predict several psychological effects, such as the acquisition of vocabulary in children, word categorisation, sentence coherence, priming effects, meaning similarity, learning difficulty of texts, etc. LSA and HAL are interesting techniques that, unlike classical propositional analysis, allow a relatively automatic analysis of texts. In addition, they are excellent predictive tools in educational and laboratory contexts. However, from a theoretical point of view they do not solve the ground problem and, therefore, do not provide a real representational theory for the spatial (or any other) domain of language (Fletcher & Linzie, 1998; Perfetti, 1998). For instance, the problem of the predicative asymmetry between target and frame relations remains unsolved. Thus, when we submitted utterances (5) to (6) to an LSA analysis, the system found the maximal similarity rate between "John in a city" and "A city in John" (rate = 1).[1] We can conclude that despite the sophistication of the analysis, LSA does not grasp the subtlety of spatial semantics.

Levels of spatial cognition

In order to explain the meaning of spatial utterances we have to know how they map our experience and actions with the environment. In other words, we have to explore how language interfaces with spatial representations (Bryant, 1997; Denis, 1996; Jackendoff, 1996). On the comprehender side, we assume that understanding locative utterances requires building the appropriate spatial representation. This spatial representation is typically more rich and detailed, as we have shown, than the coarse-grained semantics of the locative terms (e.g., the preposition). Therefore, the comprehender has to infer how the spatial relation is instantiated in this case, based on his/her knowledge of the sensory-motor or geometric features of the target and frame. On the speaker's side, we assume that producing a locative expression requires starting with a spatial partition of the environment in order to encode the appropriate statement verbally (Levelt, 1996). Thus, the speaker who says "The cow is behind the fence" in a real perceptual environment presumably starts by perceiving the target (the cow), then selects a frame in the current environment (the fence), and computes the topological relation between him/herself, the cow, and the fence.

In both comprehension and production, we must deal with the problem of how the language system and the spatial representation system interface. The

---

[1] LSA is supported by a World Wide Web site by which users can interact with the system: http://samiam.colorado.edu/~lsi/

issue of the interface has frequently been analysed in the literature, although the problem is quite ill defined and different authors seem to refer to different things when they explore the connections between language and spatial representations. One difficulty derives from the identification of the systems that interface. Spatial cognition is a complex multilevel system and we must be careful to identify which of the several subsystems have functional connections with language. Let us describe briefly some levels of spatial cognition that have been described in the literature:

Visuo-spatial perception. Our visual system analyses the segregating perceptual entities in a three-dimensional layout (Marr, 1982). Thus, from the flow of visual information in the environment we perceive distinctively the "spoon" and the "bowl". Although visual perception is the most important source of spatial information, haptic and auditory inputs can also provide complementary (or alternative) spatial information (e.g., we sense the shape of the spoon when we touch it, and we hear its sound when it drops to the floor).

The sensory-motor system. We use sensory-motor schemas as a way to connect our body with the objects and events built by our spatial perception systems. Sensory-motor schemas allow us to manipulate objects and to orient ourselves and navigate in the environment (e.g., Piaget, 1951). For instance, we develop specific sequences of hand and arm motion to manipulate the spoon into the bowl, or we find our way between the dining-room and the office. These sensory-motor schemas take benefit from some primitive image-schemas such as support, container relationships, or object animacy (e.g., Lakoff, 1987; Mandler, 1992).

The spatial conceptual system. The information of the perceptual and the sensory-motor levels is "digitalised" into a few topological categories by the conceptual system. For instance, the image-schema of containment allows the building of a more abstract categorisation of "inside" and "outside" regions in containers; the support schema allows us to distinguish between "above" and "below" areas, or the body schema permits us to categorise the "front", "back", "right", and "left" of intrinsic frameworks. The spatial meaning is considerably simplified by the conceptual system. Thus, the containment schema (and the corresponding sensory-motor actions) can be reduced to the propositional representation of "putting the spoon into the bowl". It is likely that, on some occasions, spatial language interfaces at this level of conceptual representations, because language itself provides discrete labels that correspond to topological categories.

The imagery system. This is a visuo-spatial representation system, which works autonomously, free from the immediate perceptual inputs. Mental images are usually thought of as fine-grained Euclidean representations that preserve

perceptual properties such as metric distances, orientations, and kinematic transformations of depicted objects (e.g., Denis, 1991; Kosslyn, 1980; Shepard &
Cooper, 1982). Unlike conceptual representations, mental images work as an
analogical code for memory as well as a generative system, which allows creating, combining, and transforming visuo-spatial representations. Thus, we can
build from memory an image of our action of putting the spoon into the bowl,
which preserves the continuous character of the original action, or even we can
simulate mentally a new sensory-motor action (not retrieved from memory),
such as putting the bowl upside down and the spoon on it.

This chapter addresses the functional connections between spatial language and
some of these subsystems of spatial representations. In particular, it describes:
(1) The studies of mental frameworks of spatial three-dimensional egocentric
layouts, constructed from descriptions that employ axial terms such as front,
back, right, etc. The proposed interface is between language and the categories
provided by the spatial conceptual system. (2) The studies on visuo-spatial images
constructed from verbal descriptions of maps, with a focus on mental scanning
paradigms. In this case the proposed interface is between language and mental
imagery. We will show that these two lines of research illustrate the mapping of
verbal utterances at different spatial levels of representation.

FRAMEWORK STUDIES

Dimension accessibility in mental frameworks

Axial terms are frequently used to describe a spatial relation between a target
and a frame.[2] These terms refer to the six canonical egocentric directions—
above, below, front, back, right, left—and they are used to describe framework
relations, involving a target and a frame (e.g., "the bottle is behind the computer"). In a seminal paper, Franklin and Tversky (1990) explored how participants
represent and update three-dimensional environments, described by means of
these canonical direction words. Participants initially studied a printed version
of a second-person narrative. For instance, in the opera theatre a loudspeaker was
located above your head, a sculpture below your feet, a bronze plaque in front
of you, a lamp behind you, and a bouquet of flowers to your right. In a second
phase, participants were given other portions of the narrative, each time reorienting
their point of view to face a particular object mentally. For each new orientation,
participants were asked to focus mentally on the object placed in a given location (e.g., behind) and to press a key as soon as they did it, which provided the
first response time (RT1); after that, they had to choose the name of the critical

---

[2] We adopt here the term "target" to refer to the object under focus whose position is described,
and "frame" to refer to the object with respect to which the target position is described. The duality
target/frame is equivalent to figure/ground (Miller & Johnson-Laird, 1976), figure/reference (Landau
& Jackendoff, 1993), referent/relatum (Levelt, 1989), or trajector/landmark (Regier, 1996).

object from among the whole list of objects presented and a new reaction time was recorded (RT2) as well as the accuracy of the response. The critical measure was RT1, which was a clue to the accessibility of spatial information, whereas RT2 was just for control. The results showed that RT1 varied systematically according to a standard pattern: The fastest responses were obtained for the head–feet dimension, followed by the front–back, and then the right–left. In addition, there was a within-dimension asymmetry: the front was faster than the back.

The differences in the accessibility of dimensions suggest that the spatial relations between a character and several surrounding objects described in a text are computed within a body-centred coordinate framework. Locations in the vertical dimension are easy to discriminate because this dimension involves two strong asymmetry cues: gravity effects and head-feet positions. Front–back is also quite easy to discriminate, as perceptual and motor activity differ in both extremes of the dimension. Finally, right–left might be the least discriminable dimension because there are no strong asymmetry cues, either in the world or in the design of the body. Egocentric frameworks do not merely represent spatial relations explicitly described in the narrative, but also are used by people to infer the pattern of spatial relations that emerges when the character of a narrative is described as reorienting to face another object, recalculating object positions according to the new point of view (Franklin & Tversky, 1990).

We may notice, however, that egocentric descriptions are not the only possibility in natural texts. Some experiments have analysed multiple (non-egocentric) perspectives, with narratives involving two characters who differed in their point of view of the same environment, and the participants were asked to judge the objects' positions shifting from one character to the other (de Vega, 1994; Franklin, Tversky, & Coon, 1992; Maki & Marek, 1997). The critical question is how participants are able to handle the two perspectives. A possibility is that participants switch between points of view, depending on which perspective the narrative requires at a given moment. Another alternative, perhaps more economic, is that participants adopt a neutral perspective, which does not correspond to any character's point of view, but includes both of them (e.g., an oblique perspective). Franklin et al. (1992), in a variant of their two-stage reaction time paradigm, obtained a dimension equiaccessibility pattern (the latencies for all directions were approximately the same) instead of the standard pattern associated with body-centred perspective. They concluded that participants had adopted a neutral perspective including the two characters.

However, different results were obtained in multiple perspective tasks with sentence verification paradigms (de Vega, 1994; Maki & Marek, 1997). In de Vega's experiments, participants were given verbal descriptions, in the second person, of an environment with objects placed in the four canonical directions of the horizontal axes. After learning the environment, participants read a text that introduced two characters (e.g., the tourist and the fisherman) who either shared a similar perspective (they looked in the same direction) or had an opposite perspective (they faced each other), although neither of them had the same perspective as that initially described for "you". In the test phase, participants were given items composed of three sentences to be read at their own pace. The first two sentences guided the reader's attention to one character ("The tourist stops for a while and puts on his coat. It is mid-afternoon and the temperature is cool"), while the third sentence described a spatial relation between a landmark and a character, either the one introduced by the previous sentences or the other one. For instance, "He [the fisherman] looks at the lighthouse in front of him". Participants had to verify whether the spatial relation was true or false. Unlike in Franklin et al. (1992) experiments, the standard dimension effect was obtained (front–back was faster than right–left), although no front–back asymmetry was observed. The lack of front–back asymmetry supports the idea that participants adopt a neutral perspective on the layout, embedding the landmarks as well as the characters (Franklin et al., 1992). However, the standard dimension effect indicates that participants "flesh out" this neutral perspective to instantiate a particular character's perspective, and to compute the specific spatial relations from that character's point of view. Participants were able to verify spatial relations from any character's perspective, although verification times were much slower when the two characters had opposite perspectives, suggesting that additional cognitive resources are necessary to instantiate a character's perspective when the reader keeps in mind two alternative points of view on the described layout. Finally, those items involving two characters (independent of whether they shared the same perspective or not) produced slower verification times, indicating that the shift of character involves cognitive resources by itself. Maki and Marek (1997) on their side, using the same sentence verification paradigm and Franklin and Tversky's three-dimensional environments, like de Vega obtained the standard pattern and even the front–back asymmetry for multiple perspective tasks.

The role of language in dimension accessibility

An important question to be addressed is what causes the standard pattern of accessibility to the three dimensions. Does the standard pattern reflect a general, modality-free feature of body-centred spatial representations? If so we may find the same standard pattern when participants represent either described or percep-tual environments. This "generality hypothesis" would correspond to the position of Bryant (1997), who claims that there is a common spatial representational system that receives input from both verbal and non-verbal modalities, but this system's format is neither linguistic nor perceptual. In line with that position is the fact that for most memory-based experiments the reaction times fit the standard pattern very well, regardless of how the layout was perceived (e.g., Hintzman, O'Dell, & Arndt, 1981) or described (e.g., Bryant, Tversky, & Franklin, 1992; Franklin & Tversky, 1990), indicating that the standard pattern is produced by the spatial representation system (or the spatial conceptual system), not by language.

Another possibility, however, is that the embodied representations of frameworks differ according to the modality of the input, because each modality interfaces with a different level of spatial representation. Let us call this the "modality hypothesis". In other words, the standard pattern may not be an effect of an invariant feature of spatial body-centred representations, but it would be bound to the verbal modality used for communicating directions. In its simplest form the modality hypothesis means that the pattern of reaction times is caused by lexical biases, for instance, encoding the words "right" and "left" may take longer than "front" and "back". Franklin and Tversky (1990) considered this possibility, and ran an elegant experiment to exclude a lexical bias interpretation. They required their participants to imagine themselves in a reclining position, so that the verbal labels were combined with the dimensions differently from the combination linked with the upright position. With this procedure the response times followed the standard ordering for dimensions, but due to the changed orientation of participants the pattern had a different rank order over the labels (front–back < head–feet < right–left).

Another version of the modality hypothesis is that the standard pattern of dimension accessibility is caused by the mapping of verbal labels onto a topological reference system rather than by lexical factors in the labels themselves (de Vega, Rodrigo, & Zimmer, 1996). According to this view, the use of a topological reference system is constrained to the verbal communication. Thus, the use of axial terms for indicating the object's positions necessarily requires establishment of a framework object, and computing the topological regions around it, in order to refer to the position of the target object. Instead, a non-verbal communication, such as pointing to objects, does not involve any encoding of topological regions around a framework object and, consequently, no standard pattern would be found.

To test this hypothesis, de Vega et al. (1996) ran several experiments contrasting the communication by axial labels and by means of pointing gestures. The rationale of the experiments was that pointing provides a contrasting element—a sort of baseline—for better understanding the modality-specific properties that may emerge in verbal communication about space. Pointing to objects and describing their position by means of axial language are similar enough to make their comparison useful, because they are two communication modalities. But also axial labelling presumably adds some specific demands, which can be revealed when one contrasts both modalities. In the first experiment, participants initially gained information about the position of objects placed in front, behind, right, and left, respectively, by means of a pointing procedure: each time they pressed one of four alternative arrow-keys they were given a sentence describing the object in the corresponding direction. Later on, they were asked on several occasions to rotate 90° to face a given object, and at each new position they were required to indicate the direction of the target object by pressing the corresponding arrow-keys. Unlike in the previous experiments with mental frameworks, in

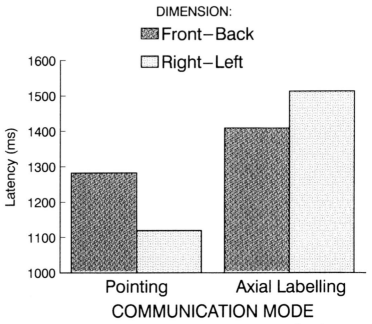

Figure 5.1. Verification times for pointing and verbal labelling. Adapted from de Vega, Rodrigo, and Zimmer (1996).

every reorientation participants were required to turn *physically* by rotating their body, the chair, and the table on which was the portable computer. In another experiment, participants performed exactly the same task except that they used, both at the learning and at the testing stage, direction labels ("front", "back", "right", and "left") to indicate the position of landmarks.

The verification times, illustrated in Figure 5.1, showed the standard pattern in the verbal labelling task (front–back < right–left) and a reversed pattern in the pointing task (right–left < front–back). Thus, we can conclude that for mental framework tasks the "standard" pattern of dimension accessibility is not a general feature of spatial representations, but it seems a modality-specific feature of verbal descriptions of layouts.

However, a simple modality-specific interpretation may be challenged by some results in the literature. Specifically, the classical paper of Hintzman et al. (1981), using a multiple-choice pointing procedure, similar to the one used by de Vega et al. (1996), showed the same standard pattern that had been obtained in language-based studies. An important feature of Hintzman et al.'s study was that participants were required to imagine themselves rotating and facing a given direction while their body remained still. By contrast, in de Vega et al.'s study participants were prompted to rotate physically and actually face a given direction.

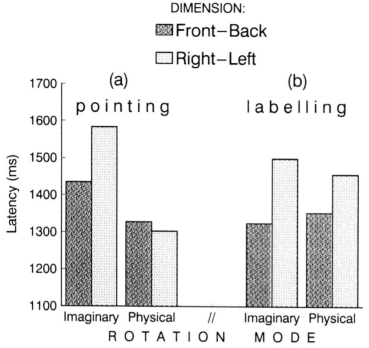

Figure 5.2. Verification times for pointing and verbal labelling with either imagined or physical rotation (de Vega & Rodrigo, in press).

Thus, it seems that both the modality of communication (verbal and pointing) and the mode of rotation (physical or imaginary) may interact to modulate the accessibility to dimensions. Recently we explored this possibility (de Vega & Rodrigo, in press). The materials and procedure were the same as the in de Vega et al. (1996) study. In addition, the modality of communication was either pointing (Experiment 1) or labelling (Experiment 2). In the two experiments, however, after the learning stage half of the participants were required to rotate "physic-ally", whereas the remaining participants were asked to "image" their rotation while their body remained still. In both cases they were tested for the position of the landmarks, from each new orientation. The results indicate that pointing was faster in the physical than in the imaginary rotation (see Figure 5.2a). This confirms previous studies with perceptual environments, in which blindfolded participants were asked to point to landmarks after physical or imaginary reorientations; and their speed and accuracy were also better under physical than imaginary rotation (e.g., Farrell & Robertson, 1998; May, 1996; Rieser, 1989). In addition, we found a different pattern of dimension accessibility for both modes of rotation: equiaccessibility in physical rotation (front–back = right–left) and standard in imaginary rotation (front–back < right–left). By contrast, the verbal modality was less influenced by the mode of rotation, and similar speed was observed under physical and imaginary rotation (see Figure 5.2b). Furthermore, the same standard pattern of dimension accessibility was obtained in both rotation conditions.

By putting together these results, we cannot conclude that the standard pattern is a modality-specific effect, contrarily to de Vega et al.'s (1996) suggestion, because it can be observed both in pointing and in labelling. However, we also have shown that the standard pattern is not general, contrary to Bryant's (1997) hypothesis, because in pointing either an equiaccessibility or a reversed pattern under physical rotation demands was obtained. The modality critically interacts with the mode of rotation and this interaction can be an important cue to understanding the specificity of the representations underlying spatial language and pointing.

We propose two kinds of embodiment for spatial representations that are compatible with our results: a first-order embodiment, which is anchored in the current sensory-motor information, and a second-order embodiment, which is detached from the current sensory-motor information. First-order embodiment takes place when people compute object-to-body relations typically in the current perceptual environment. This occurs when people navigate, avoid obstacles, reach for objects, look in the direction of an object, etc. A main feature of this first-order embodiment is that the updating of object-to-body relations, as the body position changes, relies on low-cost sensory-motor routines. Proprioceptive cues of the body motion automatically reallocate object-to-body positions (Farrell & Robertson, 1998; May, 1996; Rieser, 1989). This updating is not confined to objects in the visual field, but also applies to hidden objects (e.g., behind one, or occluded) and large-scale environments whose landmarks are not immediately perceived (Easton & Sholl, 1995). In any case, the object-to-body spatial relations are computed directly on the physical body position. De Vega and Rodrigo's (in press) results strongly suggest that pointing involves this sort of first-order embodiment, as performance in pointing was better when the rotation of the current body position facilitated the sensory-motor updating, than when the imaginary rotation of the body made this updating irrelevant.

Second-order embodiment, on the other hand, occurs when people compute spatial relations according to an entirely representational framework, which includes the landmarks as well as the self (or any other entity used as framework). The canonical coordinates of the represented self serve as topological regions into which the object positions are mapped. This represented self is "disengaged" from the current body position, and its "motions" are mental transformations (e.g., mental rotation) rather than physical motions. Consequently the updating of the layout following each "motion" does not benefit from the sensory-motor routines, but involves a high-cost mental computation of the new target-to-frame relations. Axial language involves this sort of second-order embodiment, as the performance was similar under physical and imaginary rotation. The actual body activity (either being still or moving) does not have appreciable effects on language-based spatial computations, which indicates that they are performed in an entirely represented framework.

What does language add to gestures?

After reviewing the experiments that directly compared verbal and gestural communication about space, we are now in a better position to explore theoretically the differences between both communication modalities, having in mind a simple question: What does language add to non-verbal communication about space? Whorfian linguists, traditionally, have tried to show that language imposes biases in our conceptualisation of the world (e.g., Bowerman, 1996; Hunt & Agnoli, 1991; Levinson, 1996). However, their main methodological strategy consisted of cross-linguistic comparisons among speakers of languages differing in some morpho-syntactic or lexical feature. Instead, the comparison of pointing and labelling involves a more basic analysis of spatial conceptualisation under non-linguistic and language-based communication.

Two main features of pointing are remarkable for our purposes: its first-order embodiment and its communication constraints. Pointing is embodied, because the direction of the gesture is governed by our body-to-object position, not by other considerations such as where the addressee is located, or the position of the target object relative to other objects in our perceptual field. If we reorient our body in the environment, our pointing gesture to a given target has to be modified correspondingly to keep the alignment arm–finger–object. Of course, we can ask participants to point to objects from an arbitrary perspective independent of their body position, trying to mimic the perspective-taking of verbal communication. However, with this rather artificial task, participants get into serious difficulties, as we have seen (de Vega & Rodrigo, in press; Hintzman et al., 1981; May, 1996; Rieser, 1989). Concerning the communicative constraints of pointing, interlocutors necessarily are co-present in the current perceptual context, because the addressee must be able to track the pointed direction visually and search for the possible target in the environment. In addition, the referred object is usually available in the immediate context visible to both interlocutors, although pointing can be extended to non-visible or concealed objects (e.g., an object behind us, inside a box, or behind a wall). In these cases, pointing becomes memory-based rather than perceptually grounded, but even in this case we point grossly to the object direction that must be projected in the perceptual "here and now".

Now we turn to the cognitive demands that axial descriptions of space "add" to the most basic pointing modality. First, axial language can be "disengaged" from the current here and now, overcoming some obvious limitations of pointing. We may produce spatial utterances to communicate not only about the current environment but also about memory-based, unknown, and fictitious environments.

In these cases interlocutors do not need to share the same environment. It is possible, even, to communicate directions verbally to an implicit or physically absent addressee (e.g., in written texts and in telephone conversations, respectively), departing from the face-to-face interaction that is necessary in pointing contexts.

Second, unlike pointing, axial language is relativistic because in order to report the position of the target, the speaker necessarily has to make explicit its relation to a frame object (Jackendoff, 1996; Miller & Johnson-Laird, 1976). This posits additional problems on the part of the speaker, who has to choose an object to play the role of frame for the particular target under consideration. Thus, if we want to describe to someone the position of the telephone in this office, we have to decide among many potential frames of reference (the table, the window, myself, my interlocutor, etc.). This choice must be based on some visuo-spatial features of the target and the frame, as well as on some pragmatic conventions. Thus, we tend to prefer as frames objects that are larger and more stable than the targets, which are close to the targets, which are visible or well known to our interlocutor, etc. (Herskovits, 1985; Landau & Jackendoff, 1993; Miller & Johnson-Laird, 1976). These differences between targets and frames determine the predicative asymmetry we mentioned in the introduction. For instance, sentences (7) and (9) are appropriate, but their reversed versions (8) and (10) are not:

(7) The telephone is on the table.
(8) The table is below the telephone.
(9) The bicycle is in front of the house.
(10) The house is behind the bicycle.

Third, axial language is "perspectivistic". A consequence of framing is that language users may have the possibility of working with different kinds of frameworks (not only with different frame objects). For instance, in English it is possible to use intrinsic, deictic, or absolute frameworks (Levelt, 1989, 1996; Levinson, 1996). Intrinsic frameworks involve frame objects (typically persons) which have distinctive direction regions, such as "front", "back", "right", and so on. The egocentric and person-centred frameworks considered in this chapter are examples of intrinsic frameworks. However, when the frame object has no intrinsic directions, such as a mountain or a tree, the meaning of axial utterances is "deictic", involving an implicit observer in the scene, in addition to the nominal target and frame. For instance, "the mailbox is in front of the tree" means that the mailbox is at some point between the tree and the speaker, rather than at any non-existent "front region" of the tree. Finally, absolute frameworks refer to a coordinate system external to the target, the frame, and/or the speaker; they are typically used to express geographical relations such as "Paris is north of Tenerife".

VISUO-SPATIAL IMAGES CONSTRUCTED FROM VERBAL DESCRIPTIONS

We turn now to the analysis of another facet of the functional connections linking language and the mental representation of visuo-spatial configurations. The situation considered here has to do with the use of language as a device for describing environments on which an observer has an allocentric point of view; that is, from a "survey" perspective (cf., Taylor & Tversky, 1992, 1996). More specifically, the issue discussed is the capacity of people to construct and inspect visual images of spatial configurations that have come to their knowledge through some indirect experience mediated by language, rather than through direct perceptual (visual) experience.

There is indeed a variety of sources from which people build visual knowledge and store it in memory, with the perspective of retrieving such knowledge in later circumstances and performing cognitive operations upon it. Until now, a great deal of the research effort has focused on imagery as a form of representation that extends perceptual experience when this experience is over. The processes of interest are those that consist of reactivating internal representations of objects while these objects are temporarily or definitely unavailable to perception. The exploration of this issue has generated paradigms designed to identify the properties of the image medium and the extent to which these properties parallel those of perceptual experience. The hypothesis that has constantly guided these approaches is that the internal events on which the experience of imagery is based are analogous transcriptions of perceptual experience, in particular as regards its structural organisation.

The idea of imagery as a surrogate to perception is an old one. In many natural circumstances where people have to retrieve information about an absent object, the best substitute for the object is a representation that preserves the object's structure and entertains high structural isomorphism with that object. This form of representation offers an advantage; that is, there is no need to invent any special processes to access information within the representation, as the representation is structured like the object and is thus open to similar processing. Therefore, it is important for researchers to develop methods that help to demonstrate the similarity of imagery to perception via the similarity of the operations executed on both of them. These methods should be applicable to both perception and imagery. When applied to imagery, they should require the subject to generate an image and execute operations on it. Most importantly, these operations should be selected for their capacity to elicit responses that would reveal the internal structure of the representation. If some properties are detected in perceptually based images, will they be similar to those obtained in perception? There is a good deal of literature giving credit to the hypothesis that such is the case (see Intons-Peterson, 1996; Kosslyn, 1980; Podgorny & Shepard, 1978). The greatest value of the method will be attained if it can be applied to a variety of types of images, in particular whatever the source of the images; that is, whether they are based on perceptual or linguistic inputs. If the properties evidenced in perceptually based images are true of verbally based images, the consequence would be of major significance, as this would support the idea that these properties are not exclusively dependent on the perceptual origin of the images, but reflect more fundamental properties of the imagery system, whether it has been fed by perceptual experience or by internal constructions derived from language.

The mental scanning paradigm and the assessment of the metric properties of images

One of the most popular methods that have been invented to test the properties shared by images and percepts is the mental scanning paradigm, which was first used by Stephen Kosslyn in the early steps of his long-range investigation of mental imagery (Kosslyn, 1973; Kosslyn, Ball, & Reiser, 1978; Pinker & Kosslyn, 1978). Mental scanning is one of the processes that a person can implement on a visual image that is temporarily activated in the "visual buffer". Other transformations may involve zooming in on the image, rotating it, adding new components to it, etc. We focus here on the process of mental scanning, which corresponds to the systematic shifting of attention over a visual image. The instructions typically call for continuous scanning, which is to be performed from a starting point of the image to a target point. The classic finding is that the time to scan mentally across an imagined object from one point to another point increases linearly with the distance separating the points. The farther a point is from the initial focus point on the imaged object, the longer it takes to scan to it in the image. Since its first report, this result has been taken as supporting the view that the metric properties of the surfaces of objects are made explicit in visual images. Thus, imagery can be validly claimed to use mechanisms that are used to encode and interpret objects during perception.

The question then consists of placing language in the theory and examining whether images constructed from linguistic descriptions of objects exhibit similar metric properties. In this investigation, it is important that the subjects are invited to construct mentally novel objects that they have never encountered before perceptually. The mental representations are built internally on the basis of exclusively verbal descriptions. In fact, a sequence of statements describes an array of objects arranged according to specific spatial relationships. What is novel is the spatial disposition of items, not the content of the individual items. The first attempt of this type was made by Kosslyn, Reiser, Farah, and Fliegel (1983), who asked subjects to construct composites of multiple objects arranged according to a description. In each scene, one object was described as "floating" some specified distance and direction with respect to another object (e.g., "The rabbit is floating 5 feet above and 5 feet left of the cup, and the violin is 6 inches below the cup"). Then, subjects heard probe phrases that contained the names of two objects. They were to focus mentally on the first object named and then to scan straight across the image until reaching the second object named. The results showed that more time was required to scan across a greater distance in the imaged scenes. The conclusion was that distances were expressed in the images, in spite of the fact that the subjects had not been exposed perceptually to a physical (pictorial) presentation of these distances at any time.

A problem with the Kosslyn et al. (1983) material was that the descriptions contained explicit metric information regarding the distances separating objects. This may be a problem if one wants to draw strong conclusions from the correlation between scanning times and distances. As was advanced by some anti-imagist theoreticians, it is possible for at least some subjects to use their explicit knowledge of the distances in order (if even unconsciously) to alter their response times to conform to what they know of the relationships existing among time, speed, and physical distance (Pylyshyn, 1981). Although this explanation has been repeatedly shown to be unable to account fully for the mental scanning effects (Denis & Kosslyn, 1999; Pinker, Choate, & Finke, 1984), it is nevertheless desirable to avoid the risk of collecting responses that may be partly contaminated by the subject's exposure to explicit metric information in the descriptions.

Such care was taken in a series of experiments conducted by Denis and Cocude (1989, 1992, 1997; Denis, Gonçalves, & Memmi, 1995; Denis & Zimmer, 1992). In these experiments, subjects received descriptions of a geographical configuration, namely a fictitious island. The description said that the island was circular in shape, and that six geographical landmarks were located on the periphery of the island. Each landmark was located at an unambiguously defined point. For this purpose, the conventional directions used in aerial navigation were used, to result in the following description: "At 11, there is a harbour. At 1, there is a lighthouse. At 2, there is a creek. At an equal distance between 2 and 3, there is a hut. At 4, there is a beach. At 7, there is a cave." Note that the statements on the positions of landmarks did not provide any information about the distances separating the pairs of landmarks. However, when subjects built a visual image of the island, the very format of the resulting representation should have revealed pieces of information that were not in the description, in particular inter-landmark distances. It is an inherent property of visual images that when any point A is located, and then any other point B, the framework in which the points are posited cannot avoid exhibiting the spatial relationship (thus, the distance) between the two points. All the relations are made explicit because the format of representation makes all of them visible. It is well known that spatial descriptions may be under-specific while remaining acceptable pieces of discourse (Mani & Johnson-Laird, 1982). However, they may well contain implicit information that a visual representation will be unable to maintain implicitly. It is mandatory for images to offer determinate views of a

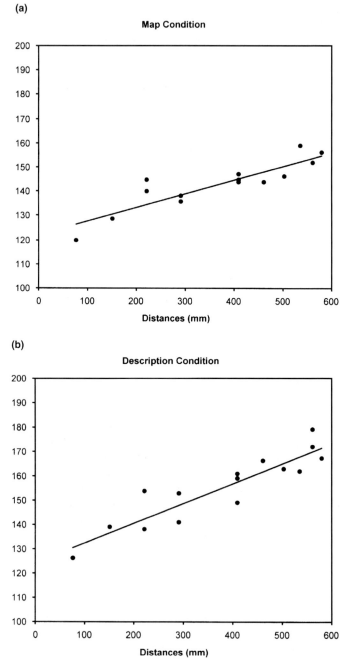

Figure 5.3. Reaction time as a function of scanning distance in the map (a) and the description (b) conditions (Denis & Cocude, 1989).

configuration of objects, due to the integration of their components into a unifying framework.

The first experiments consisted of looking for evidence of mental scanning effects when subjects scanned over an image constructed from the verbal description just quoted. Subjects listened to the description six times and were strongly encouraged to visualise the shape of the island and locate each landmark at its specific position. When they were tested in the mental scanning task, their response times proved to be positively correlated with the corresponding distances (which were entered in the computations as their ratios to the diameter of the island). The pattern of response times was compared to the pattern produced by control subjects who had learned the positions of the six landmarks from inspecting a map of the island. Figure 5.3 shows that the time–distance correlation was quite similar for subjects who performed mental scanning after either verbal or perceptual learning. Thus, one concludes that in the conditions of this experiment, a verbal description was actually used to create a visual image in which spatial distances were expressed in a veridical manner. As these distances had not been experienced perceptually, it means that they were experienced in the form of an internal representation which possessed structural properties that did not differentiate it from a perceptually based representation.

Does the structure of a verbal description affect the structure of the resulting visual image?

The reader may have noticed that the description used in the study just reported was presented according to clockwise order. This was intended to provide the subjects with optimal conditions for integrating successive pieces of information sentence after sentence. It is obviously easier to posit items one after the other if some continuity of the description is preserved. It is well known from studies on spatial mental models that the construction of a representation is sensitive to the care taken by the describer in preserving the continuity of his/her description. Discontinuous descriptions, or descriptions conveying information according to atypical or unexpected orders, have been shown to result in much cognitive difficulty for the on-line construction of internal spatial representations, and hence their memorability (Denis, 1996; Denis & Denhière, 1990; Ehrlich & Johnson-Laird, 1982). So, in the previous study, clockwise order was thought to contribute to building a coherent, integrated image of the configuration by the subjects.

A new set of experiments was devoted to analysing the effects likely to result from the processing of poorly structured descriptions, by comparing the clockwise descriptive sequence used previously with a random one. This new version might affect the metric quality of the representation under construction, with detrimental effects on the scanning performance. Additional effects could also appear, such as lengthening of the time necessary for learning the description. It is likely that more learning trials are necessary for memorising the image of a configuration that is constructed by following an unexpected sequence. For this reason, it was decided to observe the effect of the structure of verbal descriptions on learning by testing the subjects in two successive mental scanning tasks. All the subjects were involved in three learning trials of the description, before performing the first mental scanning task. They then resumed learning for three more trials, and performed a second scanning task.

The subjects who processed the clockwise description produced scanning responses that showed good integration of landmark positions as early as the first scanning task. This was attested by a significant positive correlation between scanning times and distances. After additional exposure to the same description, the subjects showed increased time–distance correlation, suggesting that the additional three learning trials helped them to attain a representation in which the metric values were still more accurately represented. However, the improvement remained rather modest, just because the first test already reflected a strong time–distance relationship. The pattern was strikingly different for the subjects who processed the random description. Their first scanning task did not reveal any correlation between times and distances, reflecting the absence of any structure within their images. Obviously, the subjects had memorised that there was a harbour at some specified location, a lighthouse at some other location, etc., but the relative positions of the landmarks were not firmly expressed in their images. As a result, no systematic relationship appeared between scanning times and distances. In addition, their response times were very long. Three more exposures to the description resulted in a marked change. In the second scanning task, subjects' response times were much shorter and there was a significant positive correlation between times and distances. The order of magnitude of the correlation was similar to the one achieved by the other group of subjects after three learning trials only.

These data confirmed that images generated from descriptions can exhibit metric properties similar to those of perceptually based images. More importantly, they demonstrated that the structure of a description affects the structural quality of the image constructed from that description. A poorly structured description is not good support for constructing an image expected to incorporate valid metric information. To be fully achieved, the process needs additional learning. Thus, the capacity of images derived from verbal inputs to reflect accurately the objects to which they refer does not appear to be an all-or-nothing property, but results from stepwise elaboration. This was clearly confirmed in a further experiment in which a more fine-grained manipulation of image elaboration was used. Subjects were exposed to the random description for the same number of trials as in the previous experiment (that is, six trials), but the timing of learning/ test alternations was different. Here, subjects were involved in a total of three scanning tests, each one intervening after two exposures of the subjects to the verbal description. The results for each of the three scanning tests are shown in

Figure 5.4. The scanning times for the first test were longer than in the second test, and the times further decreased between the second and third tests. No correlation between scanning times and distances was found for the first test, but the coefficients reached significance for the second and third tests. Thus, the first test did not reveal any structure in the image under construction. Two learning trials were not enough for subjects to construct an accurate image from a verbal description, and mental scanning showed no sign of any metric properties in the imagined configuration. The next two trials changed the situation dramatically. The chronometric pattern attested that metric information was now specified in the images, and two more trials indicated still further improvement in the internal structure of the image. Furthermore, the scanning times decreased progressively, suggesting that the internal structure of the images, as accessed by the scanning processes, was more readily available.

Semantic effects and individual differences

The analysis of the results just reported focused on the spatial (metric) properties of the objects represented. No attention was paid to the semantic content of the landmarks. The words "harbour", "lighthouse", etc., were used only to label points of interest. In other words, only the geometry of the configuration was considered, and no effect connected with the semantic content of the landmarks' nouns was expected. However, it is well known that the memory of real-world spatial configurations is affected by knowledge, experience, and value attached by the subjects to the landmarks. For instance, distances to infrequently visited landmarks tend to be overestimated, whereas distances to familiar landmarks are underestimated (Byrne, 1979; Moar & Bower, 1983).

Denis and Cocude (1997) examined the sensitivity of the mental scanning paradigm to verbal descriptions in which some landmarks were rendered more salient than others. The objective was to determine whether such a manipulation would lead to systematic biases, as is the case in real-world configurations. Mental scanning was used again, in order to tap the differential availability of the landmarks, if any, as reflected by differences in the scanning time patterns. The experiment involved having half of the landmarks processed in a rather special way. Not only did the description of each landmark give information about its location (as in the previous experiments), but in addition it provided a short narrative containing a number of concrete details about it. For instance, this is the narrative that was designed to increase the salience of the lighthouse: "At 1, there is a lighthouse. This strange lighthouse is painted red and white. It has been famous ever since the storm when a luxury liner ran into the cliffs nearby, with more than two hundred casualties. Since this catastrophe, jewellery and precious objects lie below the waves at the foot of the lighthouse." The other half of the landmarks were described in a neutral fashion. For the purpose of comparison, the neutral description of the lighthouse read as follows: "At 1,

(a)

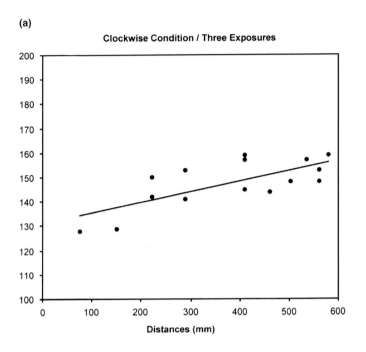

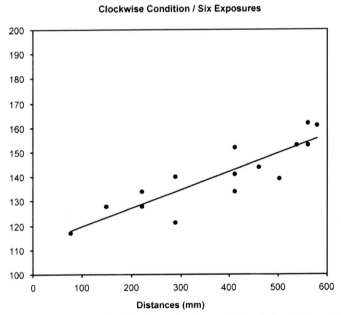

Figure 5.4.   Reaction time as a function of scanning distance in the clockwise (a) and the random (b) conditions (Denis & Cocude, 1992).

(b)

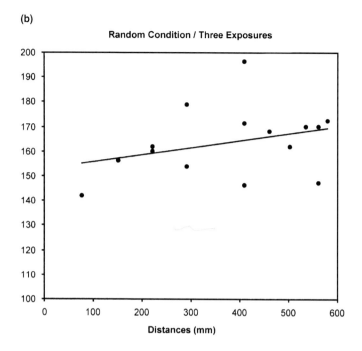

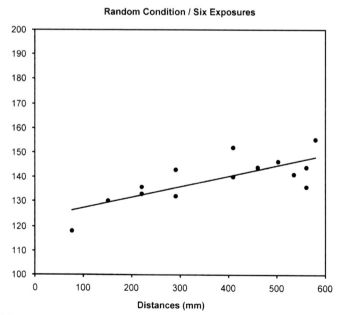

Figure 5.4.   (*continued*).

there is a lighthouse. This granite lighthouse, built fifty years ago, raises its lofty grey silhouette at the edge of the coast. From the top, twenty-five metres up, its powerful beam guides boats through the night. When fog sets in, its halo in the mist is extremely useful to ships who have lost their way." The results showed unambiguously that there was no difference at all between response times when scanning was directed towards either salient or neutral landmarks, nor between the time–distance correlations, whatever the direction of scanning. Apparently, the locations of the landmarks, not their semantic content, governed the scanning times in this task, suggesting that the metric of the representation was not affected by the semantic content of the landmarks.

The structural quality of visuo-spatial images, as assessed by mental scanning measures, was also examined from an individual differences point of view. More specifically, the issue was to determine whether people known as "good imagers" show better ability at incorporating accurate metric in images constructed from descriptions. People differ in their mental scanning performance (Dror, Kosslyn, & Waag, 1993). Would it be the case that people scoring high on tests tapping visual imagery capacities demonstrate special capacities in the construction of visual images from descriptive language? Denis and Cocude (1997) compared subjects scoring high or low on the Minnesota Paper Form Board (MPFB; Likert & Quasha, 1941) in the mental scanning test following three exposures to the clockwise description of the island.

The results proved to be quite different for the two groups of subjects. The subjects with high visuo-spatial capacities produced the typical mental scanning results; that is, their scanning times were positively correlated with distances. They thus showed that their images had reached a stable state, with the distances accurately represented. In contrast, the subjects with the lowest visuo-spatial capacities did not show any evidence that their images had such structural properties. Their scanning times were about one-third longer than those of the other subjects, and there was no relationship between times and distances. This pattern indicated that subjects identified as poor imagers on the basis of standard tests were confirmed as poor imagers in terms of the accuracy of the images they constructed from descriptions. People with the highest capacities, on the other hand, attested that they could use language to create images whose spatial metric was well represented and maintained under control during scanning tasks.

CONCLUDING REMARKS

This chapter has examined how the meaning of spatial utterances should be explained in terms of a language-to-representation interface. We have argued that theoretical approaches that do not deal with this interface are unsuitable as psychological explanations. Thus, neither formal semantic approaches nor mathematical analysis relying on word co-occurrence are sufficient, because they neglect how words refer to spatial representation. Alternatively, we reviewed two lines of research that clearly demonstrated that people who understand spatial descriptions are able to build quite detailed representations of spatial layouts in their memory.

The first line of research examined how people build mental frameworks with an egocentric point of view, when they learn verbal descriptions of layouts involving axial terms. These mental frameworks are updated by the participants when the text requires them to shift their point of view. In addition, some dimensions become more accessible than others as a result of our conceptual and sensory-motor experience with the world. When mental frameworks learned in the context of either pointing or axial descriptions were compared, specific profiles for the two kind of representations emerged. Pointing is anchored in the physical body and usually refers to objects in the current perceptual environment; consequently it uses the proprioceptive system of navigation to update objects' positions. By contrast, axial labelling is disengaged from the current "here and now", involving more functional autonomy than pointing: we can describe layouts independent from the current environment and use an arbitrary point of view, independent of our body position.

The second line of research showed how people understand map descriptions and how their spatial representations preserve in an analogical fashion the metric properties of the described maps. The experiments tested the features of these mental images generated from descriptions, by means of a verbal—rather than perceptual—variant of the classic mental scanning paradigm. The rationale of such studies is that the larger the correlation between scanning time and distance in the layout, the more accurate is the spatial representation elaborated by the participants. In all cases the correlation was high and significant, but also several factors were found to contribute to the accuracy of the mental image. Thus, the quality of the description, the amount of training, and the participants' spatial skills were factors that increased the time–distance correlation.

The interface between language and spatial representation is a complex issue, which is not exhausted by this chapter. However, we have provided sufficient empirical evidence that people who deal with spatial descriptions may be able to build representations that are embodied surrogates for experience, and preserve the topological and metric properties of layouts. This is a remarkable performance, as the structure of the linguistic code (linear and governed by arbitrary syntactic rules) differs entirely from the structure of the resulting spatial representation.

REFERENCES

Bierwisch, M. (1996). How much space gets into language?. In P. Bloom, M.A. Peterson, L. Nadel, & M.F. Garrett (Eds.), *Language and space* (pp. 31–76). Cambridge, MA: MIT Press.

Bowerman, M. (1996). Learning how to structure space for language: A crosslinguistic perspective. In P. Bloom, M.A. Peterson, L. Nadel, & M.F. Garrett (Eds.), *Language and space* (pp. 385–436). Cambridge, MA: MIT Press.

Bryant, D.J. (1997). Representing space in language and perception. *Mind and Language, 13,* 239–264.

Bryant, D.J., Tversky, B., & Franklin, N. (1992). Internal and external spatial frameworks for representing described scenes. *Journal of Memory and Language, 31,* 74–98.

Burgess, C., Livesay, K., & Lund, K. (1998). Explorations in context space: Words, sentences, discourse. *Discourse Processes, 25,* 211–258.

Byrne, R.W. (1979). Memory for urban geography. *Quarterly Journal of Experimental Psychology, 31,* 147–154.

Denis, M. (1991). *Image and cognition.* New York: Harvester Wheatsheaf.

Denis, M. (1996). Imagery and the description of spatial configurations. In M. de Vega, M.J. Intons-Peterson, P.N. Johnson-Laird, M. Denis, & M. Marschark, *Models of visuospatial cognition* (pp. 128–197). New York: Oxford University Press.

Denis, M., & Cocude, M. (1989). Scanning visual images generated from verbal descriptions. *European Journal of Cognitive Psychology, 1,* 293–307.

Denis, M., & Cocude, M. (1992). Structural properties of visual images constructed from poorly or well-structured verbal descriptions. *Memory and Cognition, 20,* 497–506.

Denis, M., & Cocude, M. (1997). On the metric properties of visual images generated from verbal descriptions: Evidence for the robustness of the mental scanning effect. *European Journal of Cognitive Psychology, 9,* 353–379.

Denis, M., & Denhière, G. (1990). Comprehension and recall of spatial descriptions. *European Bulletin of Cognitive Psychology, 10,* 115–143.

Denis, M., Gonçalves, M.-R., & Memmi, D. (1995). Mental scanning of visual images generated from verbal descriptions: Towards a model of image accuracy. *Neuropsychologia, 33,* 1511–1530.

Denis, M., & Kosslyn, S.M. (1999). Scanning visual mental images: A window on the mind. *Current Psychology of Cognition, 18,* 409–465.

Denis, M., & Zimmer, H.D. (1992). Analog properties of cognitive maps constructed from verbal descriptions. *Psychological Research, 54,* 286–298.

de Vega, M. (1981). Una exploración de los metapostulados de la psicología contemporánea: El logicismo [An exploration of the metapostulates of contemporary psychology: Logicism]. *Análisis y Modificación de Conducta, 7,* 345–376.

de Vega, M. (1994). Characters and their perspectives in narratives describing spatial environments. *Psychological Research, 56,* 116–126.

de Vega, M. & Rodrigo, M.J. (in press). Updating mental frameworks mediated by pointing and labeling under physical and imaginary rotation. *European Journal of Cognitive Psychology.*

de Vega, M., Rodrigo, M.J., & Zimmer, H. (1996). Pointing and labeling directions in egocentric frameworks. *Journal of Memory and Language, 35,* 821–839.

Dror, I.E., Kosslyn, S.M., & Waag, W.L. (1993). Visual-spatial abilities of pilots. *Journal of Applied Psychology, 78,* 763–773.

Easton, R.D., & Sholl, M.J. (1995). Object-array structure, frames of reference, and retrieval of spatial knowledge. *Journal of Experimental Psychology: Learning, Memory, and Cognition, 21,* 483–500.

Ehrlich, K., & Johnson-Laird, P.N. (1982). Spatial descriptions and referential continuity. *Journal of Verbal Learning and Verbal Behavior, 21,* 296–306.

Emmorey, K. (1996). The confluence of space and language in signed languages. In P. Bloom, M.A. Peterson, L. Nadel, & M.F. Garrett (Eds.), *Language and space* (pp. 171–210). Cambridge, MA: MIT Press.

Farrell, M.J., & Robertson, I.H. (1998). Mental rotation and the automatic updating of body-centered spatial relationships. *Journal of Experimental Psychology: Learning, Memory, and Cognition, 24,* 227–233.

Fletcher, C.R., & Linzie, B. (1998). Motive and opportunity: Some comments on LSA, HAL, KDC and Principal Components. *Discourse Processes, 25,* 355–362.

Franklin, N., & Tversky, B. (1990). Searching imagined environments. *Journal of Experimental Psychology: General, 119*, 63–76.

Franklin, N., Tversky, B., & Coon, V. (1992). Switching points of view in spatial mental models. *Memory and Cognition, 20*, 507–518.

Glenberg, A.M. (1997). What memory is for. *Behavioral and Brain Sciences, 20*, 1–55.

Harnad, S. (1990). The symbolic grounding problem. *Physica, 42*, 335–346.

Herskovits, A. (1985). Semantics and pragmatics of locative expressions. *Cognitive Science, 9*, 341–378.

Hintzman, D.L., O'Dell, C.S., & Arndt, D.R. (1981). Orientation in cognitive maps. *Cognitive Psychology, 13*, 149–206.

Hunt, E., & Agnoli, F. (1991). The Whorfian hypothesis: A cognitive psychology perspective. *Psychological Review, 98*, 377–390.

Intons-Peterson, M.J. (1996). Integrating the components of imagery. In M. de Vega, M.J. Intons-Peterson, P.N. Johnson-Laird, M. Denis, & M. Marschark, *Models of visuospatial cognition* (pp. 20–89). New York: Oxford University Press.

Jackendoff, R. (1996). The architecture of the linguistic–spatial interface. In P. Bloom, M.A. Peterson, L. Nadel, & M.F. Garrett (Eds.), *Language and space* (pp. 1–30). Cambridge, MA: MIT Press.

Johnson-Laird, P.N., Herrmann, D.J., & Chaffin, R. (1984). Only connections: A critique of semantic networks. *Psychological Bulletin, 96*, 292–315.

Klima, E.S., & Bellugi, U. (1979). *The signs of language*. Cambridge, MA: Harvard University Press.

Kosslyn, S.M. (1973). Scanning visual images: Some structural implications. *Perception and Psychophysics, 14*, 90–94.

Kosslyn, S.M. (1980). *Image and mind*. Cambridge, MA: Harvard University Press.

Kosslyn, S.M., Ball, T.M., & Reiser, B.J. (1978). Visual images preserve metric spatial information: Evidence from studies of image scanning. *Journal of Experimental Psychology: Human Perception and Performance, 4*, 47–60.

Kosslyn, S.M., Reiser, B.J., Farah, M.J., & Fliegel, S.L. (1983). Generating visual images: Units and relations. *Journal of Experimental Psychology: General, 112*, 278–303.

Lakoff, G. (1987). *Woman, fire, and dangerous things*. Chicago: University of Chicago Press.

Landau, B., & Jackendoff, R. (1993). "What" and "where" in spatial language and spatial cognition. *Behavioral and Brain Sciences, 16*, 217–265.

Landauer, T.M., & Dumais, S.T. (1997). A solution to Plato's problem: The Latent Semantic Analysis theory of acquisition, induction, and representation of knowledge. *Psychological Review, 104*, 211–240.

Levelt, W.J.M. (1989). *Speaking: From intention to articulation*. Cambridge, MA: MIT Press.

Levelt, W.J.M. (1996). Perspective taking and ellipsis in spatial descriptions. In P. Bloom, M.A. Peterson, L. Nadel, & M.F. Garrett (Eds.), *Language and space* (pp. 77–108). Cambridge, MA: MIT Press.

Levinson, S.C. (1996). Frames of reference and Molyneux's question: Crosslinguistic evidence. In P. Bloom, M.A. Peterson, L. Nadel, & M.F. Garrett (Eds.), *Language and space* (pp. 109–169). Cambridge, MA: MIT Press.

Likert, R., & Quasha, W.H. (1941). *Revised Minnesota Paper Form Board (Series AA)*. New York: The Psychological Corporation.

Maki, R.H., & Marek, M.N. (1997). Egocentric spatial framework effects from single and multiple points of view. *Memory and Cognition, 25*, 677–690.

Mandler, J.M. (1992). How to build a baby: II. Conceptual primitives. *Psychological Review, 99*, 587–604.

Mani, K., & Johnson-Laird, P.N. (1982). The mental representation of spatial descriptions. *Memory and Cognition, 10*, 181–187.

Marr, D. (1982). *Vision*. San Francisco: Freeman.

May, M. (1996). Cognitive and embodied modes of spatial imagery. *Psychologische Beiträge, 38*, 418–434.

Miller, G.A., & Johnson-Laird, P.N. (1976). *Language and perception*. Cambridge, MA: Cambridge University Press.

Moar, I., & Bower, G.H. (1983). Inconsistency in spatial knowledge. *Memory and Cognition, 11*, 107–113.

Perfetti, C.A. (1998). The limits of co-occurrence: Tools and theories in language research. *Discourse Processes, 25*, 363–377.

Petitto, L.A. (1993). Modularity and constraints in early lexical acquisition: Evidence from children's early language and gesture. In P. Bloom (Ed.), *Language acquisition: Core readings* (pp. 95–126). New York: Harvester Wheatsheaf.

Piaget, J. (1951). *Play, dreams, and imitation in childhood*. New York: Random House.

Pinker, S., Choate, P.A., & Finke, R.A. (1984). Mental extrapolation in patterns constructed from memory. *Memory and Cognition, 12*, 207–218.

Pinker, S., & Kosslyn, S.M. (1978). The representation and manipulation of three-dimensional space in mental images. *Journal of Mental Imagery, 2*, 69–83.

Podgorny, P., & Shepard, R.N. (1978). Functional representations common to visual perception and imagination. *Journal of Experimental Psychology: Human Perception and Performance, 4*, 21–35.

Pylyshyn, Z.W. (1981). The imagery debate: Analogue media versus tacit knowledge. *Psychological Review, 88*, 16–45.

Regier, T. (1996). *The human semantic potential: Spatial language and constrained connectionism*. Cambridge, MA: MIT Press.

Rieser, J.J. (1989). Access to knowledge of spatial structure at novel points of observation. *Journal of Experimental Psychology: Learning, Memory, and Cognition, 15*, 1157–1165.

Shepard, R.N., & Cooper, L.A. (1982). *Mental images and their transformations*. Cambridge, MA: MIT Press.

Talmy, L. (1983). How language structures space. In H.L. Pick, Jr., & L. Acredolo (Eds.), *Spatial orientation: Theory, research, and application* (pp. 225–282). New York: Plenum.

Taylor, H.A., & Tversky, B. (1992). Spatial mental models derived from survey and route descriptions. *Journal of Memory and Language, 31*, 261–292.

Taylor, H.A., & Tversky, B. (1996). Perspective in spatial descriptions. *Journal of Memory and Language, 35*, 371–391.

CHAPTER SIX

Language, spatial cognition, and navigation

Michel Denis, Marie-Paule Daniel, and Sylvie Fontaine
LIMSI-CNRS, Université de Paris-Sud, Orsay, France

Francesca Pazzaglia
Università degli Studi di Padova, Italy

INTRODUCTION

Language is an essential source for human beings to construct internal representations. When people are exposed to verbal descriptions of configurations of objects or spatial scenes, it is a common experience for them to create representations of the described entities and their spatial relations. Visual imagery is a privileged mode for expressing these relations, by reflecting the topology of the scene, and in some cases detailed metric aspects. Visual images may be used as inputs for spatial reasoning. For instance, they may be used for computing topological relations among objects or landmarks that have been left implicit in a text or a piece of discourse, or for performing some mental simulation on an imagined configuration, as in mental scanning (Denis & de Vega, 1993; Johnson-Laird, 1996). The cognitive processes involved in the creation and use of internal visuo-spatial representations from verbal descriptions formed the essence of Chapter 5 of the present volume.

Complementary to the issue of comprehension, language must also be considered from the point of view of the speaker (or writer), for its capacity to express internal spatial knowledge and convey it to other people. Language production is the object of the present chapter, the objective of which is to account for the mechanisms by which a speaker (or writer) generates verbal outputs with the intention of having an addressee (or reader) build a representation of a spatial environment.

Descriptions of spatial entities are quite common in daily communication. The cognitive difficulties inherent in the generation of spatial descriptions should not be overlooked. It is impossible to be exhaustive in the description of any visual scene in the environment. Contemporary literature provides examples of writers who have imposed on themselves the task of pushing description to its limits. A famous example is H.P. Lovecraft's attempts at describing in the most extensive manner every street, corner, square, and building of Quebec City. The 200 pages devoted by the writer to this almost obsessional exercise provide an example of a description that, in principle, should be never-ending, inasmuch as it is always possible to introduce new details or to adopt a new perspective for describing objects that have already been described. A similar example is available from the French literary school known as "Nouveau Roman", whose promoters engaged themselves in developing writing techniques for in-depth, detailed description of every aspect of even quite simple scenes.

Beyond these literary exercises, which would prove to be tedious and unmanageable in most natural communicative contexts, the obvious fact is that description, first, requires a *selection* of what is to be described. Furthermore, describing entails selecting the *order* in which selected pieces of information should be arranged to be transmitted. The order of presentation, obviously, commands the order in which the units will be processed by the addressee, and there are good reasons to expect that some sequences are more "friendly", or easier to process, than others, especially if they follow an order that is expected by the listener (Daniel, Carité, & Denis, 1996; Denis, 1996). The number of possible orders in which even a small number of items can be described may be very large, although constraints normally restrict the actual number of orders produced by a sample of describers. Such constraints have been shown to occur in the description of very simple scenes, such as patterns made of a few coloured dots connected by linear segments (Levelt, 1982). Chronometric measures of description latencies have been shown to reflect differential availability of the orders in which these dots can be described (Robin & Denis, 1991). Again, in the domain of literature, such hesitations as regards the optimal sequence for describing a scene characterise the writing process. The 14 successive versions of the first paragraph of the original manuscript of the short story *Hérodias* have revealed how Gustave Flaubert tried every possible combination of just a few sentences to describe the fortress in which the story is going to take place (Grésillon, Lebrave, & Fuchs, 1991).

There is a large variety of kinds of spatial discourse and of situations in which discourse is produced. In this chapter, we will concentrate on one specific type of discourse or text that describes space, namely the description of routes, and the cognitive conditions in which this discourse or text is produced. One particular aspect of this form of discourse is its ecological value. Everyone generates and processes such discourse almost daily. Furthermore, this type of spatial discourse is closely connected to the natural environment of people who produce or process it. It does not refer to imaginary or virtual environments, and provides descriptions from the point of view of the person who is to travel through real environments. Indeed, the concept of perspective has become central in the study of spatial cognition and spatial discourse (de Vega, 1994; Taylor & Tversky, 1992, 1996). Another interesting feature of route directions is their dynamic content, and consequently the fact that some features of spatial descriptions have to be reconsidered. In particular, contrary to the description of static spatial configurations, the description of routes includes a temporal component, which places constraints on the order in which information is delivered. The order in which pieces of discourse are delivered matches the order inherent in the entities to be described, which alleviates the processing load to a large extent. However, selectivity remains paramount, and it is still important for the researcher to tackle it, along with variability of discourse.

In this chapter, we will focus on the cognitive processes involved in the production of route directions. Central to the chapter will be the issue of the mental representations which code spatial information in memory and are accessed by the processes implemented in direction giving. The visual content of these representations, as expressed through mental imagery, will be underscored. Analyses regarding the features of "good descriptions" will be reported, as well as empirical data aimed at testing the actual informational value of descriptions in assisting navigation.

LANGUAGE, WAYFINDING, AND NAVIGATIONAL AIDS

Language is one among a variety of means designed to help a person in need of assistance in unfamiliar or unknown environments. It requires that some conditions are fulfilled; first of all, that people who ask for help are able to process the verbal message that will be delivered to them. If this condition is not fulfilled (for instance, if the person does not master the language used for the description, or if the age or cognitive capacities of the person make it unlikely that he/she will be able to memorise the entire set of instructions), the most efficient procedure simply consists of physically leading the person to his/her desired destination. This procedure has an advantage; it "models" the sequence of steps accomplished by the person on the nominal sequence accomplished by the guide, and thus ensures that the person proceeds securely to the target point. Actually, the verbal outputs that are considered in the present chapter will consist of sets of instructions, the execution of which should have the effect of making the person perform a succession of steps in such a way that they bring him/her to the target point. The advantage is obvious: the guide delivers actual assistance, but this has no cost in terms of actual execution of a displacement. However, the efficiency of the verbal procedure relies on two conditions. One is that the message provided by the guide has actual informational value, and the other is that the message is processed by the user efficiently.

A second class of methods to provide assistance by avoiding a guide's actual navigational involvement consists of delivering information in some graphic or cartographic form. In this case, assistance relies on a symbolic mediation, which requires that the two interacting people master the use of the symbols involved. In particular, they should share the codes by which three-dimensional environments are expressed in the form of two-dimensional survey representations. They should also have similar procedural knowledge on how map information can be used to plan navigation in an environment that normally offers frontal views when it is traversed. They should master the graphic symbols used to represent paths and buildings, how these symbols are combined with written verbal information, and how symbols for directional instructions (such as arrows) are to be interpreted (Habel, 1997; Tversky & Lee, 1999; Ward, Newcombe, & Overton, 1986). It is well established that maps are appreciated by people in need of navigational assistance (provided a physical medium is available for displaying that information), although people who produce route directions tend to deliver exclusively verbal instructions (Wright, Lickorish, Hull, & Ummelen, 1995).

A third class of methods for navigational assistance relies on language as a device for the production of route directions. Like maps, language has the value that its use is compatible with situations in which people discussing routes are physically remote from the location being discussed. This feature is of great value in the context of planning navigational behaviour. In many circumstances, language is also used in combination with gesture, which has a deictic function in the specification of directions to follow, when directions are given on the spot. But there are many cases in which language encapsulates all the information, such as in remote written assistance or assistance via telephone. This is the case we consider here primarily. The "extreme" situation in which language only is used to convey spatial information is of special interest, in that it forces a cognitive system to generate linguistic outputs that appropriately describe a spatial environment and the way to navigate in it, with the ultimate objective that a user will reconstruct a representation containing both visual and procedural components. The visual component is important inasmuch as it makes the user of the description construct a visuo-spatial internal model (presumably involving visual imagery) and code the set of actions to be taken in the represented environment. The situation in which linguistic and non-linguistic components of a cognitive system are forced to interact is an especially interesting one to test the functional efficiency of the system as a whole (Bloom, Peterson, Nadel, & Garrett, 1996; Landau & Jackendoff, 1993; Maass, 1995).

Another notable aspect of this situation is that it usually takes place in an interactive context, involving a person in need of information (the questioner) and another who delivers that information (the answerer). Direction giving involves the establishment of common grounds, and the answerer's consideration of the questioner's goals. Establishing common grounds is accomplished through the use of counter-questions that verify the common knowledge of the questioner and the answerer. The perception of the questioner by the answerer (in particular of his/her actual knowledge about the environment) affects the mode of questioning, as well as the content of the information delivered (Golding, Graesser, & Hauselt, 1996). The interactional scheme of giving directions is reflected by the fact that in addition to providing descriptive and instructional information, the answerer's discourse also includes comments (for instance, on the difficulty of the route), securing statements (repeating or paraphrasing instructions), interactive expressions (to check whether the questioner has got the message), etc. (Couclelis, 1996; Klein, 1982; Wunderlich & Reinelt, 1982).

CHARACTERISTICS OF SPATIAL LANGUAGE IN DESCRIBING ROUTES

Route directions are a type of discourse with a clear objective; that is, they provide a person with instructions about the actions to take in order to reach a target point. This means that route directions belong to the more general category of procedural discourse (Dixon, 1987; Glenberg & Robertson, 1999). Thus, first of all, route directions prescribe a set of *actions*. These actions, however, are not context-independent. They are to take place in a specific environment. Thus, part of discourse includes some form of description of this environment. As a result, route directions are a type of discourse (or text) that is not "pure", but combines prescriptive and descriptive statements. In particular, they include descriptions of scenes (the state of the environment that comes into view at key points on the route). These descriptions are intended to help the user verify that he/she has reached a given subgoal along the route. They also allow the user to check the correct alignment of his/her trajectory with specified landmarks of the environment. Furthermore, not only are relations among landmarks described, but also the appearance of the landmarks and of the ways to be followed. Route directions may also contain metric or temporal information, as well as comments. To summarise, there is a variety of types of statements, and there is a need for their classification.

According to Allen's (1988; Vanetti & Allen, 1988) taxonomy, a direction-giver produces four main types of communicative statements in response to requests for information. *Directives* are action statements reducible to "Go to . . ." and "Turn" statements (for example, "Walk to the end of the block", or "Turn left at the corner"). *Descriptives* are statements typically containing a form of the verb "to be" in which a spatial relationship between two features of the environment or between the traveller and one environmental feature is specified (for example, "The pharmacy is across the street from the post office"). *State-of-knowledge queries* are questions posed by a direction-giver to ascertain the knowledge state of the person requesting assistance (for example, "How well do you know the downtown area?"). Lastly, *comprehension queries* may be asked by direction-givers to make sure that the person requiring assistance has understood directions. Communicative statements contain pieces of information that constrain, define, or provide their focus. These "delimiters" are of two types. One type consists of objects or places in the environment that serve as points of origin, destinations, or reference points, such as landmarks (buildings, etc.) and choice points (e.g., intersections). The other type consists of constructs that qualify or quantify another delimiter or a communicative statement, such as distance designations, direction designations, and relational terms.

The classification introduced by Denis (1997) is mainly based on the two key components of route directions, namely, *reference to landmarks*, and *prescription of actions*. The crucial role for landmarks in route directions lies in their functional value in helping users to create visuo-spatial models of the environment. Landmarks have a variety of functions. One is to signal the sites where actions are to be accomplished, or where ongoing actions are to be modified (for instance, turning left). Landmarks also help to locate other landmarks (for instance, a speaker will refer to a prominent landmark to locate a less visible, but functional one). Landmarks also serve the function of confirmation, during a lengthy segment of the route. As to prescriptions, they apply to two main classes of actions: changing orientation, and proceeding. A specific type of prescription may also be found, namely prescriptions of positioning, which allow users to check that their current orientation matches the intended one.

The classification then considers three possible combinations of landmarks and actions. First, actions can be prescribed without reference to any landmark, such as "Turn left" or "Walk straight ahead". In some cases, metric information is associated with the prescription ("Proceed for 500 metres"). The second case combines an action and a landmark. A predicate asserts the prescribed action, while an argument refers to the landmark to which the action applies. For instance, "Cross the parking lot", "Turn right at the pharmacy", "Go past the swimming pool". Here, it is made explicit that the action must be implemented at a point that is best described as a visual landmark of the environment. The third case is the introduction of landmarks without referring to any associated action. Typically, the expression consists of positing a new landmark which comes to view while proceeding through the environment ("There is a bookshop", "Then you come across a church"). In addition to these three classes, a fourth one covers the descriptions of landmarks, such as naming ("The name of the bar is The Last Minute") or description of visual features ("It is a big pink-coloured building"), and a fifth one includes commentaries ("It will not take long").

Beyond the specificities of each classification, the general feature that emerges is the major role assigned to landmarks in spatial discourse. Progression is only rarely defined by distances to be covered and angles to be taken at reorientation points. Instead, the description takes into account the perceptual environment in which it is to take place. This is as if, beyond the objective of delivering a set of instructions for actions, the speaker's intention was to have the addressee construct an advance internal model of the environment through which he/she will move. The underlying assumption of the speaker is that progression will profit from prior knowledge of the visual environment that is to be experienced.

Three operations are supposed to be required to provide adequate assistance to a person in need of route instructions. The first operation for the speaker comprises *activating an internal representation* of the territory in which the proposed displacement will be made. People have a repertoire of representations of spatial environments. In order to satisfy a request for assistance, the speaker first has to circumscribe and activate the relevant subset of this repertoire. Internal spatial representations are likely to include procedural information learned from the moves that the speaker has experienced in previous displacements, but they also contain visual aspects of the environment, as explored from the subject's egocentric perspective (McNamara, Halpin, & Hardy, 1992; Sholl, 1987; Thorndyke, 1981; Thorndyke & Hayes-Roth, 1982). Visuo-spatial imagery has been shown to contribute to the elaboration of internal representations of environments learned from maps as well as from verbal descriptions (Denis & Cocude, 1997; Denis & Denhière, 1990; Thorndyke & Stasz, 1980). The notion that route descriptions use visuo-spatial representations as inputs is supported by the study of specific neuropsychological deficits. For instance, not only do neglect patients "ignore" the left part of visual scenes that they reconstruct from memory, but they also have more difficulty in thinking about leftward re-orientations when describing routes in a familiar environment (Bisiach, Brouchon, Poncet, & Rusconi, 1993). The assumption that route descriptions reflect spatial knowledge activated in the form of visuo-spatial representations can be tested empirically in normal subjects, by examining the effects of visual imagery on the content of route descriptions.

The next operation consists of *planning a route* in the subspace of the mental representation currently activated. Defining a route means defining a sequence of segments that connect the starting point to the destination and are to be followed by the moving person. The succession of route segments will directly command the succession of actions to be undertaken by the user of the description. Note that the speaker's objective is not to communicate to the addressee his/her whole representation of the environment wherein the displacement is to take place. A restriction on the representation is executed, resulting in the activation of the relevant part of spatial knowledge. The definition of a specific route results from a selection among a set of variants. It is based on criteria like the shortest route, or the route with the smallest angular discrepancy with respect to the goal at each intersection, and so on (Cornell, Heth, & Alberts, 1994; Gärling, 1989; Golledge, 1995; Pailhous, 1970). In principle, linguistic factors are not relevant for this set of operations. However, if route planning is mainly a preverbal operation, the choice of some specific routes or segments of routes may be constrained by criteria linked to their communicability. For instance, a detour may be easier to describe than a shortcut devoid of distinctive landmarks. As a consequence, the definition of a route not only takes into account the ease of its execution, but also the fact that the route has to be described verbally.

The last operation consists of *formulating the procedure* that the user will have to execute to move along the route and eventually attain its end. This operation results in a verbal output, which reveals the intimate interfacing achieved between the speaker's spatial knowledge and his/her linguistic capabilities. It is virtually never the case that describers refer exhaustively to the whole sequence of visual scenes and landmarks that will appear along the route. In practice, the person describing a route produces a limited number of statements (if only because he/she takes into account the limited processing capacities of the addressee). The objective of the speaker is to make the user progress along segments of appropriate length and execute reorientations at critical points, according to appropriate angles. In fact, the formulations in a route description never come down to a succession of prescriptions of progress and reorientation (which in principle could be expressed in purely metric terms), but give central importance to the mention of landmarks to be encountered along the route. A critical problem is then the selection of the landmarks. Only a few of the very large number of buildings, signs, and other landmarks that punctuate a route are eventually mentioned. The selection may be guided by the intrinsic value of some objects in the environment, such as their visual salience (Conklin & McDonald, 1982), but also by their informative value for the actions to be executed. In particular, those parts of the route where reorientations are needed are expected to be those where more landmarks are mentioned.

Contrary to descriptions of static entities, the descriptions of routes are constrained by the temporal succession of their components. Exceptions are backtrack statements, and rather infrequent macrodescriptions prior to the step-by-step descriptions. Thus, typically, route descriptions adhere to the chronology of the operations to be executed and to the order in which the environmental features are to be encountered. Nevertheless, although highly constrained as regards their sequential order, route descriptions reflect large interindividual variations. Consider, for instance, the two descriptions shown in Table 6.1. They are extracted from a set of responses from 20 students on a university campus asked to describe how to go from the train station to the university dorms (Denis, 1997). The steps to be followed by users of the two descriptions are exactly the same. It is interesting to note that in order to elicit the very same navigational behaviour, one participant felt it necessary to produce a description three times as long as the other participant. Note also the large difference between the two descriptions in their richness in visual landmarks. The most talkative participant posits landmarks at every point where crucial actions are to be taken, but also along linear segments.

One may reasonably suspect that variations among descriptions' contents should have an impact on the value of the descriptions as navigational aids. Too much information may create cognitive overload that will be detrimental to the processing. In contrast, too little information will create uncertainty at crucial points. Is it possible to identify features that determine the communication value of descriptions? This question can be expressed in another form: Is it possible to

TABLE 6.1
Two descriptions of routes

Informant #1
"Cross the railroad tracks. Then, continue to walk down the street. You reach an intersection. Continue along a footpath. Continue walking to a little bridge. There, it will be the building just to the left."

Informant #10
"Go through the train station. There is a bar just opposite. Walk down the street. To the right, there is a photocopy shop. At the bottom of the street, there is a bar on the street corner. Cross the street. To the left, there is a church. To the right, there is a driving school. Walk down the path without turning left or right. Keep on the same path. There is a residence on the right and a long slope. Walk down to the little bridge that passes over the Yvette river. There, you will see two buildings on the left. Go towards them. It is not the first building, but the second to the left. This is Building 232."

generate optimal forms of spatial discourse, and if this is the case, what are the features of good descriptions, and what are the criteria establishing that a description is a "good" one?

Measures of the quality of individual descriptions may first be found in ratings provided by users of these descriptions. Empirically, a simple procedure consists of asking people to "judge" a set of descriptions on a rating scale, ranging from a value for descriptions enabling a reader to build easily a clear representation of the route and reach the goal without error or hesitation, to a value for poor descriptions containing insufficient information or more information than is necessary, and which do not enable the reader to build a consistent representation. The distribution of ratings reflect that even in a homogeneous sample of participants (such as university students), the protocols differ dramatically, from a subset of very good to a subset of very poor descriptions, with a majority of medium-level descriptions. In general, the descriptions that receive the highest ratings are compact descriptions, with landmarks explicitly positioned, and a limited number of very specific instructions. In contrast, low-rated descriptions do not refer to key landmarks. They are either extremely simplified descriptions, with very few landmarks, or they reflect overspecification, introducing a volume of information that is far beyond most users' processing capacities.

The significant agreement among the judges, as well as the fact that their ratings result in highly correlated values within subjects tested on several descriptions, indicates that although based on subjective evaluations, the ratings actually capture the key features of the descriptions. The judged communicative value of the descriptions is thus a consistent feature, and it is relevant to look for correlation between judges' ratings and objective measures likely to account for them. One candidate measure is the richness of the descriptions, indicated by the number of propositions contained in corresponding protocols. Obviously, a description must be informative, and information is correlated with the number of items in a speaker's output. On the other hand, the sheer number of items in a description is probably of limited value, as a description may be numerically very rich and at the same time contain false or irrelevant information. Actually, there is no correlation between the judges' ratings and the number of propositions in individual protocols. Another candidate predictor of the judges' ratings is the number of landmarks mentioned in the descriptions. There is in fact no correlation between the rated quality of descriptions and the number of landmarks. Obviously, it is not the number of selected landmarks that makes for a good description, but more likely their relevance. Thus, "good" descriptions cannot be accounted for simply in terms of their size or their richness in landmarks. More sensitive measures may be needed, in particular those reflecting the similarity of individual descriptions to nominal (or optimal) descriptions.

How then can we obtain an "optimal" version of a route description that contains the essential prescriptions and landmarks useful to a traveller, while standing midway between the two extremes of excess or lack of information? One possibility would be to call for experts, but there is no way to define the "expertise" in this domain. Furthermore, one should prefer a method that exploits the rich set of data contained in natural descriptions by ordinary people. Denis (1997) used a simple statistical procedure to abstract "skeletal descriptions" and objectively test their informational value. The method consists, first, of compiling all the pieces of information that have been given by all the participants of a sample. The union of all individual descriptions for a given route results in what is called a "megadescription", that is, the addition of every statement that was actually produced by all the subjects about this route. The next operation consists of collecting judgements from a new group of participants on the relevance of each item in the megadescription. Participants are asked to cross out all those items that they consider to be superfluous or unnecessary. Only the pieces of information necessary and sufficient to guide a walking traveller must be kept, so that the traveller reaches his/her goal without any help other than this information. The participants' responses result in frequencies of choice for each item of the megadescriptions. A stringent exclusion criterion is used. Usually, only items selected by at least 70% of the participants are considered to contribute to the construction of skeletal descriptions. In the case of the route mentioned earlier, 25% of the items comprising the megadescription are kept in the corresponding skeletal description (see Table 6.2).

It is worth emphasising that a skeletal description is a *construct*, which does not correspond to any output of a specific participant's behaviour. Nevertheless, it reflects the essence of a route, distilled from actual descriptions. A skeletal description does not yield a random patchwork of unrelated items. In the example reported earlier, it is fully informative, while containing the minimal set of landmarks and instructions needed to navigate appropriately. It contains a large proportion of items that combine an action prescription and reference to a landmark. In short, it contains the essential elements of the navigational procedure,

TABLE 6.2
A skeletal description of a route

Cross the rail track.
Walk down the street.
Continue to the bottom.
You reach an intersection.
To your left, there is a church.
To your right, there is a driving school.
There is a footpath between the two.
Take the path.
Continue walking down to a little bridge.
Cross the bridge.
There are two buildings on the left.
These are Buildings 231 and 232.
Cross the road.
Proceed toward the leftmost building.
It is Building 232.

without any extra embellishment. More importantly for our purpose, a skeletal description can be considered as close to an "optimal" description, and used as a reference point for evaluating individual protocols and quantifying the "distance" between individual protocols and that reference.

In order to test the hypothesis that the similarity of an individual description to the skeletal description predicts the rated quality of the description, two measures may be considered. The first is the proportion of items in a description that belong to the set of items in the corresponding skeletal description. The assumption here is that the more items of a skeletal description are in an individual description, the higher its value would have been rated by the judges. The second index reflects the extent to which skeletal elements saturate an individual description, by measuring the proportion of skeletal items in each individual protocol. The capacities of both indices to predict the evaluations made by the judges can then be examined. Actually, there is a strong positive correlation between these indices and the judges' ratings (Denis, 1997). Thus, objective measures reflecting the resemblance of individual protocols to the skeletal description predict the judged quality of the descriptions. These analyses also validate the construct of skeletal description, a concept that proves to be a meaningful one in that it reflects the essential components of a good description.

Are there any individual characteristics that affect the quality of descriptions produced by these individuals? More specifically, are there individual cognitive features that explain that people differ in their capacities to generate good route descriptions? Undoubtedly, verbal capacities are a prerequisite for the quality of verbal productions, and people with high verbal capacities will be expected to produce better verbal outputs. But this is probably true for every type of verbal production. In the case of spatial discourse, it is relevant to make hypotheses about the link between the content of spatial descriptions and the internal representations from which they are presumably generated.

The framework outlined at the outset of this section postulates that the long-term cognitive representations recruited for generating spatial discourse contain visuo-spatial components of subjects' spatial knowledge. People are known to differ from each other in the richness and/or accessibility of such visuo-spatial representations (McKelvie, 1995; Paivio, 1986; Poltrock & Brown, 1984). The question is whether these individual differences are reflected in subjects' verbal expressions of their spatial knowledge. Because high imagers are more likely to access their internal visual knowledge than their counterparts, this would also be true when they access their spatial representations to describe routes. This bias towards visuo-spatial representations would then be reflected in more frequent references to the visual components of routes described by high visuo-spatial imagers (mainly landmarks).

Vanetti and Allen (1988) collected descriptions of routes from participants in four groups based on their combination of spatial and verbal abilities. High spatial participants produced descriptions that proved to be more efficient according to independent navigational measures. Also, people with low spatial and low verbal abilities produced a lower proportion of environmental features such as landmarks and choice points, especially near the arrival point. Thus, spatial ability is important in the production of efficient route directions, but verbal ability plays another important role in facilitating the effective translation of spatial knowledge into verbal outputs.

To assess the hypothesis that high visuo-spatial imagers would include more reference to visual landmarks, the participants of the Denis (1997) study were divided into two groups as a function of their scores on two visuo-spatial tests. There was no significant difference between the high and low visuo-spatial imagers in the rated quality of their descriptions, but the high imagers' descriptions contained significantly more information than did those of low imagers, and this effect was mainly due to the larger number of propositions that introduced visual landmarks. Thus, people most likely to retrieve visuo-spatial information from their memories refer more frequently to this type of information in their verbal descriptions. The fact that high visuo-spatial imagers mentioned more landmarks in their descriptions although their protocols did not receive higher ratings than those of poor imagers clearly suggests that a high imager may also be a poor describer.

Another way of approaching individual differences in route descriptions involves comparing protocols produced by men and women. The literature on gender differences offers numerous indications that spatial cognition is sensitive to such differences. Several experiments on route descriptions have indicated that female subjects tend to mention more landmarks than their male counterparts, whereas males are more inclined to process metric and directional information (Galea & Kimura, 1993; McGuinness & Sparks, 1983; Miller & Santoni, 1986).

In giving directions from maps, males use more mileage estimates and cardinal directions than do females (Ward et al., 1986).

The analysis of the data reported by Denis (1997) did not reveal any systematic differences in the rated communicative value of men's and women's descriptions. But women tended to produce descriptions that contained a larger number of propositions than did men. The clearest contrast between the groups was in the number of propositions introducing landmarks. Women referred to significantly more landmarks than did men, a finding that confirms previous reports that women describing routes devote more attention to landmarks than men. Another finding was that female participants produced descriptions that were significantly more similar to the skeletal descriptions than males. This is consistent with the systematic tendency of women to produce richer descriptions than men.

THE CONTENT AND STRUCTURE OF ROUTE DIRECTIONS

Route directions belong to the domain of spatial discourse, with the specific feature of having an intrinsic temporal dimension that imposes itself onto their structure. Descriptions of static environments leave a number of sequences possible for describing them, depending on the priority that the describers give to specific landmarks or subsets of landmarks. Some kinds of environments, however, are traversed in a highly predictable fashion, and thus are described according to a sequence commanded by a virtual movement through them. This is the case for apartments, as was shown by Shanon (1984). Very few people will describe their apartment by first describing the main room (living room), but typically will match the description to the sequence of steps made by a visitor (starting from the entrance door, then describing the entrance or corridor, then the first room served by the corridor, etc.). Similarly, the description of rooms typically follows the sequence commanded by a "gaze tour" following the walls of the room (Ehrich & Koster, 1983; Ullmer-Ehrich, 1982).

In the case of route directions, the order in which the environment is described matches the order in which the environment will be explored. This is closely dependent on the procedural nature of this form of discourse. Typically, when a procedure is described, the steps of the procedure are described in the order in which they will have to be accomplished. This means that the description may include not only the steps of the procedure, but also, as preliminary information, the macrostructure of the procedure; that is, the overall plan to be followed when executing the procedure. Such advance information may be found in describers of routes, especially those who devote much effort to providing their addressees with explicit information (for instance listing first the main intermediate goals), but this strategy is an exception. The great majority of descriptions of routes simply start with the obvious starting point, and describe the route in a stepwise fashion.

However, this apparently low-level description does not mean that describers are not following an overall plan. The analysis of most route directions makes it easy to detect that they obey a form of planning, with an underlying structure in goals, subgoals, sub-subgoals, etc. However, this hierarchical structure is very rarely stated explicitly in the discourse. It generally remains implicit, and it is one of the aims of researchers in this domain to make it explicit.

The first important task is obviously the description of the starting point of the route. The speaker must define this point unambiguously and give every indication so that the addressee places him/herself cognitively at this point. The speaker must also orientate the addressee in the correct direction, for example by using a visible landmark as a precursor to progress. As a consequence of the gradual change of the person's position, the visual scene around the person changes and new features appear in his/her visual field. These features are potential landmarks for describing the next actions to take. The describer selects those landmarks that should be used as a signal of termination of progress, or as reference points to reorientate the person. Mention of landmarks may be associated with the more detailed local view of an important node: "You will reach an intersection [mention of landmark]; there are buildings on the right, and a park on the left [description of local view]". In such a case, the local description has a function of confirmation.

At specific points on the route, reorientation must be performed. Reorientations are very rarely prescribed in terms of angular quantities. More usually, they are carried out by using the landmark just attained and its alignment with further landmarks, which will be used as reference points for progression along the new segment. Most descriptions of routes can be accounted for by iteration of a triplet of instructions at the end of any segment: prescribe reorientation; prescribe progress along segment s+1; announce landmark (which both signals the end of progress and site for the next reorientation). Descriptions end by mentioning the ultimate landmarks at the arrival point, optionally with additional descriptions of landmark properties to discriminate the ultimate landmark from other similar ones (Denis, 1997; Golding et al., 1996).

Obviously, landmarks have a critical role in monitoring the progression of the person through the environment, mainly at nodes where reorientation takes place. In environments where pathways have proper names (like streets in cities), reference to landmarks is not so critical. But in open environments (a university campus) or suburban environments, where the network of pathways is more open, it is important to remove any ambiguity. The sites for reorientation are those where walkers will have to pay much attention to the environment, and where describers will devote more effort to describing the environment unambiguously. To return to the route mentioned earlier (examples of descriptions were given in Table 6.1), the frequencies of landmarks mentioned in successive portions of the route showed that landmarks were distributed quite unevenly throughout the descriptions and concentrated where they could play a role in

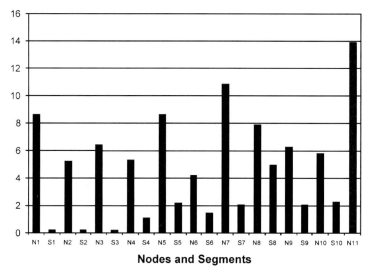

Nodes and Segments

Figure 6.1.   Number of landmarks mentioned along a route involving underground and overground sections (Fontaine & Denis, 1999). The abscissa shows the alternation of nodes (N) and connecting segments (S). N1 is the starting point (platform of the subway station "Place d'Italie"). N5 is the last node of the underground section of the part of the route (street intersections). N11 is the arrival point (the entrance door of a school).

reorientation. Landmarks were mostly mentioned at nodes (91%), while the remaining 9% were mentioned along segments that connected nodes (Denis, 1997). In some environments, however, lengthy progression along extended linear segments may call for confirmation landmarks. The speaker will then mention landmarks situated along the route, to provide confirmation that the person is still on the right route (Lovelace, Hegarty, & Montello, 1999).

The fact that landmarks are more likely to be mentioned at reorientation points of a route seems to be quite a general phenomenon, which may be found in descriptions of a variety of environments. Even in a very special type of urban environment (the city of Venice), 81% of buildings mentioned and other three-dimensional landmarks occurred at critical nodes, and the remaining 19% were mentioned along the segments connecting the nodes. While the former are thought to contribute to orienting the mover at decision points, the latter are essentially intended to confirm that the mover is walking in the correct direction (Denis, Pazzaglia, Cornoldi, & Bertolo, 1999). Another study investigated route directions in different environments, such as underground ones, and even when the described route is a composite of underground and overground. People were asked to describe the route from the platform of a subway station in Paris to the station exit, then the way to proceed along the streets of Paris from the subway station to a specific target. Figure 6.1 shows that in both underground and outside environments, nodes involving a choice among several directional options were

TABLE 6.3

Average number of propositions for five classes of statements in control and concise conditions

	Control condition	Concise condition	Size of effect
Prescription of actions without reference to landmarks	5.7	3.4	−40%
Prescription of actions with reference to landmarks	14.2	7.4	−48%
Introduction of landmarks	9.6	2.6	−73%
Description of landmarks	4.4	0.8	−82%
Commentaries	0.9	0.2	−83%

the places where landmarks were mentioned the most frequently (Fontaine & Denis, 1999). Thus, landmarks are concentrated where they are expected to help orientation or reorientation. These findings clearly indicate that landmarks are not included in descriptions simply as adjunct or anecdotal items, but for their actual information value, mainly when reorientation is needed.

As we have pointed out, descriptions of routes reflect large interindividual differences, in terms of their length, richness in landmarks, similarity to skeletal descriptions, etc. Descriptions are also sensitive to constraints that may occur during production. One of these constraints is the requirement to be concise. From the user's point of view, concise messages are preferred, inasmuch as they lower the processing load and make the core information more directly available, by eliminating superfluous or redundant information. On the part of the describer, an invitation to be concise should increase the amount of his/her attention devoted to selecting information. Daniel and Denis (2000) compared the protocols of participants who were invited to produce written descriptions of a route in concise wording (descriptions should not exceed five lines) and those of participants who worked in standard, unconstrained conditions. Not surprisingly, the constrained condition resulted in shorter descriptions (with an average of 14.4 propositions versus 34.8 in the control condition). But the most interesting part of the study consisted of evaluating the differential impact of being concise on the different parts of route instructions. Table 6.3 shows the average number of propositions for five classes of statements based on the classification mentioned earlier (Daniel & Denis, 1998; Denis, 1997). Clearly, concise descriptions were implemented in quite different ways among the five classes considered. The number of action prescriptions was substantially reduced (mainly by eliminating unnecessary prescriptions of straight progression), but the most dramatic reduction affected the introduction of new landmarks and their description. The strong reduction in references to landmarks did not result in incoherent descriptions. It reflected the fact that in unconstrained conditions, people tend to mention landmarks beyond what is just necessary, to make the described scenes

TABLE 6.4
Average number of propositions for five classes of statements as
produced in a group condition

	Group condition	Size of effect
Prescription of actions without reference to landmarks	3.0	−47%
Prescription of actions with reference to landmarks	13.6	−4%
Introduction of landmarks	3.3	−65%
Description of landmarks	0.5	−88%
Commentaries	0.7	−27%

richer in visual information. When constrained to restrict the amount of information actually delivered, they shorten those passages that are more saturated with non-critical landmark information. Lastly, commentaries, which in any case were very few in the control condition, were almost totally eliminated under instructions to be concise.

Similar effects were also obtained in conditions intended to enhance concise content, although by a different manipulation. For instance, a context likely to favour selectivity and a concise content is the task of having route directions generated by small groups of participants, instead of individually. The common endeavour created by social context usually facilitates confrontation of solutions and assessment of relevance of selected information. It increases the likelihood that any proposed solution receives immediate feedback and that inadequate solutions are rejected early. Thus, inviting people to work together in small groups of three or four might create a social context likely to generate better descriptions, containing more carefully selected information, and thereby more concise descriptions. Table 6.4 shows the results obtained from groups of people, each of which was assigned the task of producing one single description based on interactive cooperation. The conciseness effect (calculated relative to the value of the control condition in the individual task) was clear. Again, number of landmarks mentioned and landmark descriptions were strongly reduced. A distinct feature, however, was that the statements combining actions and landmarks were not reduced. This suggests that these items tend to be preserved given the valuable package of information that they represent.

TESTING EFFICACY OF DIRECTIONS BY MEASURES OF NAVIGATIONAL PERFORMANCE

A sensible feature of individual route directions is their similarity to nominal directions based on skeletal descriptions. Such indices as ratings of communicative value and measures of similarity to skeletal descriptions provide effective hints that the closer an individual protocol is to purportedly "ideal" descriptions, the higher it is rated by judges. The ultimate confirmation that individual descriptions have different value for communication and navigation, depending on their proximity to nominal descriptions, should be sought in behavioural studies, where navigational performance is measured in response to various types of route directions. Will a description eventually serve the objective for which it has been generated, that is allow the person who uses it to execute navigational performance in satisfying conditions? Beyond criteria of (rated) quality of spatial descriptions, behavioural criteria should be used as well.

The first study on this subject was conducted in a complex urban environment, namely the city of Venice (Denis et al., 1999). It is important, indeed, to extend this type of research to a variety of environments. The special interest of the city of Venice is that it offers an environment with narrow, mostly winding streets. Venice also has two superimposed networks, the streets and the canals. When people are walking, the canals act as barriers to their progress, and pedestrian navigation requires knowledge of the location of bridges to cross the canals. Lastly, the particular structure of the streets often implies that the final, or even an intermediate, goal is not visible until the very last moment. The absence of any wide open view to the horizon makes it difficult to create a survey representation and probably favours the use of "route representations" based on successions of landmarks.

Three itineraries in Venice were selected (for instance, from the Rialto fish market to Campo San Salvador) and descriptions were obtained from a sample of inhabitants. Detailed analysis of the verbal protocols resulted in skeletal descriptions for each itinerary. Table 6.5 shows the skeletal description for one route. In addition, based on judges' ratings, a good and a poor description were selected. The navigation task then involved a sample of participants who had never been in Venice before. They were undergraduate students from Italian cities who were attending courses at the University of Padova. Each participant received a description in a written form at the starting point of the corresponding route and read it on the spot. Then the participant started walking along the designated route. An experimenter escorted the participant along the entire length of the route and kept a record of signs likely to reflect any difficulty on the part of the participant. When participants took a wrong turning, the experimenter called them back and repositioned them at the intersection, informing them that the direction they had followed was not correct. The participants were asked to walk in a relaxed manner while avoiding pauses and to ask for assistance from the experimenter if necessary.

The number of directional errors and number of requests for assistance from the experimenter were recorded. Hesitations were scored as 1 every time participants stopped for more than 5 seconds, and 0.5 for shorter stops. Table 6.6 shows the average numbers of directional errors, hesitations, and requests for assistance per route for each type of description. As the overall scores were very low, the

TABLE 6.5
Skeletal description of a route in Venice

You are in Campo de la Pescaria.
Stand with your back to the Grand Canal.
The fish market is under arches.
Walk along the entire length of the fish market.
You will find a little square.
Turn to the left.
Go straight along a street.
You will arrive at a crossroads.
Go straight ahead.
You will go through the fruit market.
You will see the steps of a bridge.
It is the Rialto Bridge.
Cross the bridge.
After the bridge there is a street.
Go straight ahead.
You will arrive in a square.
It is Campo San Bartolomeo.
In the middle, there is a monument.
Turn right.
You are in a large street.
Go along it for 100 metres.
You are in Campo San Salvador.
There is a column in the middle of the square.

TABLE 6.6
Average error scores during navigation per route for each type of description

	Good description	*Poor description*	*Skeletal description*
Directional errors	0.25	0.69	0.12
Hesitations	0.06	1.31	0.56
Requests for assistance	0.51	0.94	0.31
Total error score	0.82	2.94	0.99

total error score was calculated by summing the three individual error scores. The analysis showed that the good descriptions resulted in better navigation than poor descriptions. Furthermore, the similarity of performance for good and skeletal descriptions indicated that the latter captured some of the essential features of the best original descriptions.

These results provide behavioural support for judges' ratings. Those descriptions that were assessed as the best for their navigational assistance indeed proved to guide navigation the most efficiently. They probably did so because they had numerous features that are characteristic of good descriptions. They were clear, unambiguous, and concise. In contrast, poor descriptions made navigation much more difficult. They clearly led participants to make more directional errors and be more uncertain, as indicated by the frequent hesitations they elicited. In contrast, participants using good descriptions almost never hesitated.

The same study examined the influence of individual differences in mental representation of space. Navigational performance of participants was analysed as a function of participants' preference for different spatial perspective. Based on their scores on a Questionnaire on Spatial Representation (Pazzaglia, Cornoldi, & De Beni, 2000), people inclined to use survey representations to solve navigational tasks were compared to those preferring to rely on visual landmarks as seen from an egocentric perspective. Both groups performed equally well when given good and skeletal descriptions, but the total error scores reflected lower performance of the survey-oriented than the visually oriented participants when they followed poor descriptions. This indicates that survey-oriented people may experience special navigational difficulties with materials having poor communicative value. People having preference for either survey or visual perspective were found to perform differently in wayfinding tasks in indoor environments (Pazzaglia & De Beni, 1997). Two learning conditions were compared: learning the route from a map or from verbal directions. As in the Venice study, the survey-oriented participants made more errors than the other group when using the verbal directions, while map learning tended to be more beneficial to visually oriented participants.

In a further study, Daniel, Tom, Manghi, and Denis (2000) investigated the navigational value of route directions. Their impact was measured not only on navigational performance (as in the Venice study), but also on navigational times. Students who were totally ignorant of the Orsay campus were invited to walk along a route after reading one of three versions of route directions: a good description, a poor description, or a skeletal description. The route was 417 metres long. The overall time to reach the destination was quite similar for people who read the skeletal and the good descriptions (13 min 7 s and 13 min 42 s, respectively), but the participants who read the poor description took significantly longer (17 min). The number of directional errors and the resulting times were larger for readers of the poor description than of either of the other two. The same was found for the number of stops and corresponding hesitation times. The poor description also created distorted representations, as attested by the fact that people who read poor descriptions (and consequently spent more time walking) overestimated the length of the route by 54%, while the error was only −16% for the skeletal description and +22% for the good description. This study confirmed the functional value of skeletal descriptions, a construct based on the assumption that individual descriptions are variants of a core structure. The concept of a skeletal description was forged to capture the idea that some pieces of information in route directions are more crucial for navigation than others. Behavioural assessments provided confirmation of these ideas.

CONCLUSION

A number of empirical studies converge on a rather new issue in the domain of spatial cognition, namely people's use of language to convey spatial information and, more particularly, provide navigational assistance to other people. Route directions are a form of procedural discourse that exploits a vast database of human knowledge, namely spatial knowledge, and provides people with opportunities of constructing knowledge to guide their action in new environments. By articulating the concept of internal representations and the concept of externalising of representations by using language, this field of research provides arguments for the value of a basic cognitive approach to resolving concrete spatial problems. A further reason for investigating route directions as a form of spatial discourse is that they offer quite a rich field for interdisciplinary research (Chown, Kaplan, & Kortenkamp, 1995; Sorrows & Hirtle, 1999). Psychology and cognitive neuroscience, but also linguistics and computer science, converge on this issue, which, beyond its theoretical interest, opens on a number of applications in the domain of human–computer systems and navigational aids.

REFERENCES

Allen, G.L. (1988). *A general approach to the study of the production and comprehension of route directions*. Technical Report, Department of Psychology, University of South Carolina.

Bisiach, E., Brouchon, M., Poncet, M., & Rusconi, M.L. (1993). Unilateral neglect in route description. *Neuropsychologia, 31*, 1255–1262.

Bloom, P., Peterson, M.A., Nadel, L., & Garrett, M.F. (Eds.) (1996). *Language and space*. Cambridge, MA: The MIT Press.

Chown, E., Kaplan, S., & Kortenkamp, D. (1995). Prototypes, location and associative networks (PLAN): Towards a unified theory of cognitive mapping. *Cognitive Science, 19*, 1–51.

Conklin, E.J., & McDonald, D.D. (1982). Salience: The key to the selection problem in natural language generation. In *Proceedings of the 20th Annual Meeting of the Association for Computational Linguistics* (pp. 129–135), Toronto, June.

Cornell, E.H., Heth, C.D., & Alberts, D.M. (1994). Place recognition and way finding by children and adults. *Memory and Cognition, 22*, 633–643.

Couclelis, H. (1996). Verbal directions for way-finding: Space, cognition, and language. In J. Portugali (Ed.), *The construction of cognitive maps* (pp. 133–153). Dordrecht, The Netherlands: Kluwer.

Daniel, M.-P., Carité, L., & Denis, M. (1996). Modes of linearization in the description of spatial configurations. In J. Portugali (Ed.), *The construction of cognitive maps* (pp. 297–318). Dordrecht, The Netherlands: Kluwer.

Daniel, M.-P., & Denis, M. (1998). Spatial descriptions as navigational aids: A cognitive analysis of route directions. *Kognitionswissenschaft, 7*, 45–52.

Daniel, M.-P., & Denis, M. (2000). *The production of route directions: Investigating conditions that favor concise spatial discourse*. Unpublished manuscript. LIMSI-CNRS, Université de Paris-Sud, Orsay.

Daniel, M.-P., Tom, A., Manghi, E., & Denis, M. (2000). *Route directions: Their impact on navigational performance*. Unpublished manuscript. LIMSI-CNRS, Université de Paris-Sud, Orsay.

Denis, M. (1996). Imagery and the description of spatial configurations. In M. de Vega, M.J. Intons-Peterson, P.N. Johnson-Laird, M. Denis, & M. Marschark (Eds.), *Models of visuospatial cognition* (pp. 128–197). New York: Oxford University Press.

Denis, M. (1997). The description of routes: A cognitive approach to the production of spatial discourse. *Current Psychology of Cognition, 16,* 409–458.

Denis, M., & Cocude, M. (1997). On the metric properties of visual images generated from verbal descriptions: Evidence for the robustness of the mental scanning effect. *European Journal of Cognitive Psychology, 9,* 353–379.

Denis, M., & Denhière, G. (1990). Comprehension and recall of spatial descriptions. *European Bulletin of Cognitive Psychology, 10,* 115–143.

Denis, M., & de Vega, M. (1993). Modèles mentaux et imagerie mentale. In M.-F. Ehrlich, H. Tardieu, & M. Cavazza (Eds.), *Les modèles mentaux: Approche cognitive des représentations* (pp. 79–100). Paris: Masson.

Denis, M., Pazzaglia, F., Cornoldi, C., & Bertolo, L. (1999). Spatial discourse and navigation: An analysis of route directions in the city of Venice. *Applied Cognitive Psychology, 13,* 145–174.

De Vega, M. (1994). Characters and their perspectives in narratives describing spatial environments. *Psychological Research, 56,* 116–126.

Dixon, P. (1987). The structure of mental plans for following directions. *Journal of Experimental Psychology: Learning, Memory, and Cognition, 13,* 18–26.

Ehrich, V., & Koster, C. (1983). Discourse organization and sentence form: The structure of room descriptions in Dutch. *Discourse Processes, 6,* 169–195.

Fontaine, S., & Denis, M. (1999). The production of route instructions in underground and urban environments. In C. Freksa & D.M. Mark (Eds.), *Spatial information theory: Cognitive and computational foundations of geographic information science* (pp. 83–94). Berlin: Springer.

Galea, L.A.M., & Kimura, D. (1993). Sex differences in route-learning. *Personality and Individual Differences, 14,* 53–65.

Gärling, T. (1989). The role of cognitive maps in spatial decisions. *Journal of Environmental Psychology, 9,* 269–278.

Glenberg, A.M., & Robertson, D.A. (1999). Indexical understanding of instructions. *Discourse Processes, 28,* 1–26.

Golding, J.M., Graesser, A.C., & Hauselt, J. (1996). The process of answering direction-giving questions when someone is lost on a university campus: The role of pragmatics. *Applied Cognitive Psychology, 10,* 23–39.

Golledge, R.G. (1995). Path selection and route preference in human navigation: A progress report. In A.U. Frank & W. Kuhn (Eds.), *Spatial information theory: A theoretical basis for GIS* (pp. 207–222). Berlin: Springer.

Grésillon, A., Lebrave, J.-L., & Fuchs, C. (1991). Flaubert: "Ruminer Hérodias". Du cognitif–visuel au verbal–textuel. In D. Ferrer & J.-L. Lebrave (Eds.), *L'écriture et ses doubles: Genèse et variation textuelle* (pp. 27–109). Paris: Editions du CNRS.

Habel, C. (1997). Discours et représentations spatiales dans la description de plans. In M. Denis (Ed.), *Langage et cognition spatiale* (pp. 103–125). Paris: Masson.

Johnson-Laird, P.N. (1996). Images, models, and propositional representations. In M. de Vega, M.J. Intons-Peterson, P.N. Johnson-Laird, M. Denis, & M. Marschark, *Models of visuospatial cognition* (pp. 90–127). New York: Oxford University Press.

Klein, W. (1982). Local deixis in route directions. In R.J. Jarvella & W. Klein (Eds.), *Speech, place, and action* (pp. 161–182). Chichester, UK: Wiley.

Landau, B., & Jackendoff, R. (1993). "What" and "where" in spatial language and spatial cognition. *Behavioral and Brain Sciences, 16,* 217–265.

Levelt, W.J.M. (1982). Linearization in describing spatial networks. In S. Peters & E. Saarinen (Eds.), *Processes, beliefs, and questions* (pp. 199–220). Dordrecht, The Netherlands: Reidel.

Lovelace, K.L., Hegarty, M., & Montello, D.R. (1999). Elements of good route directions in familiar and unfamiliar environments. In C. Freksa & D.M. Mark (Eds.), *Spatial information theory: Cognitive and computational foundations of geographic information science* (pp. 65–82). Berlin: Springer.

Maass, W. (1995). How spatial information connects visual perception and natural language genera-tion in dynamic environments: Towards a computational model. In A.U. Frank & W. Kuhn (Eds.), *Spatial information theory: A theoretical basis for GIS* (pp. 223–240). Berlin: Springer.

McGuinness, D., & Sparks, J. (1983). Cognitive style and cognitive maps: Sex differences in repres-entations of a familiar terrain. *Journal of Mental Imagery, 7*(2), 91–100.

McKelvie, S.J. (1995). The VVIQ as a psychometric test of individual differences in visual imagery vividness: A critical quantitative review and plea for direction. *Journal of Mental Imagery, 19*(3–4), 1–106.

McNamara, T.P., Halpin, J.A., & Hardy, J.K. (1992). The representation and integration in memory of spatial and nonspatial information. *Memory and Cognition, 20*, 519–532.

Miller, L.K., & Santoni, V. (1986). Sex differences in spatial abilities: Strategic and experiential correlates. *Acta Psychologica, 62*, 225–235.

Pailhous, J. (1970). *La représentation de l'espace urbain: L'exemple du chauffeur de taxi*. Paris: Presses Universitaires de France.

Paivio, A. (1986). *Mental representations: A dual coding approach*. New York: Oxford University Press.

Pazzaglia, F., Cornoldi, C., & De Beni, R. (2000). Differenze individuali nella rappresentazione dello spazio e nell'abilita di orientamento: Presentazione di un questionario autovalutativo [Individual differences in spatial representation and in sense of direction: A self-rating scale]. *Giornale Italiano di Psicologia, 27*, 241–264.

Pazzaglia, F., & De Beni, R. (1997). *Different modalities of representing space*. Paper read at the final meeting of the project "Imagery, Language and Mental Representation of Space: A Cognit-ive Approach", Saint-Malo, France, 22–23 September.

Poltrock, S.E., & Brown, P. (1984). Individual differences in visual imagery and spatial ability. *Intelligence, 8*, 93–138.

Robin, F., & Denis, M. (1991). Description of perceived or imagined spatial networks. In R.H. Logie & M. Denis (Eds.), *Mental images in human cognition* (pp. 141–152). Amsterdam: North-Holland.

Shanon, B. (1984). Room descriptions. *Discourse Processes, 7*, 225–255.

Sholl, M.J. (1987). Cognitive maps as orienting schemata. *Journal of Experimental Psychology: Learning, Memory, and Cognition, 13*, 615–628.

Sorrows, M.E., & Hirtle, S.C. (1999). The nature of landmarks for real and electronic spaces. In C. Freksa & D.M. Mark (Eds.), *Spatial information theory: Cognitive and computational founda-tions of geographic information science* (pp. 37–50). Berlin: Springer.

Taylor, H.A., & Tversky, B. (1992). Spatial mental models derived from survey and route descrip-tions. *Journal of Memory and Language, 31*, 261–292.

Taylor, H.A., & Tversky, B. (1996). Perspective in spatial descriptions. *Journal of Memory and Language, 35*, 371–391.

Thorndyke, P.W. (1981). Distance estimation from cognitive maps. *Cognitive Psychology, 13*, 526–550.

Thorndyke, P.W., & Hayes-Roth, B. (1982). Differences in spatial knowledge acquired from maps and navigation. *Cognitive Psychology, 14*, 560–589.

Thorndyke, P.W., & Stasz, C. (1980). Individual differences in procedures for knowledge acquisi-tion from maps. *Cognitive Psychology, 12*, 137–175.

Tversky, B., & Lee, P.U. (1999). Pictorial and verbal tools for conveying routes. In C. Freksa & D.M. Mark (Eds.), *Spatial information theory: Cognitive and computational foundations of geographic information science* (pp. 51–64). Berlin: Springer.

Ullmer-Ehrich, V. (1982). The structure of living space descriptions. In R.J. Jarvella & W. Klein (Eds.), *Speech, place, and action* (pp. 219–249). Chichester, UK: Wiley.

Vanetti, E.J., & Allen, G.L. (1988). Communicating environmental knowledge: The impact of verbal and spatial abilities on the production and comprehension of route directions. *Environment and Behavior, 20*, 667–682.

Ward, S.L., Newcombe, N., & Overton, W.F. (1986). Turn left at the church, or three miles north: A study of direction giving and sex differences. *Environment and Behavior, 18*, 192–213.

Wright, P., Lickorish, A., Hull, A., & Ummelen, N. (1995). Graphics in written directions: Appreciated by readers but not writers. *Applied Cognitive Psychology, 9*, 41–59.

Wunderlich, D., & Reinelt, R. (1982). How to get there from here. In R.J. Jarvella & W. Klein (Eds.), *Speech, place, and action* (pp. 183–201). Chichester, UK: Wiley.

CHAPTER SEVEN

Actions, mental actions, and working memory

Robert H. Logie
University of Aberdeen, UK

Johannes Engelkamp and Doris Dehn
Universität des Saarlandes, Germany

Susan Rudkin
University of Aberdeen, UK

When we interact with the world, the ability to maintain some form of mental representation of our environment is crucial. If you were now to close your eyes and attempt to reach out and pick up small objects nearby, you would have little difficulty in doing so. This strongly suggests that our interaction with objects in the environment does not necessarily require visual input for successful interaction. It also suggests that we can mentally represent fairly accurately the location as well as the identity of objects in our immediate environment. This ability to represent visual and spatial aspects of our surroundings has been widely studied within the working memory framework and there is now converging evidence for a distinction between a visual temporary store and a spatial/movement-based system. We will discuss some of the evidence for this distinction before looking at the spatial/movement-based system in more detail. This system appears to be involved in the planning and execution of physical movement, as well as the mental representation of paths between objects in the environment.

We will also consider mental actions in the form of mental manipulation of components of images. In this context we will discuss research on mental synthesis, a task that involves transforming, manipulating, and combining distinct parts of an image into novel forms. This research is discussed in terms of representation in working memory and the association with stored knowledge in long-term memory.

Finally we will discuss the link between physical actions and temporary memory for action phrases. There is a body of evidence which indicates that the enactment of a verb phrase enhances later retrieval. This effect is discussed in terms of the additional information available through enactment of a phrase.

Therefore, throughout the chapter we will draw on several distinct approaches to the mental representation of actions, including temporary memory for movements and movement sequences, mental actions involved in the transformation and manipulation of images, and the role of enactment in temporary memory for action descriptions. The chapter will end first with an indication of how we might draw on each of these cognate but distinct approaches to provide insight into how the representation of space is linked with memory for movements, their planning and execution, and second, how the findings that we discuss may contribute to an understanding of how working memory might support acquisition of new knowledge through interaction with physical objects and mental manipulation of images.

THE VISUAL CACHE AND INNER SCRIBE OF WORKING MEMORY

There is now a body of evidence to suggest that temporary memory for visual information may be somewhat distinct from temporary memory for paths between objects or targeted movement sequences. In an attempt to investigate this possible distinction, Logie and Marchetti (1991) examined two contrasting memory tasks. One of these involved presentation of a sequence of squares appearing one after another in different random locations on a computer screen, with recognition memory for the sequence tested after a retention interval of 10 seconds during which the screen was blank. A second task involved presenting an array of squares each in a different hue of the same basic colour (e.g., shades of blue). During the retention interval, in one condition subjects were required to tap out a regular pattern. In another condition, the retention interval was filled with presentation of a random sequence of line drawings of objects in the same location. Presentation of the line drawings disrupted retention of the colour hues but did not disrupt retention of the sequence of squares. In contrast, tapping out a pattern disrupted memory for the sequence of squares in different locations, but did not affect memory for colour hues. These data pointed to a separation between a visual temporary memory system and a spatial/movement-based memory system.

Further evidence for this distinction came from a developmental study by Logie and Pearson (1997) in which groups of children aged 5, 8, and 11 were tested on their memory span for a block sequence task (based on De Renzi & Nichelli, 1975) and on their memory span for visually presented matrix patterns. The two forms of memory span correlated very poorly within each age group, and memory span for the static visual matrix patterns increased with age much more rapidly than did memory span for the sequence of movements to random blocks. This technique, known as "developmental fractionation" (Hitch, 1990) indicates that the cognitive systems responsible for these two tasks seem to develop at different rates and to have little overlap within a given age group.

A further source of support arises from studies of brain-damaged individuals who appear to show selective deficits of visual working memory in the absence of a spatial deficit, while other patients show the converse. For example, Farah, Hammond, Levine, and Calvanio (1988) described a patient who had great difficulty with mental imagery tasks that involved judgements about visual appearance such as "Which is darker blue, the sky or the sea?". However this same patient had no difficulty with imagery tasks that involve mental actions such as imaging and recalling a path between targets. More recently, Wilson, Baddeley, and Young (1999) have described a female patient who is a professional sculptress but who, following brain damage, is unable to visualise patterns or shapes, and to imagine the potential appearance of her sculptures. In contrast, Beschin, Cocchini, Della Sala, and Logie (1997) described a patient suffering from pure representational unilateral spatial neglect. This patient was unable to describe the spatial layout of familiar scenes, leaving out details from what would be his imagined left. He also had significant difficulty with a task that involves following and remembering a path around an imagined matrix (Brooks, 1967). However he had no difficulty in describing visual properties of scenes, and has no general visual or spatial perceptual problems.

These cases offer examples of the body of evidence (for more comprehensive reviews see Logie, 1995; Baddeley & Logie, 1999) for the distinction between a temporary store for visual information such as form, colour, and static layout of objects, which we shall refer to as a "visual cache", and a separate system that is linked to temporary memory for movements and movement sequences, which we shall refer to as an "inner scribe". Note that thus far we have referred to a spatial/movement-based system. This dual labelling has been deliberate in an attempt to disambiguate the use of the term "spatial". Sometimes the term is used to refer to the layout or arrangements of objects in a scene. Other times it refers to representation of a sequence of movements between objects. Here, and elsewhere in the chapter, we shall focus on the link with movements, mental and physical, in the spirit of the views of Bain (1868, p. 366) who suggested that the very meaning of space lies in its scope for movement: "The possibility of a certain amount of locomotion is implied in the very idea of distance" (see also James, 1902, p. 281). In this chapter we will argue further that the representation of space in working memory allows scope for mental actions to be planned, executed, and encoded for later recall, topics we now turn to in more detail.

MENTAL PATHS AND PHYSICAL ACTIONS

Some of the best-known studies on the planning and execution of physical movement have explored the use of physical action in studies of dual task performance. For example, Baddeley and Lieberman (1980) required experimental participants to imagine a four by four square matrix pattern. Participants were then required to imagine placing consecutive numbers in a series of adjacent squares following a path around the matrix. After the "number path" had been described, the participants were then asked to recall verbally the sequence of imagined movements required to reproduce the imagined path. In one experimental condition the participants were blindfolded and were given a flashlight with which they had to follow the motion of a swinging pendulum. A tone signalled whether the flashlight was shining on or off the pendulum. Therefore subjects were performing concurrently two distinct tasks; generating the mental image of a path and moving their arm back and forth in time with a metronome. The mental imagery task involved only auditory input and vocal recall, while the movement task involved auditory feedback from the tone and controlled tracking movement of the hand and arm. Neither task involved visual input. Under these circumstances, participants' recall of the matrix paths was significantly impaired relative to performing the imagery task without concurrent movement.

One possible reason for the deterioration in recall performance that Baddeley and Lieberman observed is that it is simply more difficult to carry out two tasks simultaneously than to perform only one. However the interference seemed to be specific to the combination of the imagined path task and concurrent movement: When the imagined path task was concurrent with visual discrimination of patches of light, recall performance was unimpaired. In other words, the cognitive processes involved in mentally imaging a sequence of locations along a path appear to overlap with the cognitive processes involved in controlling arm movement. The fact that subjects were blindfolded in the movement condition indicates that this overlap in processing resources is linked to spatial representations and movement control rather than relying on the visual system.

A similar pattern of results was obtained by Quinn and Ralston (1986) where again volunteer participants were required to imagine a path around a square matrix and carry out concurrent movement. In their procedure, the movement involved the volunteer using one hand to tap a regular pattern on a table top, but with the hand hidden from view. As with the Baddeley and Lieberman experiments, recall of the imagined path was disrupted by concurrent arm movement. In subsequent experiments Quinn (1994) varied the procedure for arm movement with one condition involving tapping areas on the table top in a random fashion. In a further condition the experimenter held the participant's hand and moved it across the table top in a random fashion. In this case the participant's hand was being moved but they had no control over that movement. Quinn found that random movement generated by the participant resulted in disruption of imagined path recall. However when the experimenter generated the movement there was no disruptive effect. In a third condition, the experimenter held the participant's hand and moved it in a regular and predictable pattern, and under these conditions the dual task disruption reappeared. In summary, when subjects were controlling the movement themselves or could predict where their hand was going next, then they had difficulty recalling the imagined matrix path. However when the participant was unable to control or predict the movement of their own arm, then they had little difficulty constructing, retaining, and recalling the imagined matrix path. This pattern of findings suggests that the planning of movement may be as, if not more, crucial than its execution for generating these disruptive effects.

Another approach has explored the use of a block sequence recall task (De Renzi & Nichelli, 1975; Logie & Pearson, 1997; Smyth, Pearson, & Pendleton, 1988), in which the experimenter taps a series of blocks arranged randomly on a board and the subject's task is to tap the blocks in the same sequence. Typically this uses a span procedure in that the number of blocks in the sequence increases until the subject can no longer successfully recall the sequences correctly. This task relies on encoding, retention, and reproduction of a sequence of arm and hand movements to a series of specified targets. As such, it should be the kind of task that is ideal for exploring the role of visuo-spatial working memory in representation and planning of actions. Smyth et al. (1988) and Smyth and Pendleton (1989) observed that recall of the block sequence was impaired if, throughout presentation of the sequence, subjects had to move their hands in a regular square pattern. This pattern of findings, then, links working memory for a path among targets in the environment and production of targeted movement. In other words, when subjects are tapping four targets in a square pattern, this involves cognitive resources that overlap with those required for maintaining a representation of a path between objects in the environment.

In further experiments Smyth and Scholey (1994) have demonstrated that a version of the block sequence task was also disrupted by concurrent shifts of spatial attention in which subjects detected and pointed to the sources of tones presented in spatially separated locations. Some disruption was also involved if the spatially separated tones were presented but required no motor response. From these and similar results, Smyth and Scholey concluded that spatial attention was crucial to the encoding and retention of a sequence of locations, but the greater decrement found when pointing was involved suggests that aspects of action planning and production also rely on the cognitive system that is responsible for temporary memory for spatial locations. This approach has recently been extended by Merat (1999) who used sound localisation with response via a directional dial rather than by pointing. Her data indicate that sound localisation has an impact on verbal serial recall tasks and tasks involving verbal memory updating, suggesting that localisation may have a general attentional load rather than being specific to spatial memory and processing.

The importance of higher-level attentional processes in memory for a sequence of targeted movements was tackled by Salway and Logie (1995) who explored the use of the imaged matrix path task employed in the experiments by Quinn and by Baddeley and Lieberman described earlier. Salway and Logie found that hand tapping in a regular square pattern disrupted memory for the imaged path around a square matrix. These results are consistent with other studies linking movement with memory for paths. However Salway and Logie found that the path imaging task was even more disrupted by concurrent oral random generation of numbers, a task that is often described as involving attentional control as well as verbal output (e.g., Baddeley, 1966; Baddeley, Emslie, Kolodny, & Duncan, 1998). This was surprising, because generation of a random verbal sequence would not appear to involve any spatial demands. A further experimental condition demonstrated that memory for the path was largely unaffected by the requirement to repeat a single irrelevant word (go go go . . .); therefore the disruptive effects of random generation could not be attributed readily to the disruptive effects of simply performing any secondary task, or to some verbal strategy that subjects might have adopted when retaining the imagined path. It appeared more that the general attentional demands of the path task were larger than had been assumed previously, and that a secondary task that draws on these attentional resources reduces the cognitive resource available for the visuo-spatial imagery task. If we consider only the specific interference with spatial imagery tasks by concurrent arm or hand movement, this leads to the conclusion that there are specialised cognitive resources for the mental representation of paths among objects, and that these cognitive resources are also required for the planning and/or execution of physical movement to targets in the environment. However, the results from Smyth and Scholey (1994) and from Salway and Logie (1995) point to the additional involvement of attentional resources. This involvement of attentional resources arises in the next section on visuo-spatial representation, imagery, and mental actions, and will recur in the concluding section of the chapter.

VISUO-SPATIAL REPRESENTATION, IMAGERY, AND MENTAL ACTIONS

In examining the representation of actions, thus far we have focused largely on memory for pathways between targets and its links with production of physical movement. Another approach is to investigate mental actions in the form of mental manipulations of components of images. There is considerable evidence that a variety of mental actions can be performed on mental images; they can be scanned, expanded, compressed, pulled apart, rotated, and combined (e.g., Kosslyn, 1994; Roskos-Ewoldsen, Intons-Peterson, & Anderson, 1993). The relevant experiments have been well documented elsewhere (see e.g., Richardson, 1999, for a recent review) and we will not reiterate their discussion here. However some recent work has explored how, in performing these various mental acts on imagery, novel discoveries may be made or problems solved. In this context some of the experimental work on such mental actions has focused on how the notion of visuo-spatial working memory might account for what has been referred to as mental synthesis. In this task, experimental participants are

LAMP

APPLIANCE USED FOR BOXING

Figure 7.1.   Example of a drawing, plus labels given before (above) and after (below) drawing generated by a participant in Barquero and Logie (1999) Experiment 1.

required to imagine separate named shapes which they are required to transform, manipulate, and combine mentally to form a complete object. Mental imagery can support the production of novel forms through combining these separate parts. For example, people can mentally fold pieces of marked paper to judge the shape of the final form (Shepard & Feng, 1972). Cooper (1991) has demonstrated that engineering students are capable of constructing three-dimensional representations of complex objects after being presented with two-dimensional drawings of the top, front, and side views. Her findings suggest that the subjects can both mentally synthesise a complete three-dimensional object, and also use this representation as a basis to make judgements about the compatibility of presented two-dimensional views. In a series of studies by Finke and colleagues (e.g., Finke, 1989; Finke & Slayton, 1988), subjects were asked to imagine letter shapes and to transform and combine the imaged letters to form an image of a familiar object (see Chapter 1 by Pearson, De Beni & Cornoldi, this volume). Helstrup and Anderson (1996) have demonstrated that it is possible to generate images of novel object shapes by mentally manipulating and combining the basic shapes of real common objects, such as a ruler, a glass, and a pineapple. Figure 7.1 shows an example of a subject production from these three shapes in experiments reported by Barquero and Logie (1999).

A similar agility with mental manipulation was demonstrated by Brandimonte and colleagues (Brandimonte, Hitch, & Bishop, 1992a, b). In their experiments, participants were presented with pictures of objects, along with a picture of one segment of the object. One of the tasks required participants mentally to subtract the segment from the image of the object and report the resulting figure. An example is shown in Figure 7.2. Most subjects could perform this task, and it is notable that the patterns resulting from the manipulation were clear only from

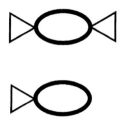

Figure 7.2. Example of the type of mental subtraction task used by Brandimonte, Hitch, and Bishop (1992a).

the geometric properties of the stimuli, and not from the semantic associates of the object shape. For example, the initial shape shown in Figure 7.2 is of a wrapped sweet. The resulting shape of a fish, following mental subtraction could not readily be predicted from what we know about confectionery. Again, this demonstrates that mental actions can be performed on mental images and that the phenomenal experience of manipulating the image is associated with functional cognition.

However, there are circumstances under which mental reinterpretation of an image is more difficult. For example, Chambers and Reisberg (1985, 1992) demonstrated that when subjects were presented very briefly with perceptually reversible figures such as the Necker cube or the duck–rabbit figure, then they were unable to reverse the figure in their image, but could do so when they later drew their image on paper (for a detailed discussion see Cornoldi et al., 1996).

In a series of experiments by Pearson, Logie, and Green (1996), the Finke and Slayton (1988) guided mental construction task was explored, with subjects required first to construct a mental image of a recognisable object, then to provide a name for the object. Next the subjects drew the object they had imagined, and finally they provided a name for their drawing. The subject productions were then assessed as to the fit between the names provided and the drawing. The second name (after drawing) tended to correspond more closely than the first name to the drawing, suggesting that there are some limitations in constructing and interpreting novel images, and that externalising these images was one way to enhance this interpretation. Similar results have been found in some more recent experiments by Barquero and Logie (1999) using more open-ended versions of the mental synthesis task with mental combinations of real object shapes (e.g., a pineapple, a glass, and a ruler) to generate recognisable objects that were different from those presented (see Figure 7.1). In both sets of experiments the name produced after subjects had drawn their image (shown below the drawing in Figure 7.1) tended to be a better fit to the constructed shape than was the name based on the image alone (shown above the drawing in Figure 7.1). In summary, subjects could perform mental actions on the object shapes, but the semantic content of the mental images of real objects somehow inhibits our ability to see these as simple shapes. When the mental image is transferred to paper, its "re-inspection" through perception aids the process of shedding the semantic associates of the constituent object shapes (the pineapple, the ruler, and the glass) and generating an interpretation for the resulting combination.

A further constraint on discovery from mental actions comes from the amount of information that we are attempting to manipulate. For example both Barquero and Logie (1999), and Pearson, Logie and Gilhooly (1999) have shown the way in which the number of elements to be mentally manipulated impacts on mental synthesis performance. They have also shown that the task most likely involves verbal rehearsal of the shape names and temporary visual storage of partial synthesis of components while forming the image, as well as manipulation of the images of the shapes. In other words, mental actions can lead to mental discoveries, but discoveries may be constrained by the semantic content of the material and the number of elements on which the mental actions are being performed. Moreover such tasks involve several aspects of the cognitive system including verbal rehearsal, visual temporary storage, and possibly executive processes to support manipulation and combination of images. A more thorough review of this literature is provided in Chapter 1 by Pearson, De Beni, and Cornoldi (this volume).

All of these experiments lead to three general conclusions; first that visuo-spatial mental representations are interpreted rather than raw sensory records. That is, the mental representation is derived from sensory input that has been pre-processed and associated with stored knowledge in long-term memory before it is available to conscious inspection and manipulation. Second, the phenomenal experience of mental actions involving the manipulation and mental inspection of images to form novel, meaningful configurations appears to reflect some functional aspect of cognition. Third, the cognition in these tasks involves executive functions of working memory possibly supported by a visual, more passive store, and a verbal rehearsal system for the names of the objects to be combined. Therefore we cannot consider that mental imagery is supported solely by specialised and independent cognitive functions such as a visual buffer or visuo-spatial sketchpad. Mental imagery relies on a range of cognitive functions, some specialised and some more general purpose. We shall return to this argument in the final section of the chapter after considering the important and related topic of how we encode and recall physical (rather than mental) actions and their associated verbal descriptions.

MEMORY, ACTIONS, AND ACTION DESCRIPTIONS

Thus far we have focused on mental actions such as in imagery manipulation and the link between memory for actions and physical movement. We have made only passing reference to the link between physical actions and the verbal descriptions of actions. However, given our argument that conscious mental representations have semantic content, it is reasonable to assume that verbal coding of actions may play an important role in directing the nature of that semantic content. For example, we noted in discussing the experiments by Smyth and colleagues that recall of action sequences may have reflected the use of verbal coding of each action. We have also focused on how the temporary representations in working memory might be formed and manipulated, but have not considered in any detail how the forming of those temporary representations might lead to encoding of an episodic trace of each trial, or how such episodic traces might be retrieved. It is clear from a large and growing literature that there is a strong link between memory for the verbal labels and memory for the actions that those labels describe. We will now review the main findings from the complementary literature on memory for action phrases, and then turn to some theoretical discussion as to how actions and mental actions might offer additional insight into the functioning of visuo-spatial working memory.

The effects of enactment

At the beginning of the 1980s, both Engelkamp and Krumnacker (1980) and Cohen (1981) observed that the enactment of a verb phrase (such as "to lift the pen") significantly enhances the probability of its later retrieval in comparison with mere verbal processing of the phrase. This basic finding is often referred to as the SPT effect (for *subject performed task*; e.g., Cohen, 1981). It has been replicated in a large number of studies (e.g., Bäckman, 1985; Bäckman & Nilsson, 1984; Cohen & Bean, 1983; Engelkamp, 1986a, b, 1988; Engelkamp & Zimmer, 1983; Helstrup, 1987, 1989; Nilsson & Cohen, 1988; Saltz, 1988; Zimmer, 1991; see Engelkamp, 1998 for a recent review).

The typical research paradigm for studying memory for simple action descriptions (e.g., Cohen, 1981; Engelkamp & Krumnacker, 1980) is as follows: Participants are given a list of unrelated action phrases (e.g., "to clap the hands", "to cut the onion", "to play the piano"), which they hear or read. All participants are instructed to learn the phrases for a later memory test. Half of the participants are told to read the phrases or to listen to them, referred to in the literature as the verbal task condition (VT). The remaining participants also are told to read the phrases or to listen to them, but additionally to enact each phrase as it is presented, for example physically to clap their hands or to mime cutting an onion or playing the piano. This is referred to in the literature as the subject-performed task (SPT) condition. For clarity in the context of this chapter we shall refer to the latter as the enacted condition or enacted task.

As both enacted tasks and verbal-only tasks involve an equivalent amount of verbal processing, differences in memory performance between the conditions appear to be attributable to the additional requirements of enactment. Broadly speaking, there are two kinds of information that can additionally be encoded in the enacted condition and, consequently, may lead to superior memory performance. First, an action needs motor or kinaesthetic information for smooth performance. Second, enacted phrases provide rich visual, and sometimes tactile, sensory information. During its execution, the individual receives visual feedback on his or her own action. If real objects are involved in the task, then further visual and tactile information is provided. In order to identify the basis for the memory-enhancing effect of enactment, empirical investigations have focused on these two types of information. All of this information plus the verbal descriptions allow for a rich representation to be formed in working memory at the time of initial presentation. We have already noted that the contents of working memory will reflect the range of information that is activated by sensory input during a task (Logie, 1995, 1996), and that working memory may have an important role in action planning (e.g., in the Quinn 1994 studies), as well as in attending to and implementing actions (e.g., Quinn & Ralston, 1986; Salway & Logie, 1995; Smyth et al., 1988). We will discuss studies that have focused on each of the two types of information associated with actions and then explore how item and relational information influence the effect of enactment.

The role of motor information

Executing an action on verbal command necessarily involves planning and then performing the action. Given that the working memory literature indicates that even planning an action may disrupt recall of a path that is unrelated to the planned action, then can action planning contribute to enhancement of memory for the planned action? Alternatively does the enactment effect result solely from physical enactment? If the effect were entirely due to planning then memory for a planned (but not performed) action should be equal to memory for this action when it is actually performed. This hypothesis was first examined by Zimmer and Engelkamp (1984) who separated the planning of an action from its execution by instructing their subjects to prepare themselves for performing a particular action. The action was then performed in only half of the trials. The results showed that memory performance was better for actions that were both planned and performed than for actions that were only planned. Hence, planning actions appears not to be the only factor that underlies the memory-enhancing effect of enactment. However the Zimmer and Engelkamp study left open the issue of whether there is an effect of planning alone.

The potential memory enhancement from planning an action compared to verbal encoding was investigated by Koriat, Ben-Zur, and Nussbaum (1990) who demonstrated across four experiments that memory for actions that had been planned, but not performed was better than memory for verbal descriptions of the actions. In a study of action planning in normal ageing, Brooks and Gardiner (1994) went a step further and compared memory performance after verbal encoding, action planning, and action performance for young and elderly participants, but failed to replicate the Koriat et al. finding. The results showed a general advantage for enactment and an effect of normal ageing with poorer performance overall for the elderly participants compared with the young. How-ever neither the elderly nor the young showed any difference in performance between the planning and the verbal alone condition.

The inconsistency in these findings with regard to the memory-enhancing effect of planning processes was addressed by Engelkamp (1997) who showed that planning an action results in better retrieval than verbal processing when the encoding condition was manipulated between subjects. When the encoding con-dition was manipulated within subjects then planning an action did not enhance memory in comparison to mere verbal processing. The discrepancy in previous findings can then be resolved at least in part by noting that Brooks and Gardiner (1994) used a within-subject design in contrast to the between-subjects design used in Experiment 3 of Koriat et al. (1990). However the issue was not wholly resolved, because Koriat et al. (1990) also observed a planning effect in their Experiments 1 and 2 in which they used a within-subject design. One possible account stems from a contrast in the list length used, in that Koriat et al. used very short lists (five items) compared to the list lengths used in the other experiments that we have discussed here. The issue merits further study, but it is clear that there may only be a modest memory advantage for actions that are planned as opposed to those that are physically performed, and that the planning advantage is vulnerable with particular forms of experimental design, encoding conditions, or list lengths. Nevertheless the data are broadly consistent with the working memory literature, showing at least some influence of action planning on the representation of action: a disruptive effect when the planned action is unrelated to the represented action, and an enhancement effect when they are closely related.

It is clear however that physical performance of the action phrase has a much greater impact on the enhanced recall of the phrase. In the working memory literature, there has been no direct comparison between the disruptive effects of planning unrelated actions and those of performing such actions. Both affect memory for movement sequences, but we do not know the relative extent of the effects of each. This issue has however been studied in some detail within the literature on recall of action phrases. Engelkamp and Zimmer (e.g., 1994a; Engelkamp, 1998) maintained that the memory enhancement observed for enacted action phrases is at least partially due to the motor information provided by execution of the action itself. Evidence for this view comes from three lines of research, namely studies on selective motor interference in free recall of action phrases, studies on assessment of motor similarity of action phrase pairs, and studies of motor similarity effects on recognition. With regard to the first approach, several studies have reported interference with recall of action phrases from concurrent, unrelated motor tasks, and this interference is much greater than that observed with concurrent, unrelated visual tasks (Cohen, 1989; Saltz & Donnenwerth-Nolan, 1981; Zimmer & Engelkamp, 1985; Zimmer, Engelkamp, & Sieloff, 1984). This result bears more than a passing resemblance to the finding reported earlier in the chapter that physical movement disrupts memory for block sequences or paths around an imagined matrix.

The second line of research has involved presenting pairs of action phrases which are rated by participants for similarity. Engelkamp and Zimmer (1984) demonstrated that when the first action phrase is performed, rather than just heard by the participant, then participants' judgements of similarity to the second action phrase is faster than when both action phrases are presented verbally. Engelkamp and Zimmer argued that the enactment of the first phrase activates or "primes" the motoric information necessary for the subsequent comparison more effectively than does the verbal description of the action. Engelkamp (1985) showed further that simply imagining the first action was not sufficient to achieve the priming effect on similarity judgements.

In the third line of research Engelkamp and Zimmer (1994b, 1995; Engelkamp, Zimmer, Mohr, & Sellen, 1994) devised contrasting sets of action phrases, for which the actions were respectively motorically similar or motorically dissimilar, and studied recognition memory for the presented action phrases. In a series of experiments, motorically similar distractors that were also conceptually similar to the targets resulted in higher false alarm rates than did dissimilar distractors.

Taken together, the evidence points to the importance of physical action in appearance of the enactment effect, and the results are consistent with our earlier discussion of the working memory literature suggesting a link between physical movement and the mental representation of sequences of movements to targets, such as in the block sequence recall task, or the imaged matrix task. The consistency in these findings is even more striking when we consider that memory for action phrases often involved retaining 15, 20 or even more phrases, which would ostensibly exceed the storage capacity of a working memory system. This raises questions as to the possible role for working memory in either encoding or retrieval of action phrases, and it is notable in this respect that the motor interference effects on action phrase memory arose during encoding of the action phrases. The impact of action similarity on action phrase similarity judgements offers additional evidence for the role of long-term stored knowledge being activated and used. This is consistent with the idea mentioned earlier that operations in working memory involve activated stored knowledge and that the contents of working memory have semantic content.

The role of sensory information

An early explanation of the memory-enhancing effect of enactment (e.g., Bäckman & Nilsson, 1984; Bäckman, Nilsson, & Chalom, 1986) pointed to the multi-modality and the sensory richness of subject-performed tasks. In some studies, the actions for recall were performed with real objects, whereas with purely verbal encoding no objects were used (e.g., Cohen, 1981, 1983; Bäckman et al., 1986; Nyberg, Nilsson, & Bäckman, 1991). The external object might thus have enriched the memory trace for enacted, but not for verbally processed, phrases. However enactment effects were also observed in studies in which no real objects were provided (e.g., Engelkamp & Krumnacker, 1980; Helstrup, 1989; Mohr, Engelkamp, & Zimmer, 1989); therefore the memory-enhancing effect of enactment cannot be ascribed to the use of real objects alone. Nevertheless, the use of real objects does enhance memory performance for action phrases (Engelkamp & Zimmer, 1983, 1996, 1997), and this effect is stronger for recall of verbally encoded phrases than it is for enacted action phrases (Engelkamp & Zimmer, 1997; Nyberg et al., 1991). That is, the employment of real objects in both verbal and enacted encoding conditions decreases the advantage for enactment. This contribution to memory performance of real object presentation indicates that sensory, and specifically visual, information plays an important role in recall, particularly in memory for verbally encoded action phrases. However, what is equally clear is that the enactment effect appears to be quite independent of the contribution from sensory information, and this cannot therefore offer an adequate account. This conclusion is further strengthened by findings from studies that compared memory for performed and for perceived actions.

Visual sensory information during enactment is also provided by an individual observing his or her own body movements. In order to control for this kind of information, an enactment condition can be compared with a condition in which the individual observes another person—usually the experimenter—performing the action. This condition is referred to in the literature as an experimenter-performed task, although in this chapter we shall refer to observed action. If the memory-enhancing effect of enactment is exclusively due to visual sensory factors, then memory performance should not differ between enacted and observed actions. However the empirical evidence suggests that enactment leads to better retrieval than does observing the action being performed by someone else (e.g., Engelkamp & Zimmer, 1983, 1997). The evidence from these same studies also suggests that using a real object results in a mnemonic advantage for both conditions, again indicating that the enactment effect is independent of the use of physical objects.

These findings demonstrate several important issues. First, it appears that at least three kinds of information contribute to the recall of action phrases, namely the visual sensory information provided by observing one's own body movement required for the action, the visual sensory information from observing the physical objects involved in the actions, and the motoric or kinaesthetic information from the movement. Second, visual sensory information from perceiving real objects improves memory; but it is not crucial for the enactment effect. Third, visual information from observing actions by other people gives rise to poorer performance than does enactment by the rememberer, and therefore the motoric or kinaesthetic information appears to play a crucial role.

So far, the discussion of the role of sensory factors in enacted tasks has focused on the contribution of visual sensory factors to memory for action phrases such as perceiving the actions of the related objects. A related question to be investigated is whether enactment increases the probability of recollecting information about the location of performed actions or the location of objects involved in those actions. Conway and Dewhurst (1995) compared memory for object arrangements that had been encoded by (a) placing objects at particular positions ("*Put object x next to object y*"), (b) imagining the placement of objects ("*Imagine object x next to object y*"), or (c) observing the placements of the objects ("*Watch object x next to object y*"). Recognition performance was tested using items that were of the form "*object x was next to object y*". Conway and Dewhurst found that recognition performance for enacted arrangements was better than performance for observed arrangements, which in turn exceeded performance for imagined arrangements. In contrast, Zimmer (1996) failed to find a difference in the free recall of object positions that were either placed by the subjects themselves or by somebody else. Koriat, Ben-Zur, and Druch (1991) tested the ability to discriminate between two study lists for enacted and observed actions. Because the study lists differed in *where* they were presented as well as *by whom* they were presented, the list discrimination task could also be considered a test for visual or location information. Koriat et al. (1991) observed that although overall recognition was better for enacted phrases, the ability to discriminate between lists was superior for observed phrases.

Thus, whether visual sensory and location information is retained better for enacted than for non-enacted phrases is still unclear. An influencing factor appears to be the relevance of the information for the execution of the action. Engelkamp (1995; Engelkamp & Perrig, 1986) argued that with regard to spatial information it is critical whether spatial information is part of the performed action (e.g., "put the shoe next to the box") or not (e.g., "put on the shoe in the train"). Whether this distinction can contribute to clarifying the role of object position is an obvious topic for future study.

In summary, we can conclude that the study of memory for action events reveals that different kinds of sensory and motor information can be identified as contributing to memory for action phrases in addition to verbal information. At the very least, we should consider visual information while observing others, visual and motor (or kinaesthetic) information when performing actions oneself, visual sensory information from the real objects involved in actions, and probably also location information related to the actions.

The role of item information and inter-item associations

The previous discussion focused on the question of what kind of visual sensory and motor information, in addition to verbal information, contributes to the encoding of enacted verb phrases. However, differences in memory performance can also be explained in terms of item information such as its semantic associates, as well as inter-item associations. In list learning, items are encoded as individual events (item information) and at the same time they become interrelated. Moreover, both kinds of information also contribute differently to different memory tests. Free recall draws on both item and inter-item information whereas recognition memory relies primarily on item information (e.g., Einstein & Hunt, 1980; Hunt & Einstein, 1981). The question then arises as to to what degree item information and inter-item associations respectively contribute to the enactment effect. The suggestion that performing an action provides item information is supported by the fact that the enactment effect is particularly robust in recognition memory (e.g., Engelkamp, Zimmer, & Biegelmann, 1993; Knopf, 1991; Zimmer & Engelkamp, 1999). The role of inter-item associations was less clear cut (e.g., Zimmer & Engelkamp, 1989; Bäckman et al., 1986). However, more recent research (Engelkamp, 1998; Engelkamp & Zimmer, 1996) has begun to shed some light on this issue, in that they have demonstrated that categorical structure is apparent in free recall of lists of action phrases. When the recalled lists are scored according to categorical grouping of the phrases, it is clear that categorisation is used for retention and recall of action phrases to about the same extent for verbal only conditions and for enacted conditions. Thus while inter-item associations within the list contribute to overall performance, there is no evidence that they contribute to the advantage for enacted phrases (see also Zimmer & Engelkamp, in press).

In sum, the recall of action phrases shares some of the characteristics that are typical of verbal free recall, in that additional visual, verbal, or semantic cues encoded at presentation can aid subsequent retrieval. Where the action phrase tasks differ is in the additional impact of enactment. This suggests that motoric or kinaesthetic codes can have an influence on episodic memory in addition to those typically considered in the verbal memory literature. The focus of the discussion within this literature has viewed memory for action phrases as an episodic memory task. However there are suggestions from this literature that working memory may have an important role in the encoding, and possibly also the retrieval, of the action phrases. There are also several findings that echo results from studies reported in the working memory literature. In the final section of this chapter, we shall examine this possible overlap and explore the implications for the role of working memory in physical and mental actions.

ACTIONS AND WORKING MEMORY: THE INNER SCRIBE?

Our survey of research on memory for action phrases demonstrates clearly that enactment of such phrases during encoding has an impact on their subsequent retrieval. The enactment is presumably having an impact on how the phrase is initially represented, in that it appears to add motoric or kinaesthetic cues to the visual, verbal, and semantic information associated with and encoded for each action. This then allows each of these cues to act as cues for retrieval. Broadly, motoric or kinaesthetic information present during encoding acts as do other forms of cue, in that it adds to the probability of retrieval. It is equally clear from the discussion of this literature that enactment may have a greater or lesser effect depending on the precise experimental conditions, and the body of literature on this topic is assisting the understanding of episodic encoding and retrieval of action phrases. However, our task in this chapter is not to explore the nature of the episodic traces, but to explore whether working memory might have some role to play, what that role might be, and whether investigation of this role might lead to some theoretical development as to the nature of working memory.

The first three sections of the chapter explored the case for working memory involvement in mental action. Is working memory involved in encoding action phrases or in supporting the process of enactment of these phrases? The fact that unrelated movement can disrupt memory for action phrases allows us to follow the logic used in dual task studies to conclude that the encoding of the action phrases requires some aspect of cognition that is also involved in generating the unrelated movement. This seems specific to movement, because unrelated visual input has no such effect. A similar finding is obtained when we consider the effect of unrelated movement on retention of movement sequences or paths between targets. This set of findings is consistent with the idea that working memory for movements might also support encoding of action phrases and allow the motoric or kinaesthetic information in enactment to be encoded along with other information about the phrase. The separation within working memory between a spatial, movement-based system (the inner scribe) and a visual temporary memory system (the visual cache) also is consistent with these findings, with the inner scribe having a role in the process of enactment.

The evidence on balance seems to support the idea that planning or imagining an action may have a beneficial effect on recall of an action phrase, even if not to the same extent as physical enactment. The working memory literature also points to planning of unrelated movements having a disruptive effect on retention of movement sequences between targets. Clearly action phrases involving objects such as "cut the onion" or "tie the shoelace" are movements that are different in nature from those involved in remembering a path around a four by four matrix of squares or between wooden cubes placed randomly on a board. The former involve real-world objects and actions that have associated meaning, and which can be encoded verbally, visually, semantically, or motorically. The latter are rather more difficult to encode verbally or semantically, although visual as well as motoric information may contribute to performance. In this sense the latter tasks are the nonsense syllables of movement memory.

Although there is considerable scope for additional cues to aid recall with action phrases, this does not prevent the use of working memory for their manipulation or encoding. The availability of these additional cues may result in the pattern of findings being more complex, and this complexity is apparent in the literature that we have discussed. Note too our earlier argument that the contents of working memory have associated semantics. In this view, working memory will draw on whatever information might be available to assist in performance of its assigned tasks, whether this be visual, verbal, semantic, motoric, kinaesthetic, tactile, olfactory, auditory, or procedural, although only a subset of such information might be employed for any one task. It was clear from our discussion of the mental synthesis tasks that there are several components of the task, and there are several components of working memory that appear to be involved to support task performance. These components of working memory act as an ensemble with well learned strategies and procedures to achieve task goals (Baddeley & Logie, 1999).

If working memory deals with interpreted representations, then it cannot act as an input filter between perception and long-term memory, as it is often portrayed in introductory textbooks on memory. It must deal with the product of activated representations in long-term memory (Logie, 1995, 1996). Where the activated information is incomplete, working memory acts as the workspace to manipulate the information and seek some means to resolve ambiguities or generate new knowledge. Indeed, this points to one possible reason why we have evolved with a working memory. If we can make sense of a sensation, scenario, or experience from our current knowledge, this can happen effortlessly by activating the relevant knowledge that allows us to act appropriately for the current context. However, if we are confronted by ambiguity, by implication this means that the knowledge activated from the long-term store of knowledge is insufficient. What knowledge is activated can be manipulated and transformed within working memory to help resolve the ambiguity. That is, working memory can generate new knowledge from old, and as such would have significant evolutionary value. This same argument can be applied to how we might start to acquire knowledge from birth. The neonate is confronted by what William James (1902, p. 7) referred to as "pure sensations", in that there is no knowledge base which can offer an interpretation of perceptual input beyond pain, pleasure, and satiation of hunger or thirst. Empirical developmental studies since James's pronouncements have indicated that babies may have rather more knowledge than he gave them credit for. However, it might be interesting to explore the concept that working memory in the neonate can generate new knowledge based on whatever information is activated in response to their current environment, thereby "bootstrapping" knowledge. Some empirical support for this idea comes from work with rather older children (age 3 and upwards): Gathercole and Baddeley (e.g., 1989) have shown that the system associated with subvocal rehearsal in working memory may play an important role in repeating speech sounds and contribute to the acquisition of vocabulary, that is, to acquiring new knowledge by manipulating the product of perception.

This role for working memory in generating new knowledge feeds into an evolutionary-based argument for its contribution to encoding, retaining, and executing action. Taking the example task given at the start of the chapter of reaching out and picking up objects, one way to supplement information in working memory is physically to manipulate objects in our environment. Another way of generating new information is to attempt mentally to manipulate objects along with associated information that we have available. Both physical and mental manipulation may generate novel associations or interpretations. Physical manipulation provides external stimulus support and avoids overloading working memory capacity. It also gives us visual, tactile, motoric, kinaesthetic, and other information about the object that we could not gain from mental manipulation, and this information may feed into new learning. Mental manipulation allows us to combine the percepts from real objects with novel variations on prior knowledge that those percepts activate.

CONCLUSION

We have examined mental actions, memory for physical actions, and the impact of enactment and of unrelated physical movement. By mental actions we have referred to manipulating representations of shapes and actions in mental imagery. We have argued that working memory plays a crucial role in supporting these mental actions and in combining the results of mental actions with planned and executed physical actions involving targets or objects. We have argued further that mental actions might involve a component of working memory that has been referred to as an "inner scribe", but that most tasks involving mental actions are likely to involve temporary retention of verbal labels for actions or objects, as well as temporary retention of visual, auditory, or other information available from stored knowledge that is activated by perceptual input. The concept is then of a working memory that functions as a system that has evolved to acquire new knowledge through mental manipulation of existing knowledge, as well as to effect temporary memory functions in support of visuo-spatial thinking.

REFERENCES

Bäckman, L. (1985). Further evidence for the lack of adult age differences on free recall of subject-performed tasks: The importance of motor action. *Human Learning, 4,* 79–87.

Bäckman, L., & Nilsson, L.-G. (1984). Aging effects in free recall: An exception to the rule. *Human Learning, 3,* 53–69.

Bäckman, L., Nilsson, L.-G., & Chalom, D. (1986). New evidence on the nature of the encoding of action events. *Memory & Cognition, 14,* 339–346.

Baddeley, A.D. (1966). The capacity for generating information by randomization. *Quarterly Journal of Experimental Psychology, 18,* 119–129.

Baddeley, A.D., Emslie, H., Kolodny, J., & Duncan, J. (1998). Random generation and the executive control of working memory. *Quarterly Journal of Experimental Psychology, 51A,* 819–852.

Baddeley, A.D., & Lieberman, K. (1980). Spatial working memory. In R.S. Nickerson (Ed.), *Attention and performance VIII* (pp. 521–539). Hillsdale, NJ: Lawrence Erlbaum Associates Inc.

Baddeley, A.D., & Logie, R.H. (1999). Working memory: The multiple component model. In A. Miyake & P. Shah (Eds.), *Models of working memory: Mechanisms of active maintenance and executive control* (pp. 28–61). Cambridge: Cambridge University Press.

Bain, A. (1868). *The senses and the intellect* (3rd Edn). London: Longman, Green & Co.

Barquero, B., & Logie, R.H. (1999). Imagery constraints on quantitative and qualitative aspects of mental synthesis. *European Journal of Cognitive Psychology, 11,* 315–333.

Beschin, N., Cocchini, G., Della Sala, S., & Logie, R.H. (1997). What the eyes perceive, the brain ignores: A case of pure unilateral representational neglect. *Cortex, 33,* 3–26.

Brandimonte, M.A., Hitch, G.J., & Bishop, D. (1992a). Influence of short-term memory codes on visual image processing: Evidence from image transformation tasks. *Journal of Experimental Psychology: Learning, Memory, and Cognition, 18,* 157–165.

Brandimonte, M.A., Hitch, G.J., & Bishop, D. (1992b). Verbal recoding of visual stimuli impairs mental image transformations. *Memory & Cognition, 20,* 449–455.

Brooks, B.M., & Gardiner, J.M. (1994). Age differences in memory for prospective compared with retrospective subject-performed tasks. *Memory & Cognition, 22,* 27–33.

Brooks, L.R. (1967). The suppression of visualisation by reading. *Quarterly Journal of Experimental Psychology, 19,* 289–299.

Chambers, D., & Reisberg, D. (1985). Can mental images be ambiguous? *Journal of Experimental Psychology: Human Perception and Performance, 11,* 317–328.

Chambers, D., & Reisberg, D. (1992). What an image depicts depends on what an image means. *Cognitive Psychology, 24,* 145–174.

Cohen, R.L. (1981). On the generality of some memory laws. *Scandinavian Journal of Psychology, 22,* 267–281.

Cohen, R.L. (1983). The effect of encoding variables on the free recall of words and action events. *Memory & Cognition, 11,* 575–582.

Cohen, R.L. (1989). The effects of interference tasks on recency in the free recall of action events. *Psychological Research, 51,* 179–187.

Cohen, R.L., & Bean, G. (1983). Memory in educable mentally retarded adults: Deficit in subject or experimenter? *Intelligence, 7,* 287–298.

Conway, M.A., & Dewhurst, S.A. (1995). Remembering, familiarity, and source monitoring. *The Quarterly Journal of Experimental Psychology, 48*A, 125–140.

Cooper, L.A. (1991). Dissociable aspects of the mental representation of visual objects. In R.H. Logie & M. Denis (Eds.), *Mental images in human cognition* (pp. 3–34). Amsterdam: Elsevier.

Cornoldi, C., Logie, R.H., Brandimonte, M.A., Kaufmann, G., & Reisberg, D. (1996). *Stretching the imagination: Representation and transformation in mental imagery.* Oxford: Oxford University Press.

De Renzi, E., & Nichelli, P. (1975). Short term memory impairment following hemispheric damage. *Cortex, 11,* 341–354.

Einstein, G.O., & Hunt, R.R. (1980). Levels of processing and organization: Additive effects of individual item and relational processing. *Journal of Experimental Psychology: Learning, Memory, and Cognition, 10,* 133–143.

Engelkamp, J. (1985). Aktivationsprozesse im menschlichen Gedächtnis. In D. Albert (Ed.), *Bericht über den 34. Kongreß der Deutschen Gesellschaft für Psychologie in Wien* (pp. 231–234). Göttingen: Hogrefe.

Engelkamp, J. (1986a). Nouns and verbs in paired-associate learning: Instructional effects. *Psychological Research, 48,* 153–159.

Engelkamp, J. (1986b). Differences between imaginal and motor encoding. In F. Klix & H. Hagendorf (Eds.), *Human memory and cognitive abilities* (pp. 205–213). Amsterdam: Elsevier (North-Holland).

Engelkamp, J. (1988). Modality-specific encoding and word class in verbal learning. In M. Gruneberg, P. Morris, & R.N. Sykes (Eds.), *Practical aspects of memory* (Vol. 1) (pp. 415–420). Chichester, UK: Wiley.

Engelkamp, J. (1995). Visual imagery and enactment of actions in memory. *British Journal of Psychology, 86,* 227–240.

Engelkamp, J. (1997). Memory for to-be-performed tasks versus memory for performed tasks. *Memory & Cognition, 25*, 117–124.

Engelkamp, J. (1998). *Memory for actions*. Hove, UK: Psychology Press.

Engelkamp, J., & Krumnacker, H. (1980). Imaginale und motorische Prozesse beim Behalten verbalen Materials. *Zeitschrift für experimentelle und angewandte Psychologie, 27*, 511–533.

Engelkamp, J., & Perrig, W. (1986). Differential effects of imaginal and motor encoding on the recall of action phrases. *Archiv für Psychologie, 138*, 261–273.

Engelkamp, J., & Zimmer, H.D. (1983). Zum Einfluß von Wahrnehmen und Tun auf das Behalten von Verb–Objekt–Phrasen. *Sprache & Kognition, 2*, 117–127.

Engelkamp, J., & Zimmer, H.D. (1984). Motor program information as a separable memory unit. *Psychological Research, 46*, 283–299.

Engelkamp, J., & Zimmer, H.D. (1994a). *The human memory. A multi-modal approach*. Seattle: Hogrefe & Huber.

Engelkamp, J., & Zimmer, H.D. (1994b). Motor similarity of movement in recognition of subject-performed tasks and verbal tasks. *Psychological Research, 57*, 47–53.

Engelkamp, J., & Zimmer, H.D. (1995). Similarity of movement in recognition of subject-performed tasks and verbal tasks. *British Journal of Psychology, 86*, 241–252.

Engelkamp, J., & Zimmer, H.D. (1996). Organization and recall in verbal tasks and in subject-performed tasks. *European Journal of Cognitive Psychology, 8*, 257–273.

Engelkamp, J., & Zimmer, H.D. (1997). Sensory factors in memory in subject-performed tasks. *Acta Psychologica, 96*, 43–60.

Engelkamp, J., Zimmer, H.D., & Biegelmann, U. (1993). Bizarreness effects in verbal tasks and subject-performed tasks. *European Journal of Cognitive Psychology, 5*, 393–415.

Engelkamp, J., Zimmer, H.D., Mohr, G., & Sellen, O. (1994). Memory of self-performed tasks: Self performing during recognition. *Memory & Cognition, 22*, 34–39.

Farah, M.J., Hammond, K.M., Levine, D.N., & Calvanio, R. (1988). Visual and spatial mental imagery: Dissociable systems of representation. *Cognitive Psychology, 20*, 439–462.

Finke, R. (1989). *Principles of mental imagery*. Cambridge, MA: MIT Press.

Finke, R., & Slayton, K. (1988). Explorations of creative visual synthesis in mental imagery. *Memory and Cognition, 16*, 252–257.

Gathercole, S., & Baddeley, A.D. (1989). Evaluation of the role of phonological STM in the development of vocabulary in children: A longitudinal study. *Journal of Memory and Language, 28*, 200–213.

Helstrup, T. (1987). One, two, or three memories? A problem-solving approach to memory for performed acts. *Acta Psychologica, 66*, 37–68.

Helstrup, T. (1989). Loci for act recall: Contextual influence on processing of action events. *Psychological Research, 51*, 168–175.

Helstrup, T., & Anderson, R. (1996). On the generality of mental construction in imagery: When bananas become smiles. *European Journal of Cognitive Psychology, 8*, 275–293.

Hitch, G.J. (1990). Developmental fractionation of working memory. In G. Vallar & T. Shallice (Eds.), *Neuropsychological impairments of short-term memory*, (pp. 221–246). Cambridge: Cambridge University Press.

Hunt, R.R., & Einstein, G.O. (1981). Relational and item-specific information in memory. *Journal of Verbal Learning and Verbal Behavior, 20*, 497–514.

James, W. (1902). *Principles of psychology* (Vol. II). London: Macmillan & Co.

Knopf, M. (1991). Having shaved a kiwi fruit: Memory of unfamiliar subject-performed actions. *Psychological Research, 53*, 203–211.

Koriat, A., Ben-Zur, H., & Druch, A. (1991). The contextualisation of input and output events in memory. *Psychological Research, 53*, 260–270.

Koriat, A., Ben-Zur, H., & Nussbaum, A. (1990). Encoding information for future action: Memory for to-be-performed versus memory for to-be-recalled tasks. *Memory & Cognition, 18*, 568–578.

Kosslyn, S.M. (1994). *Image and brain*. Cambridge, MA: MIT Press.

Logie, R.H. (1995). *Visuo-spatial working memory*. Hove, UK: Lawrence Erlbaum Associates Ltd.

Logie, R.H. (1996). The seven ages of working memory. In J.T.E. Richardson, R. Engle, L. Hasher, R.H. Logie, E.R. Stoltzfus, & R.T. Zacks (Eds.), *Working memory and human cognition* (pp. 31–65). New York: Oxford University Press.

Logie, R.H., & Marchetti, C. (1991). Visuo-spatial working memory: Visual, spatial, or central executive? In R.H. Logie & M. Denis (Eds.), *Mental images in human cognition*, (pp. 105–115). Amsterdam: Elsevier Science Publishers BV.

Logie, R.H., & Pearson, D.G. (1997). The inner eye and the inner scribe of visuo-spatial working memory: Evidence from developmental fractionation. *European Journal of Cognitive Psychology*, *9*, 241–257.

Merat, N. (1999). *The role of working memory in auditory localisation*. Unpublished Ph.D. thesis, University of Leeds, UK.

Mohr, G., Engelkamp, J., & Zimmer, H.D. (1989). Recall and recognition of self-performed acts. *Psychological Research*, *51*, 181–187.

Nilsson, L.-G., & Cohen, R.L. (1988). Enrichment and generation in the recall of enacted and non-enacted instructions. In M.M. Gruneberg, P.E. Morris, & R.N. Sykes (Eds.), *Practical aspects of memory: Current research and issues* (Vol. 1) (pp. 427–439). Chichester, UK: Wiley.

Nyberg, L., Nilsson, L.-G., & Bäckman, L. (1991). A component analysis of action events. *Psychological Research*, *53*, 219–225.

Pearson, D.G., Logie, R.H., & Gilhooly, K.J. (1999). Verbal representation and spatial manipulation during mental synthesis. *European Journal of Cognitive Psychology*, *11*, 295–314.

Pearson, D.G., Logie, R.H., & Green, C. (1996). Mental manipulation, visual working memory, and executive processes. *Psychologische Beträge*, *38*, 324–342.

Quinn, J.G. (1994). Towards a clarification of spatial processing. *Quarterly Journal of Experimental Psychology*, *47*A, 465–480.

Quinn, J.G., & Ralston, G.E. (1986). Movement and attention in visual working memory. *The Quarterly Journal of Experimental Psychology*, *38*A, 689–703.

Richardson, J.T.E. (1999). *Imagery*. Hove, UK: Psychology Press.

Roskos-Ewoldsen, B., Intons-Peterson, M.J., & Anderson, R.E. (Eds.) (1993). *Imagery, creativity and discovery – A cognitive perspective*. Amsterdam: Elsevier.

Saltz, E. (1988). The role of motoric enactment (M-processing) in memory for words and sentences. In M.M. Gruneberg, P.E. Morris, & R.N. Sykes (Eds.), *Practical aspects of memory: Current research and issues* (Vol. 1) (pp. 408–414). Chichester, UK: Wiley.

Saltz, E., & Donnenwerth-Nolan, S. (1981). Does motoric imagery facilitate memory for sentences? A selective interference test. *Journal of Verbal Learning and Verbal Behavior*, *20*, 322–332.

Salway, A.F.S., & Logie, R.H. (1995). Visuo-spatial working memory, movement control and executive demands. *British Journal of Psychology*, *86*, 253–269.

Shepard, R.N., & Feng, C. (1972). A chronometric study of mental paper folding. *Cognitive Psychology*, *3*, 228–243.

Smyth, M.M., Pearson, N.A., & Pendleton, L.R. (1988). Movement and working memory: Patterns and positions in space. *Quarterly Journal of Experimental Psychology*, *40*A, 497–514.

Smyth, M.M., & Pendleton, L.R. (1989). Working memory for movements. *Quarterly Journal of Experimental Psychology*, *41*A, 235–250.

Smyth, M.M., & Scholey, K.A. (1994). Characteristics of spatial memory span: Is there an analogy to the word length effect, based on movement time? *Quarterly Journal of Experimental Psychology*, *47*A, 91–117.

Wilson, B., Baddeley, A.D., & Young, A.W. (1999). A person who lost her mind's eye. *NeuroCase*, *5*, 119–127.

Zimmer, H.D. (1991). Memory after motoric encoding in a generation–recognition model. *Psychological Research*, *53*, 226–231.

Zimmer, H.D. (1996). Memory for spatial location and enactment. *Psychologische Beträge, 38,* 404–417.

Zimmer, H.D., & Engelkamp, J. (1984). Planungs- und Ausführungsanteile motorischer Gedächtniskomponenten und ihre Wirkung auf das Behalten ihrer verbalen Bezeichnungen. *Zeitschrift für Psychologie, 192,* 379–402.

Zimmer, H.D., & Engelkamp, J. (1985). An attempt to distinguish between kinematic and motor memory components. *Acta Psychologica, 58,* 81–106.

Zimmer, H.D., & Engelkamp, J. (1989). Does motor encoding enhance relational information? *Psychological Research, 51,* 158–167.

Zimmer, H.D., & Engelkamp, J. (1999). Level-of-processing effects in subject-performed tasks. *Memory & Cognition* (in press).

Zimmer, H.D., & Engelkamp, J. (in press). What type of information is enhanced in subject-performed tasks? A comment to Kormi-Nouri and Nilsson (1998). *European Journal of Cognitive Psychology.*

Zimmer, H.D., Engelkamp, J., & Sieloff, U. (1984). Motorische Gedächtniskomponenten als partiell unabhängige Komponenten des Engramms verbaler Handlungsbeschreibungen. *Sprache & Kognition, 3,* 70–85.

Author Index

Subject Index